CONFLICT AND COEXISTENCE

CONFLICT AND COEXISTENCE

Nationalism and Democracy in Modern Europe

~

Essays in honour of Harry Hearder

Edited by
ROBERT STRADLING, SCOTT NEWTON
and DAVID BATES

UNIVERSITY OF WALES PRESS
CARDIFF
1997

© The Contributors, 1997

British Library Cataloguing-in-Publication Data
A catalogue record for this book is available from the British Library.

ISBN 0-7083-1404-X

All rights reserved. No part of this book may be reproduced, stored in a retrieval system, or transmitted, in any form or by any means, electronic, mechanical, photocopying, recording or otherwise, without clearance from the University of Wales Press, 6 Gwennyth Street, Cardiff CF2 4YD.

Typeset by Action Typesetting, Gloucester
Printed in Great Britain by Dinefwr Press, Llandybïe

Contents

List of contributors — vii

1. Introduction: Democracy, Nationalism and Varieties of Patriotism
   ROBERT STRADLING and SCOTT NEWTON — 1

2. 'The Lucifer of Music': Rossini and German Music Nationalism in the Nineteenth Century
   MEIRION HUGHES — 19

3. Administering the Constitutional Pill: Britain, Italy and the Italian Policy of Lord Malmesbury
   NICK CARTER — 49

4. Europe's Quest for International Peace, 1870–1914
   MATTHEW ANDERSON — 66

5. Joseph Chamberlain and Tariff Reform: British Radicalism, Modernization and Nationalism
   SCOTT NEWTON — 84

6. Democracy and Nationalism in Wales: The Lib-Lab Enigma
   CHRIS WILLIAMS — 107

7. History and the Triumph of Art: Manuel Azaña's Vision of Spanish Democracy
   ROBERT STRADLING — 132

8. The Myths of José Antonio Primo de Rivera
   PAUL PRESTON — 159

9 'Primitive Rebels' in Spain: Historians and the Anarchist
  Phenomenon
  EDDIE MAY   196

10 Harry Hearder: An Appreciation
   DAVID BATES (with additions by NICK CARTER and
   ROBERT STRADLING)   219

Index   223

List of subscribers   227

Contributors to this Volume

Matthew Anderson, Emeritus Professor of History, London School of Economics

David Bates, Professor of Medieval History, University of Glasgow

Nick Carter, Lecturer in History, Simon de Montfort University, Leicester

Meirion Hughes, sometime Leverhulme Research Fellow, University of Wales, Cardiff

Eddie May, Tutor in History, University of Leicester

Scott Newton, Senior Lecturer in History, University of Wales, Cardiff

Paul Preston, Prince of Asturias Professor of Spanish History, London School of Economics

Robert Stradling, Reader in History, University of Wales, Cardiff

Chris Williams, Lecturer in History, University of Wales, Cardiff

~1~
Introduction: Democracy, Nationalism and Varieties of Patriotism

ROBERT STRADLING AND SCOTT NEWTON

Keywords

The three keywords that denominate our introduction have all taken different and even starkly contrasting forms. They are ever-shifting and often vague concepts, yet, despite radical shifts in the modes and mores of history, they remain basic to our understanding of the past. The essays which follow explore some of these facets from a variety of standpoints. The individual reader may see the collection as a rainbow or as a kaleidoscope, depending (perhaps) on whether her or his own intellectual perspective is positivist or post-structuralist (or neither). At any rate, from our viewpoint, the book sets out to illustrate some subtle chromatic shifts in what is too often seen in the textbooks as a diatonic subject. The ever-changing relationships between democracy and nationalism ('Conflict and Coexistence') occurring both within and between political communities, have often been modulated by profound feelings of patriotism which have provided a common – even elemental – agenda. Readers who may be dubious, about either the number of patriotism's varieties or the revived urgency of its importance, need only be reminded of the United Kingdom general election campaign of 1997. Evidently unafraid of attracting use of Dr Johnson's famously dismissive dictum, the leaders of all six of the largest parties in the House of Commons (Conservative, Labour, Liberal Democrat, Irish Unionist, Scottish National Party and Plaid Cymru) each passionately attested to their own version of the faith and derided those of their rivals.

In Alfred Hitchcock's film *Notorious* the heroine ('Alicia Huberman') initially rejects the hero's suggestion that reasons of patriotism should move her to accept the FBI's commission to spy on Nazi agents in Brazil. 'I don't go for patriotism ... waving a flag with one hand and picking pockets with the other – that's your patriotism.' But, of course, the good-time girl is really a patriot after all, and when the chips are down she is willing to take risks and make sacrifices for the community which has adopted her.[1] War is the acid test of elemental ethnocentric feelings but also produces an unnaturally high rate of response. It might be argued, too, that war or rumours of war has been the normal condition of twentieth-century societies. But our contention is that, despite its epiphenomenal character, patriotism is a ferment working away in the political magma of all communities. It is a feature of power and politics which can have a context far wider than nationalism, or one which is much narrower; it can seem eternal in one moment, ephemeral in another. It is at once the most atavistic and the most metaphysical of political drives.

Such a denominator might be seen as simply an (untheorized) synonym for Gramsci's 'cultural ensemble'.[2] In practice, Marxist experts have generally found nationalism an uncomfortable topic, whilst insistently regarding patriotism as little other than its local habitation and name. Certainly both concepts suffer from the lack of theoretical provenance which, in the former case, Benedict Anderson points to as the chief source of intellectual distrust.[3] But in addition, we suspect, patriotism has not been a favoured concept with social scientists precisely because it is a populist phenomenon in which most intellectuals (at least in Britain) do not personally partake and in which they have limited interest.[4] To us, however, the fact that patriotism is no more epiphenomenal than nationalism or democracy makes it worthy of study alongside them. It is empirically evident that none of these three descriptive zones are mutually exclusive of each other: the same person can espouse all three simultaneously and even with equal commitment.

Yet patriotism seems to be the catalytic element in this trinity. It can be metonymically imagined as a bridge stretching between democracy and nationalism. Individuals, nations and international power-groups constantly position and re-position themselves on the bridge, at different times nearer to one side than the other (rarely dead in the centre) – the diametrically opposed left and right banks of the river of time. In the USA, broadly speaking, patriotism has historically exerted a downward pressure on nationalism, whether indigenous or expatriate European, and provided support for democratic projects, both national and international. There are signs that in post-1945 Europe itself, a populist patriotism in this quasi-American sense is beginning to take root – even if one too often based on negative reaction to US 'colonialism' in its multifarious modes. In other places and circumstances, patriotism has asphyxiated (or seriously retarded) democracy and promoted nationalism: Germany – in successive metamorphoses – between 1848 and 1989, France during the Dreyfusard decades, Britain in its imperialist phase and dimension, all these nations during the years of total war. In this light it may be argued that patriotism is a major cultural catalyst of the two binary 'opposites', and thus potentially challenges the ideological duopoly which has dominated the political mind-set of westerners for over a century; but it is one which remains invisible and unaffected precisely because of its resistance to ideology. It is probably for this reason that, despite its rich semantic and political resonances, it is absent from that indispensable handbook of cultural criticism, Raymond Williams' *Keywords*.[5]

The Two Faces of Nationalism

Most studies of contemporary Europe have followed their own version of the Whig interpretation of history, an intellectual culture which subliminally incorporates a patriotic pride in European political civilization. In this story, the eruption of two catastrophic world wars has been explained as the direct result of uncontrollable nationalist tensions whose final expression were the nightmares of Nazism and Stalinism. However, (so the story goes) the years since 1945 have seen a conscious rejection of nationalism by governments throughout the continent. Undoubtedly more progress was made in western Europe, with the European Coal and Steel Community (1951) becoming the first stage in a carefully negotiated progress towards the European Union of the 1990s.[6] Even in eastern Europe old tensions disappeared, asphyxiated under the weight of Soviet hegemony. As the Cold War drew to a close, Europe seemed not so much a collection of nation-states as two separate blocs. Each was characterized by internal organizations designed to promote political, economic and strategic co-operation across national frontiers: the European Community, the European Free Trade Association, and the North Atlantic Treaty Organization in the west, Comecon and the Warsaw Pact in the east. During the Gorbachev era, it was easy to hope that the post-war trend to collaboration could be reinforced by the removal of the iron curtain: the prize of a democratic Europe without internal barriers, united to the Ural mountains, glittered on the horizon.[7]

It is at this point that the Whig interpretation of European history ends. The vision of Europe united to the Urals turned out to be a mirage. Nationalism has made a comeback. Throughout eastern Europe nationalist tendencies have reappeared, sometimes leading to civil war, as in the former Yugoslavia in the period 1991–5. For many liberals events in and around the city of Sarajevo symbolized a bewildering and depressing turn of events, a collapse back to square one – the inescapable destiny of Europe, represented to any onlooker with a sense of history by the same atavistic attitudes in the same city and the cataclysm they engendered eighty years earlier. Ideals of multinationalism and international co-operation once again seem to be under siege by xenophobia and ethnocentrism. Even in western Europe ethnic minorities have suffered harassment and physical, even murderous abuse at the hands of hyperpatriotic political groupings. Meanwhile the onward march of the European Union slows down in the face of widespread concern to protect the customs, laws, and economic independence of the nation-state from the federalist designs lurking in Brussels.

Yet a closer study of the historical record suggests that nationalism never actually went away. The war against the Nazi New Order, against Japan's East Asia Co-Prosperity Sphere and against Italian expansionism, was a war fought – much more fully than that of 1914–18 – for self-determination and independence. It is true that a gathering of resistance leaders, meeting in Switzerland in 1944, produced a declaration favouring post-war European unification. But the loyalties of both governments-in-exile and of most resistance groups on the ground were in the first place simply patriotic: their *raison d'être* was the restoration of the nation-state. How many fought or otherwise sacrificed for the United Nations first and their own country second? Indeed the

Nazis and Collaborationist governments such as the Vichy and Quisling régimes were quicker than the Allies to use the rhetoric of pan-Europeanism in an effort to rally public enthusiasm for Hitler's New Order. Meanwhile the impact of German aggression produced an ideological volte-face on the part of the Soviet Union: Mother Russia came to eclipse the Internationale, and the Comintern failed to survive the war.[8]

Of course, the nationalism of 1939–45 was different from the liberal variety which had figured so prominently in nineteenth-century Europe. Mid-twentieth-century nationalism stressed human social and economic rights as well as state sovereignty and international recognition The post-war nation-state was a response to the traumas of a thirty-year period characterized by war, imperialism, racism, genocide, mass unemployment and mass destruction. Accordingly, throughout Europe governments embarked on policies of reconstruction designed to protect national security and to guarantee all citizens a job, a house, secondary education at least to the age of fifteen and medical treatment free at the point of need.

The new welfare states were not paternalist gestures on the parts of old élites desperate to retain power. They were established in response to popular demand – from organized labour and from farming interests above all – made on the assumption that only the nation-state could guarantee both self-government and social security. Keynesianism was in the ascendant: this doctrine facilitated the socializing of nationalism[9] by teaching that only state intervention could guarantee economic growth and full employment. The new economics appeared to demonstrate that the aspirations of ordinary people for a better world were not simply noble but also realistic: and in pursuit of them post-war governments embraced national economic planning.

How could an international organization such as the European Economic Community have appeared against such a background? The European Whigs avoided this problem by exaggerating the internationalism of the anti-Nazi forces and by drawing a direct line from the declaration of the resistance leaders in Switzerland to the signature of the Rome Treaty in 1958. An explanation which seems closer to the historical record has, however, been offered by Alan Milward in *The Rescue of the European Nation-State*. Milward's argument is that post-war integration was created by the European nation-states for their own purposes. And in the circumstances of the 1950s, these all derived from the commitment to maintain reconstruction. Full employment, growth, and a basic agricultural income in France, West Germany and Italy and in the Benelux countries, could only be sustained by the creation of a Coal and Steel Community, a customs union, and a common agricultural policy. The European Union of the 1990s may be more extensive than the EEC of the Six – but is there any reason to suppose that the nation-states who were late signatories to the Rome Treaty joined up purely out of international idealism?

If the construction of post-war western Europe was in large part a nationalist project, the recrudescence of nationalism, in Eurosceptic or in more sinister form, becomes less surprising. After 1945, the discourse of nationalism was never replaced at a popular level by one of Europeanism because 'Europe' was supposed to guarantee the survival of a socialized nationalism. But during the 1980s and 1990s the post-war settlement began to unravel throughout western Europe: economic uncertainty, mass unemployment and alarming levels of social inequality returned in response to the globalization of capital. During the 1960s, the average level of unemployment in western Europe was 1.5 per cent; by 1993 it had risen to 11 per cent.[10] Pro-European left-wing governments were in power for much of this period in France and Spain, but they were unable to prevent these developments. Given this failure to hold off the return of insecurity, the growth of Euroscepticism was unsurprising: 'Europe' was not working.

What was the alternative? For the liberal Right it was the speeding up of integration into the world economy. This course of action was logical enough for the forces of capital, located in banks, pension funds, unit trusts and transnational corporations. By the end of the twentieth century, few of these owed any loyalty to the nation-state, requiring instead a world economy uncluttered by restrictions to the free movement of people, goods and money. But such a strategy was likely to intensify the difficulties faced by nation-states seeking to protect their citizens from the destabilizing effects of market forces. In these circumstances it was unsurprising that many middle- and working-class voters embraced the rhetoric and the politics of nationalist parties – a development seen in the rise of far Right activity within Germany, of the National Front in France and of two competing groups in Italy: the post-fascist National Alliance and the regionally-based Northern League.

The nationalism of the 1990s could not be of the progressive and socialized variety which had flourished half-a-century before. First, its institutional and political vehicles, namely the trade unions and socialist or social-democratic parties, had themselves been weakened by the capitalist offensive (or counter-offensive) of the 1980s and by internal ideological differences concerning the best way to combat this. Secondly, contemporary nationalism could not be associated with any struggle for democracy against Fascism. Its inspiration was derived instead from resentment of the consequences of economic internationalism. All too often the popular coalitions which were mobilized around this issue were unified by fear of foreigners, immigrants and groups whose ethnic origins differed from the majority of those in the host community. The resonance of this xenophobia has been at its most powerful in the former Yugoslavia. But Gypsies in Slovakia, Hungarians in Romania, Algerians in France and Asians in Britain have also experienced its violent consequences.

Does all this mean that a noble experiment in supranationalism, which formed the foundation of an unprecedented era of peace – and of prosperity for the people of western Europe – has come to an end? Is nationalism to be the dominant political ideology of the new century, with all the concomitant evils which marred the old? The historian cannot provide straightforward answers to these questions. To begin with, the international economic and political co-operation of the 1945–90 era was itself rooted in nationalism. But beyond this, the experience of the last hundred years suggests that the phenomenon is the 'modern Janus'[11] – a creature with two faces, one democratic and one non- (or even anti-) democratic. Which is to predominate in the future? A liberal view might be that the coexistence of the peaceful-prosperous years with Keynesian policies and social-democratic structures suggests that the answer will be determined by the success or failure of efforts to restore public authority over international market forces. Whether such an attempt will be made depends on how long relative economic stagnation lasts and how painful the condition becomes before it gets better. All this may not presage the end of history; unless the return of communist governments in Poland and Russia – albeit this time democratically elected – were to trigger off the apocalypse warned of by the Virgin Mary when she appeared to Portuguese peasant children at Fatima in 1917, apparently in order to warn the world against Bolshevism. But it seems almost certain to mark the end of a massively powerful, almost hegemonic, project in which 'history' and 'politics' collaborated; the end – that is – of the Grand Narrative of Liberal Positivism.

History's Endings

Yet the current 'crisis of post-modernism' is not the first time that such a hermeneutic terminus seemed to have been reached. George Orwell once recalled a conversation with Arthur Koestler which took place in or around 1939. The Spanish Republic, the world's most celebrated failed experiment in democracy, was about to be overwhelmed by the forces of nationalism. It was a moment that was both elegiac and epiphanal for millions. Orwell offered the opinion that 'History ended in 1936'; Koestler, apparently knowing exactly what his companion meant, agreed; according to Orwell's text, he did so without adding comment, caveat, or gloss.[12]

But what *did* Orwell mean? And what was the rhetorical nature of his statement? Was it a parataxic announcement, like that of the Evangelists?; a prophecy, like those of Elijah?; or a guideline for survival in the wasteland, like the laws of Moses? We do have something (though not a lot) to go on here. Since Orwell took the trouble to recall and record his words after such a lapse of time we may assume they were not merely a poetic hyperbole, inspired by the terrible disappointment of Franco's victory. We know that Orwell had an exaggerated respect for History, and that he went on to dedicate the remainder of his writing life to saving it from some imagined extinction. By 'History' he certainly meant what most intellectuals would have meant in those days: unbroken and infallible recording of the past through 'scientific' research. But subliminally (perhaps) he also meant a history written from the point of view of himself (and of most intellectuals); a strongly idealistic and ethically cosy history – a value-laden discourse which was, to use one of Orwell's favourite words, 'decent'.[13]

This brings us back to *The Whig Interpretation of History*. In Orwell's day, the influence of Herbert Butterfield's book with this title (first published in 1931) was producing an awareness, in academic circles, of how mainstream historians privileged the liberal discourse.[14] It was this 'History' – elevated to the status of Universal Truth – which Orwell (in *Nineteen Eighty-Four*) was striving to preserve from 'Propaganda' (= Lies) in the assumed persona of Winston Smith, functionary of the Ministry of Truth in the Super-State of Oceania. It was the Spanish War and not Professor Butterfield which opened Orwell's eyes to the possibilities of a ruthless historical relativism engineered by and for a political project. But, being imbricated in modernism, he remained utterly blind to the fundamental reality of his own inflexible perspective. To Orwell, as to Butterfield, the given of liberal positivist History was a patriotic essential, not even a concept. In the epistemological mirror of 1950 – the year of Koestler's *The God that Failed* – the seeker after truth could only see the superficially recognizable image of his own culture, an image which (like all mirror-images) was simultaneously both true and false.[15] Winston Orwell did not need to learn to love Big Brother: he already was Big Brother.

Nevertheless, having something to go on does not guarantee that our response to Orwell's claim about history and 1936 is reliable or definitive. Indeed, stepping for a moment outside the intellectual's ring of responsibility, it may ultimately be safer for the world to conclude that Koestler's mute agreement was the only possible response. This might mean the end of interpretation, at least in the monolithic scientific/academic domain, not necessarily the end of history. But (nervously, to step back in) the trouble with agreement is that it tends to elide disagreement, and thus meaning. We can only know – describe the meaning of – what we agree about, by first knowing what we disagree about. Since in Orwell's text, no disagreement took place, we cannot reliably access what he meant. After this lapse of time, it may appear to us that it was Koestler's mute act of agreement, rather than the death of the Spanish Republic, which represents the end of history. This is because post-structuralism (a movement in philosophy and criticism which is having an increasing impact on history teaching and writing) has replaced the mirror with a window. Like all windows it only looks in one direction – in this case, back towards Nietzsche – and, by definition, we should not delude ourselves that the window is perfectly transparent. But at least (i) connecting with Nietzsche, the

Janus of 1900, permits us to reconcile synchronically opposed perspectives; and (ii) we recognize that the hegemony of propaganda in history is necessary but not sufficient, a realization which, uniquely and ubiquitously, allows some escape from that hegemony. The latter point represents a medium of universal liberation. To explain this in common parlance, because most people know what is meant by 'politically correct' language, and recognize it when they hear or read it, they are enabled, via a consciously critical encounter, either to use it or not.

It is important here to point out that Orwell and Koestler did not specify 1939 as the end of history, but rather 1936. This was the year that dissent actually ended in Spain. In both zones, rigorously authoritarian regimes gradually stamped out all resistance. Both claimed the patriotic high-ground, – metaphorically and in hundreds of cases, literally – and soaked it with the blood of martyrs, whilst calling on Spaniards to cleanse the fatherland of alien ideas and invaders. In the peninsular ring, two grim totalitarian systems – to use a popular discourse of the decade – slugged it out mercilessly for nearly three years. From the corners, the seconds watched, yelled advice and (when the ref wasn't looking) inserted horseshoes in gloves.

In 1939, the main bout began; the heavyweight championship. The Nazi–Soviet alliance at last officially linked together, on the strategic-military level, two international systems, the Axis and the Comintern, which had always been deeply cognate on the cultural plane. On 1 September 1939, 'in one of the dives / On fifty-second street', W. H. Auden announced the end of the 'low, dishonest decade' of the 1930s. Some of the British ruling class – Neville Chamberlain, Lord Londonderry, Unity Mitford – were caught on the hop. Others, more marginalized, like Oswald Mosley and Harry Pollitt (the latter after a little 'assisted' reflection) condemned 'this imperialist war' against the Nazis. They knew how to adjust in mid-step when the bandleader changed from a waltz to a foxtrot. Some did not, like Manuel Azaña and Leon Trotsky, both caught in no-man's-land and duly eliminated in 1940. By then, the European ruling class had made the necessary adjustment, and on balance felt it was better to join the party and make peace with the Nazi–Soviet Axis.[16] In France, gendarmes grateful not to be manning the Maginot Line against the Nazis, were happier still to round up the communists and place them in custody, where the incoming

Gestapo conveniently found them a few months later, after the fall of France. Meanwhile, in the USSR, communist exiles of German (and other) origins were rounded up and delivered gift-wrapped to Berlin. Just as Stalin and Hitler had agreed on the end of History in Eastern Europe, so Marshal Pétain and Hitler – comrades in the *fronterlebnis* of the Western Front – agreed on the end of History in Western Europe. 'So all the isms are wasms', as one British civil servant said after hearing about the Nazi–Soviet Pact. It took the simultaneous megaton shock of Hiroshima and the Holocaust to set the clock of history going again in 1945. And not until 1989, fifty years after the Koestler–Orwell Pact, did the dust from Nagasaki settle alongside the ashes from Auschwitz, the combined fallout threatening to jam the clockwork once again. Thus Francis Fukuyama emerged to breathe new life into the Whig Interpretation of History, precisely via the tendentious assertion that it had achieved its world-historical political objective.

The History Travellers

It is History's obvious reluctance to conform to any grand narrative which allows us to acknowledge the very different, but often parallel roads leading towards the existential freedom of 1940. Some history travellers took more than one road simultaneously; others shifted from one road to another on one definitive occasion; and yet others shifted back and forth more than once, and/or experimented with several roads, at different points of the journey.

Though a patriotic Italian, Gioacchino Rossini was so neither in the Johnsonian nor the French Revolutionary sense. He admired – and once worked for – Bonaparte, but dissented from his fellow-expatriate in the conviction that Italy could never become a united, leave alone a democratic, nation. Nearly two centuries later, to judge by the persistent failure of Italians in both aspirations, though (on the whole) remaining his recognizably relaxed and tolerant descendants, Rossini's judgment seems to have been vindicated. Harry Hearder's feelings on this subject were strong, but not unambiguous: he loved beauty and Italy equally, admired democracy almost without reservation, and had an abiding mistrust of the nation-state. Meirion Hughes' essay is perhaps the most direct of our tributes to their 'onlie begetter', in that, placing a certain emphasis on Italy, it examines a case-study in the formation of cultural relations between competing and evolving 'national' schools. Following this overture, Nick Carter takes up the baton to explore the haunting fears and deep divisions in British government circles which complicated, and almost crippled, an ideologically coherent approach to Italian unification. It shows (*inter alia*) how the British, not themselves having a popular nationalist tradition, found it hard to come to terms with this potentially violent phenomenon on the continent, even when it promised benefits to which British political traditions were palpably committed.

Harry Hearder, who respected Cavour, sympathetically considered and illuminated these issues from his earliest research years. But his feeling for the memory of Mazzini, which almost amounted to devotion, not just respect, meant that his driving inspiration was the hope in world government. Matthew Anderson reflects this by reconstructing the framework of what might almost be a 'counter-factual' or 'alternative' history of the late nineteenth century. Hindsight compels us to acknowledge that an apparently dominant 'international anarchy' necessarily involved a reaction – opposite but unfortunately not equal. How could peace be maintained against a background of expansionism, social Darwinism and national aggression? Was it a prototype European patriotism, underpinned by capitalist humanism? Professor Anderson's contribution illustrates the development of a utopian, non-ideological internationalism – a spirit to which, however little historians tend to associate it with his period, Harry Hearder was always deeply committed.

Scott Newton's essay elucidates the aims of the first British statesman to appreciate the meaning and anticipate the consequences of such internationalism on the macro-economic level. Joseph Chamberlain was not a radical who turned imperialist with the coming of political maturity. On the contrary, throughout his career, both as Liberal and as Liberal Unionist in uneasy alliance with the Conservatives, he challenged *laissez-faire* economics and the complex of commercial interests which stood behind the 'Nightwatchman State'. He did this at first through the 'unauthorised programme', and then via the Tariff Reform campaign. In the latter, he sought to mobilize a cross-class alliance of employers and workers around a popular nationalism which elevated national power and welfare to the apex of the

State's priorities. It was an analysis which flew in the face of the liberalism which identified Britain's self-interest with the free movement of people, goods and capital.

The programme advocated by 'Radical Joe' appealed to many substantial citizens of Wales – especially south Wales, where hectic industrialization in the middle decades of the nineteenth century had produced a powerful class of manufacturers with a range of interests in common with their workers, a range wide enough for it to be almost possible to speak of a 'cultural ensemble' in the generation before *c.* 1900. In this area, the relationship between Cardiff and its industrial hinterland is arguably a case-study in the failure of Tariff Reform – the triumph of cosmopolitan Cardiff, the locus of finance-capitalism, over manufacture-centred Merthyr adumbrating the long-term decline, both of the British economy and of industrial democracy itself.

Alongside this, Chris Williams highlights another dichotomy, one of greater relevance to issues of nationalism and democracy in the specifically Welsh context. Industrialization in south-east Wales swung the demographic-cultural balance against the traditional Welsh-speaking communities of small farming, rural towns and local industry. Welsh nationalism was derived from the same Romantic roots – Herder, as opposed to Hearder – as many another European example. As in Catalonia and Bohemia, nationalists sought to privilege ethnically-exclusive linguistic discourses, spoken and literary. But the Wales anglicized (or britonized) by abstract forces of change produced a fiercely democratic politics, in whose crucible the old culture had diminishing chances of survival, leave alone supremacy. Already by 1914, to be a patriotic Welshman – regardless of class (if not of caste) – was precisely to exhibit internationalist rather than nationalist sympathies. Chris Williams explores this intermeshing of class, community and national identities, along with the representative forms and practices generated by a society in flux. The Lib-Labs, often dismissed and even derided by historians, emerge as neither dupes of a supposedly hegemonic Welsh Liberalism nor as unreflective enthusiasts for the radical nationalism of the Cymru Fydd movement. Rather, these miners' leaders prided themselves on being authentic representatives of 'Labour' – an essentially occupational category that increasingly cut across cultural-linguistic lines as between Welsh and English workers. The Lib-Labs, and their charismatic leader 'Mabon', saw their main tasks as reflecting the aspirations and advancing the material interests of their democracy – responsibilities they wished to fulfil by working within both the wider British Labour movement and the Imperial Parliament.

Manuel Azaña was another exponent of the charisma with which his generation seems to have been so generously (in some respects fatally) endowed. He seemed the ideal head of that utopian Spanish 'Republic of Professors', the overthrow of which was mourned by Orwell and Koestler, and by our whole intellectual culture ever since. But Azaña's vision of the future was so utopian-patriarchal that it might be seen as more autocratic in a Tolstoyan sense – that is, informed by an essentially noble paternalism – than genuinely democratic. To him, the humanistic, imaginative creativity of writing was infinitely superior to (and more real than) the humdrum responsibilities and tawdry compromises of democratic politics. History, Drama and Political Science were the media of an aesthetic world which he desired all Spaniards to enter. He wished to deconstruct the genetic assumptions of Spanish history, placing Juan Luis Vives and Francisco Goya on the pedestals of popular patriotism hitherto occupied by Philip II and the Virgin Mary. Though never himself an academic, Azaña was quintessentially professorial – his whole project was didactic as well as Mosaic. He was an apostle of a species of artistic absolutism, a philosophy of Cultural Imperialism positing the privilege of art over politics which was subscribed to by many contemporaries. Yet at the same time, his actual (mundane) political gifts were undeniably brilliant. Robert Stradling argues here that his promiscuous exercise of a monomania hidden from (or justified to) most historians by his elevated intellectual culture, was a significant cause of the Spanish Civil War.

During the 1996 Spanish general election campaign, the conservative leader's claim that his party were Azaña's spiritual heirs fractured the long-standing agreement (*Pacto de Olvido*) which had hitherto kept the Civil War safely off the agenda of the new democratic process. The outraged reaction of the socialist leader, Felipe González, to Manuel Azaña's statement led to bitter quarrels in press and TV coverage. The ex-Francoist historian, Ricardo de la Cierva, had recently produced a new study of the war, in which he suggested that – sixty years on – its bloody ghost had at last been laid. Now, his response was to add a postscript to the introduction of his book, angrily reinvoking all the old fury and fire.[17] It seems that if the polemical struggle (hopefully, no more) is going to break out anew, then Manuel Azaña, one of the modern masters of polemic, will appropriately be at the centre of the storm.

One of Azaña's most dedicated enemies was the equally brilliant and cultured young extremist, José Antonio Primo de Rivera. Though a true intellectual, José Antonio defended many of the ideas Azaña attacked. By no means simple reaction, he nurtured a more traditionally patriotic vision of his country's future; not dissimilar, in its populist economic imperialism, to that advanced for Britain by Joseph Chamberlain. As we see from Paul Preston's contribution, this loyal son of the ex-dictator Miguel Primo de Rivera had a smooth patrician charm and a cultivated 'European' demeanour. His background hardly fitted him for the role of leader of a mass fascist party, and it was fortunate for his reputation that he did not survive into a later period of the movement he founded. Moreover, his personal courage was of the physical kind that readily embraced violence and the clichés of Spanish *pundonor*.[18] At once traditional in inspiration and reflecting the pugilistic political culture of the 1930s, it underpinned a policy which led directly to hundreds of sordid deaths on the streets of Spanish towns, even before the outbreak of civil war in July 1936. And in pushing the army towards rebellion, José Antonio never seems to have suspected that he and his movement would simply end up as stalking-horses for another military dictatorship.

Some aspects of the social teaching of Spanish Fascism have been seen by political commentators as touching hands with its apparent opposite and nemesis, anarchism. This was the revolutionary doctrine which Orwell came closest to espousing in 1937, because it seemed to him (probably rightly) the popular expression which was most Spanish and (perhaps wrongly) least dirtied by compromise. Eddie May argues here that the essential nature and aspirations of this mass movement, utterly unique as it was in European historical experience, may have been seriously misunderstood. The trajectory of anarchism has been characterized as non-modern or even anti-modernist by using points of comparison with normative or 'conventional' socialist directions which should now be regarded as hopelessly insecure. At the same time, there seems no doubt that much anarchist commitment was founded on a uniquely meaningful local patriotism – love of a *patria chica* – more intense in Spain than in most other countries. Anarchists never rejected the nation, but they did object violently to every manifestation of the impersonal nation-state, and posited against it a microdemocratic organism which was collective and utopian.

So it seems that throughout the period covered by the essays here western Europeans could – and in millions of cases did – move from conservative-nationalist to liberal to radical imperialist to fascist to social democratic to communist; and back again. Each of these discourses, at least for a time, in Althusser's neologism 'interpellated' them as subjects. As individuals and as groups they exercised power and influence over others in every metamorphosis; and (this book tends to plead) at every stage sought to further a patriotic project.[19] These actions and reactions were the result of reading the signposts marking the route – telling the travellers where they were, where they were going, and the distance to their destination. These signs represented the semiology of culture, mediating the people's feelings about material desire, social belonging and political aspiration. On the signs appeared keywords like 'nationalism', 'revolution', 'class', 'patriotism', 'religion', and 'democracy'. This book is about the complex interaction between people, roads, bridges and signs, and takes a medium- to long-term perspective on the crisis of the mid-twentieth century from a point located not far from the battlefield of Waterloo.

Notes

1   In *Notorious* (1946), Alicia was played by Ingrid Bergman and the FBI agent, Devlin, by Cary Grant. Both stars were reputed to be keenly anti-Nazi in their private opinions. On the expression of Hitchcock's own patriotism in his wartime films, see J. R. Taylor *Hitch: The Authorised Biography of Alfred Hitchcock* (London, 1981), 127ff.
2   See A. Gramsci, *Selections from the Prison Notebooks* (London, 1971) and the discussion in K. Thompson, *Beliefs and Ideology* (London, 1986), esp. 98–100.
3   B. Anderson, *Imagined Communities* (London, 1983), esp. 13–14. For a survey of recent studies of nationalism from a historical perspective, see H. Koenigsberger, 'The Past and Future History of Nationalism', *European History Quarterly* 26 (1996), 591–602.

4　This observation is more supported than otherwise by the various studies in R. Samuel (ed.), *Patriotism: The Making and Unmaking of British National Identity* (3 vols., London, 1989).
5　R. Williams, *Keywords: A Vocabulary of Culture and Society* (London, 1979).
6　A. W. Lovett, 'The United States and the European Coal and Steel Agreement', *Historical Journal* 39 (1996), 425–55, illustrates how idealistic plans for European Union arose from the ethnocentric motives of Jean Monnet's initiative and the hard-nosed negotiations which followed.
7　See R. Mayne, *The Recovery of Europe* (London, 1970); J. Monnet, *Memoirs* (London, 1979); J. Palmer, *Europe without America* (London, 1988), for histories of post-war integration. The literature is discussed at some length in the first chapter of A. S. Milward, *The European Rescue of the Nation-State* (London, 1992).
8　See E. Hobsbawm, *Age of Extremes: The Short Twentieth Century, 1914–1991* (London, 1995), chs. 14 and 16, for a discussion of these points.
9　The phrase is taken from D. Thomson, *World History from 1914 to 1950* (Oxford, 1954), 117.
10　See Hobsbawm, *Age of Extremes*, 406.
11　See T. Nairn, *The Break-Up of Britain* (London, 1981), ch. 9.
12　G. Orwell, 'Looking back on the Spanish war' (1943), included in *Homage to Catalonia* (Harmondsworth, 1966), 233–4. Both men narrowly escaped death during the war. Koestler was rescued from a Francoist firing squad by Marcel Junod of the Red Cross; see the latter's *Warrior without Weapons* (London, nd ?1948), 124–5. Orwell was horribly wounded by a sniper's bullet which went through his throat but missed the artery.
13　See R. A. Stradling, 'Orwell and the Spanish Civil War: A Historical Critique', in C. Norris (ed.), *Inside the Myth: Orwell, Views from the Left* (London, 1984), 103–25.
14　For an in-depth analysis of the intellectual resonances of this discourse, see J. W. Burrows, *A Liberal Descent: Victorian Historians and the English Past* (Cambridge 1981).
15　See A. Koestler *et al.*, *The God that Failed: Six Studies in Communism* (London, 1950) Three of these 'true confessions' of dedicated communists or eminent fellow travellers (those of Koestler himself, Louis Fischer and Stephen Spender) placed central emphasis on the Spanish War as the crux of both commitment and disillusion.
16　See S. Newton, *Profits of Peace: The Political Economy of Anglo-German Appeasement* (Oxford, 1996), esp. 133ff.
17　R. de la Cierva, *Historia esencial de la Guerra Civil Española. Todos los problemas resueltos, sesenta años después*. The first edition of this book (published by Editorial Fénix, Madridejos) dates from

March 1996. The new material referred to appeared in the third, published in October of the same year (see x–xv).
18 *Pundonor*: a specifically Spanish code of aristocratic sensibility, enshrined in its literature since medieval times.
19 A suitable case in point is the composer of the European Union's anthem, Ludwig van Beethoven, whose intricate political odyssey, and the various political interests which subsequently exploited it, are charted in D. B. Dennis, *Beethoven in German Politics 1870–1989* (New Haven and London, 1996), see esp. 22–31.

~2~
'The Lucifer of Music': Rossini and German Music Nationalism in the Nineteenth Century

MEIRION HUGHES

Above all, make a lot of Barbers. (Beethoven to Rossini, Vienna 1822).[1]

Whether compliment or jibe, recommendation or rebuke, Beethoven's assessment of Rossini's talent has, apparently, stood the test of time. Was this a self-fulfilling prophecy? Did Beethoven's magisterial position in German music endow his utterance with what turned out to be lasting validity? This essay will argue that Rossini's ultimate reputation as a one-masterpiece composer was not a matter of coincidence so much as a conscious process. The apogee of Rossini's working career in the 1810s and 1820s coincided with the rise of German political and musical nationalism, for both of which the development of a German national opera was of paramount importance. In Germany, as elsewhere in Europe, opera was still overwhelmingly 'Italian'. For many German musicians, the defeat of Italian opera came to mean, as it were, the overthrow of Rossini, a composer whose sensational success in the years after Waterloo seemed to point to a continuation of Italian hegemony in opera. For them, his defeat seemed as necessary a precondition of nationhood as that of Napoleon himself had been. Thus Rossini came under attack, first in the German operatic world and, subsequently, in the musical press. Critics and writers belonging to the German-speaking lands – many of whom were also composers – sought to limit, even to eradicate, his influence. They mounted such an assault on Rossini's reputation that, ultimately, the composer's place in the pantheon of music was only maintained by the quick wits of his Figaro.

Given Rossini's huge contemporary renown, the decline of his reputation thereafter can only be a matter for wonderment. Nothing better illustrated this decline than the Rossini bicentennial year of 1992, which was, even in Italy, a humble affair – especially when compared to the worldwide Mozart celebrations of the previous year. Yet, at the height of his career, Rossini was regarded as a daring innovator in opera. Many agreed with Stendhal that the composer was a 'new conqueror' who had shaken music with a Napoleonic force.[2] In his life and inspiration Rossini was often classed with the leading figures of the Romantic Age; to Balzac, for example, 'a romantic hero should be devoted to Byron's poetry, Géricault's painting and Rossini's music'.[3]

The condition of Rossini's posthumous reputation in England is indicative of the slump in the composer's stock. The first edition of Grove's *Dictionary of Music and Musicians* (1879–89) asserted that Rossini 'had more gaiety than propriety, more wit than dignity, more love of independence than good taste'.[4] It conveys the impression of a flawed artist, a composer from the Latin south, who never managed to transcend his origins as 'the son of the jolly trombadore of Pesaro'.[5] By the last quarter of the nineteenth century, Rossini was stigmatized as a *bon viveur* and society figure who was even capable of mocking his own music. In 1892, the Royal Opera House Covent Garden, instead of marking the centenary of Rossini's birth, put on a complete cycle of Wagner's *Ring* conducted by Gustav Mahler. By 1934, the composer's standing was so low that the Rossini enthusiast, Francis Toye, author of the first biography of the composer by an Englishman for over seventy years, actually began his book with the bizarre admission: 'To the best of my belief there is no demand whatever for a life of Rossini in English.'[6] Apart from the evergreen *Barber of Seville* and the orchestral overture to *William Tell* – and leaving aside his gastronomic creation, 'Tournedos Rossini' – few people knew, or apparently wanted to know, about his subject.[7] Nearly sixty years later the *Musical Times* bicentenary issue contained only one article on Rossini – that on *Il Barbiere*. Thus spake Beethoven!

As the above implies, the key to the demise of Rossini's reputation lies in the politics of Germany in the first half of the nineteenth century, and the climate of shifting cultural values they produced. The context of this essay is the emergence of the idea of Germany and the need for the Germans to emphasize their music, especially opera, in the early decades of the nineteenth century.

Strange Meeting

> Poor Weber! He came to see me in Paris on his way to London; he looked so weak and ill that his making such a journey was inconceivable to me. He hoped, as he told me, to gain something respectable for his family – he should have preserved himself for them.[8]

Four years after the Rossini–Beethoven encounter in Vienna, another meeting took place – this time in Paris between Rossini and Carl Maria von Weber. On the face of things, the two composers had much in common: they were roughly the same age; primarily composers of opera who revered the Viennese style; and raised as Roman Catholics. Perhaps the most telling affinity was that both had attempted to reform and renew opera in their respective countries. Yet appearances were deceptive. This was, in fact, one of the most unexpected encounters in the history of music.

In 1826, Rossini was at the height of his career. For over a decade he had enjoyed a global renown. After making his name at the Bourbon court in Naples, he moved to Paris having been 'headhunted' by the French court to become the musical director of the Théatre-Italien. His appointed task was to reform French opera along Rossinian lines. He was the most exciting operatic composer of the age who had breathed new life into Italian opera by challenging many ossified norms and production values, the net effect of which was that opera became, for the first time, a widespread preoccupation of the European middle classes. For their part, the ruling élites had no trouble in accepting Rossini whom they saw as safe and conservative, a composer who was prepared to work with the architects of Restoration Europe rather than against them. Despite the composer's consistent disavowals of an interest in politics, his career was inescapably a 'political' one, not least in its sources of patronage – which included King Ferdinand I of the Two Sicilies, Prince Metternich, Louis XVIII and Charles X of France – not to mention the Holy See.

In 1826, therefore, the contrast between Weber and Rossini could hardly have been more pronounced. The German composer arrived in Paris in the last stages of consumption, with only three months to live. In artistic terms also, Weber was at a low ebb, having for years struggled (almost single-handedly) to create a German national operatic tradition, with only limited success. He had only managed to compose one successful opera, *Der Freischütz* (1821), and although this work had achieved popularity in Germany, its impact had been uneven, with much critical opinion ranged against it.[9] For our purposes, the key difference between Rossini and Weber was that the latter was an intensely nationalist composer, whereas for the former the question of a relationship between national identity and music did not arise. In this respect, it was a meeting of the old and the new, on the frontier between the cosmopolitan eighteenth century and the nationalist nineteenth century.

Through his operas Weber wished to harness music to his nation's interest. For him, music was part of a struggle for the German soul, an aspiration which was as every bit as political as artistic. Weber resented the domination of opera by Italians. Like so many other German artists, he had been politicized by the national uprising of 1812 against the French, a point on which Sir Julius Benedict, his pupil and biographer, was quite specific: 'Now for the first time he was initiated to higher aspirations and brought into contact with the best of his countrymen in every condition of life'.[10] Thereafter, Weber fought against Italian hegemony in opera. His objections were twofold: that Italian domination was obstructing the growth of a native German opera tradition; and that its obsession with entertainment revealed little learning and spiritual content. Weber made no secret of his dislike of Rossini's operas, and consciously intended that *Der Freischütz* should usher in a new epoch in German opera. The two composers were rivals, but this was a rivalry perceived only on Weber's side; as even his son, Max von Weber, was later to admit: 'the antipathy between the two was not so passionate in Rossini, and that was because of the generous feelings of the more fortunate of the two'.[11]

Given this antipathy, we are entitled to ask: why did Weber visit Rossini in Paris? He was clearly apprehensive over the prospect, going as far as to ascertain in advance whether he would be welcome. Max von Weber states that it was only at Cherubini's prompting that his father 'summoned up the courage' to make the visit. Max suggests to his readers that it was a meeting of equals, initiated by Weber 'from an urge to make his peace with everyone in this world'.[12] According to Rossini's account, Weber was indeed in a conciliatory mood, and was especially concerned about critical articles that he had written about Rossini's music in the past.[13] In fact, Weber's visit was that of a supplicant and it was the weak and consumptive visitor who had to climb the stairs to the Italian's luxury apartment. Rossini's welcome was so warm that Weber paid a second visit specifically to request letters of introduction for his trip to London – probably the main purpose of the whole initiative. Rossini, who had enjoyed great success in London two years earlier, gladly obliged with a 'letter of presentation' to King George IV and other leading figures in London society.[14] It is surely significant that this important encounter was not recorded in Grove's *Dictionary*, since neither Philip Spitta (on Weber) nor Gustave Chouquet (on Rossini) chose to mention it. As it turned out, Weber did not return alive from London that summer and his body was laid to rest in Moorfields Chapel, Finsbury, on 21 June 1826.

Yet, although Rossini seemed in 1826 to be all-powerful, and was seen as patronizing Weber, these positions were to be diametrically reversed in the eyes of music history. For posterity, it was Weber and not his 'rival' who triumphed. Rossini was soon to witness the erosion of his reputation at the hands of his foes. Thoughts evoked by Weber's wretched death in exile and failure in London exerted a powerful influence over German musicians and critics in the years to come. Weber was increasingly seen as a heroic martyr who gave his life fighting foreign domination of German music. According to the school of German music criticism – within a generation to achieve a hegemonic position in European terms – Weber had the leading place in the pantheon of German music. Fifty years later, Spitta could confidently assert that 'the historian of German music in the nineteenth century will have to take Weber as his starting-point. His influence was even greater than that of Beethoven.'[15] In stark contrast, during Rossini's bicentenary year, the *Musical Times* confirmed the perceived wisdom on Rossini handed down to us by his German adversaries:

> Of all Rossini's works history had accorded *Il Barbiere di Siviglia* a special place – the only one of his operas to have a continuous record of

performance from its premiere to the present day; the only one which even today secures its position in the repertoire of every opera house.[16]

'Le Dieu de l'harmonie'

I went there on the invitation of Prince Metternich, who wrote me a most amiable letter. Being *le dieu de l'harmonie*, as the letter expressed it, I must not stay away when harmony was so important![17]

Nothing better expresses Rossini's importance on the political stage than Metternich's invitation to Rossini to attend the Congress of Verona (1822). It was almost as though the composer had become a great power in his own right. Despite his later disavowals Rossini was the composer who best expressed the spirit of the Restoration in music: through his patronal relations, politics flowed into his creative process. For a generation after Waterloo his music represented one expression of a resurgent ideology. Rossini epitomized 'Restoration Europe' in music, a loyal servant of European dynasties and chancellories who conveyed their glories to the new opera-going public.

Despite Europe's revolutionary upheavals, Italians had never relinquished their domination of opera. Even in France, they maintained their influence during the Directory and the First Empire.[18] Italian opera showed how well it could adapt to the needs and tastes of a revolutionary epoch, and still further success beckoned after Waterloo, with the emergence of a new young leader: Rossini, who looked set to extend the hegemony of musical Italy well into the new century. This situation was particularly galling in Germany, where there was an increasing demand for a native operatic tradition, free of the language and traditions of Italy. The first stirrings of opera as a German national art-form can be detected in Mozart's *Die Entführung aus dem Serail* (1782) and *Die Zauberflöte* (1791). Yet even Mozart, a self-declared 'German' artist, had to confront the rivalry between German and Italian opera in the Vienna of Joseph II.[19] The most famous occasion was in 1786 when, in an opera 'competition' (a kind of duel) staged between Salieri and Mozart, the result was a decisive Italian victory.[20] After this public setback, Mozart set his face against writing opera in German and, for the next five years, composed only in Italian: *Le Nozze di Figaro, Don Giovanni, Cosi Fan Tutte* and *La Clemenza di Tito*.

In the generation which followed the Mozart–Salieri encounter, German opera hardly stirred, despite the best efforts of German princely patrons and court-conductors.[21] German musical patriots failed to understand how their nation could be so deficient and disorganized in opera. Beethoven's *Leonora* (1805–6, revised as *Fidelio* 1814) was the only German opera to emerge from this general gloom, But even in its final form it failed to build upon its initial success in Vienna. Meanwhile, in 1812, the 'national' uprising against the French focused German national pride as never before and, more than ever, the influence of Italian opera was resented as an alien presence in Germany and was seen as a barrier to national progress and a denial of the nation's musical prowess.

All this should be viewed in the context of the growth of a distinctive form of German Romanticism which marked philosophy and letters. This phenomenon had many characteristics, including a fascination for the German past and folk-tales and legends, which were viewed as a storehouse of the *Volk*. Disagreement arose over a political agenda: while some German Romantics held to conservative values of monarchy and aristocratic authority, others wanted radical transformation. Yet all could agree on the rejection of the cultural cosmopolitanism of the past, and on a new culture as the starting-point of the *Volk*'s resurgence. The importance of music (especially folk-music) in the national renewal was continually stressed.

It was precisely when musical Germany was in ferment that Rossini appeared as a powerful new force. He was perceived as a versatile and 'contemporary' artist, who put the issues of the day onto the operatic stage. He was immediately acknowledged as a force for change and renewal, a characteristic expression of the 'romantic' spirit. He was young, amiable and good-looking; his interest in the 'poetic' aspects of the medieval, together with his fluency, flamboyance and highly personal style, were all deemed to be hallmarks of a new sensibility.[22] But the spread of Rossini's influence was regarded with dismay by German music nationalists. Disarmingly, Rossini espoused much that was 'German'; even as a young student in Bologna, he was known for his admiration of Haydn and 'German' harmony. However, for him, the patron – whether prince or banker – was a client who paid for a commercial transaction in a free market.

Indeed Italy's forces of reaction welcomed the new operatic lion as a someone with whom they could do business. Rossini quickly reached an accommodation with the restored order through the Neapolitan impresario, Domenico Barbaja.[23] Having signed a contract to direct the two royal theatres in Naples, Rossini proved himself to be a powerful weapon in the hands of King Ferdinand. The success of *Elisabetta regina d'Inghilterra* (1815), *Otello* (1816) and *La donna del lago* (1819) reflected well on the royal patron. Beneath the brilliant music and its stage production, Rossini's work underpinned such conservative notions as the magnanimity and wisdom of monarchs (*Elisabetta*), and the futility of rebellion and the mercy of kings (*La donna del lago*). In addition, Rossini wrote 'official' music for the Court; for example, the Cantata *Omaggio umiliato* (1819), to mark the king's recovery from illness. Rossini's reputation was enhanced by success elsewhere in the peninsula, not least in Rome, with *Il barbiere di Siviglia* (1816). This setting of Beaumarchais' play again confirms its composer's conservative instincts. Light-years away from Mozart's setting of Beaumarchais' sequel *Le nozze di Figaro* – the play which Napoleon described as 'the first stone flung in the French Revolution' – in Rossini's opera, Count Almaviva pursues marriage rather than seduction, seeking to confer title and wealth rather than to ruin a reputation. In all, the eponymous barber is the count's accomplice, not his opponent, his joyous helper in smoothing the path of true love. Rossini's *Barbiere* lives in that 'apolitical' world of eighteenth-century art, where masters and servants know their place and acknowledge only one enemy – boredom.

One of the reasons for the enduring popularity of Rossini and Italian opera was the power of the so-called 'cult of the south'. This was most strongly manifested in Germany where, after the publication of Goethe's *Travels in Italy* (1786–8) many German intellectuals succumbed to the allure of a land replete with history and art, whose people were sensual and spiritually at ease. Fashionable Italy worked to the advantage of its opera composers. Rossini had a quintessentially Italian perspective, which stressed that music should, above all, be pleasing and beautiful. For many Germans it encapsulated the passion, brilliance, easy sociability and irrepressible naturalness of the peninsula. Rossini's success in Germany began with *L'Italiana in Algeri* in

Munich (1816) which brought the composer the support of Prince Metternich, the Austrian Chancellor, who was already 'infatuated with the Italians, [and] with bel canto'.[24]

Yet many German intellectuals refused to be swept away by what came to be known as 'Rossini Fever'. The influential E. T. A. Hoffmann thought his music to be 'contaminated', and urged that it should be 'dispossessed by true artists'.[25] He particularly despised Rossini's trivialization of music in the pursuit of ephemeral pleasure. Who then would dare lift the standard of German opera? To many contemporaries, only one candidate had the will and the confidence: Carl Maria von Weber. The young Weber had already excited nationalists with patriotic songs, and his cantata *Kampf und Sieg* (1815) – written in commemoration of the victory at Waterloo. He seemed determined to take the field and challenge the Italian operatic domination in the name of 'young Germany'.[26] Yet as a composer, Weber had still not made his mark. He had attempted several opera projects, but none had been performed before his one palpable success, *Der Freischütz* (1821).

Weber's views about opera invested its dramatic ideal with a morally imperative status. Like other German Romantics, he regarded art as a 'divine revelation, a language of the soul requiring a devout approach from artist and audience alike'.[27] One of Weber's first actions on arrival as court composer at Dresden was to publish an article in *Abendzeitung,* the city's influential literary journal, setting out his intentions for fostering German opera on the Elbe:

> The Italians and French have fashioned for themselves a distinct form of opera, with a framework which allows them to move with ease and freedom. Not so the Germans. Eager in the pursuit of knowledge, and constantly yearning after progress, they endeavour to appropriate anything which they see to be good in others. [...] With the rest of the world the gratification of the senses is the main object; the German wants a work of art complete in itself, with each part rounded off and compacted into a perfect whole.[28]

Such thinking had no place for 'Italian frenzy', which celebrated 'meaningless ornamentation' and valued charm and skill before content. Weber's commitment to a German operatic art free from the taint of Italian triviality made him into a fervent anti-

Rossinian. The German composer was also perfectly aware that Rossini, by dint of his sheer popularity, could set back the progress of German opera for many years. As one of the characters in Weber's unfinished novel observed:

> At the present moment the danger lies with the scirocco of Rossini blowing from the south. His warmth will quickly disappear; for just as the bite of the tarantula makes people dance, it is not long before they sink exhausted to the ground – cured.[29]

Weber's perception of Rossini lies in the fear of the parching, corrupting, seductiveness of the south, complete with undertones of 'primitive' Africa. As his son, Max, recalled

> Since he had achieved recognition, Weber had battled against the Italians. He was the first one who took up the struggle for the pure German spirit in opera, as a musician of equal standing.[30]

Weber was prepared to challenge Rossini not just in terms of composition, but with a new weapon which was a German invention. Musical criticism was evolving to a recognizably modern form in Germany and Weber was among the first to grasp its potential.[31] He wrote for several newspapers and journals including J. F. Rochlitz's pioneering *Allgemeine Musikalische Zeitung*. As early as 1810 he founded the *Harmonischer Verein*, a society whose members were both musicians and literary men, committed to 'the elevation of musical criticism by musicians themselves'.[32] Sixty years after the composer's death, Spitta identified music criticism as a crucial aspect of his originality:

> Our great composers from Handel to Beethoven did not meddle in authorship. In this respect, as in so many others, Weber was the first of a new generation of artists. It pleased him to reveal the ideas with which his mind was crowded in words as well as in music.[33]

For all this, Weber's main armament was deployed in the opera *Der Freischütz*. He announced that the première (in Berlin, 18 June 1821) was 'a day hailed as of good omen' since it was the anniversary of the battle of Waterloo.[34] One is tempted to see the opening action of the opera, Kilian's musket-shot shattering its target-star, to the people's shout of 'Victory!', as a metaphor for the first blow struck in a new battle of the operas. German music historians sympathetic to the aspirations of the 'young Germany' applauded *Freischütz*. As the composer's son, Max, later wrote 'Weber had achieved, in June 1821, for the German opera, what Blucher had done, in June 1815, for German independence'.[35] *Freischütz* was indeed enough of a success to establish Weber as the standard-bearer of a national opera. But the acclaim was by no means universal: one dissenting voice was that of Franz Schubert, who declared that *Freischütz* contained 'only one musician-like piece'.[36]

Yet as *Freischütz* was being hailed as an opera of national importance, Rossini arrived in Vienna, for a season of his works performed at the Kärntnertortheater (April–June 1822). This was the outcome of Barbaja being appointed general-director of the theatre. The festival staged no fewer than five Rossini operas, using the Naples forces and proved a sensational success with the Viennese musical public. This was despite 'the anti-Rossinian writings of jingoistic, anti-Italian, pro-Teutonic critics'.[37] The *Allgemeine Musikalische Zeitung* commented that 'this is a true epidemic, against which no physician could discover a preventative'.[38] The 1822 season made Rossini's reputation in Vienna, placing his operas at the heart of the Imperial capital's musical life for years to come. Even Friedrich Hegel became a convert, writing to his wife (in 1824):

> As long as I have money to go to the Italian opera and pay for my return trip, I shall remain in Vienna! ... These artists have voices, spirit, and warmth that are theirs alone. Now I understand why Rossini's music is denounced in Germany.[39]

The stir which Rossini's season caused in Vienna, also, as we have seen, put the composer in a position successfully to seek an interview with the elusive and cantankerous Beethoven. As Rossini reported to Wagner many years later, the point of his visit was simply to express 'admiration for his genius' and gratitude for allowing him into the presence.[40] Rossini also reported how deeply upsetting he had found the destitution and privation in which Beethoven lived. So moved was the Italian composer that, the same evening, at a gala dinner given in his honour by Prince Metternich, he felt able to criticize members of the Austrian court for neglecting Beethoven and for allowing him to live in degrading squalor. These strictures, however, met only with aristocratic coolness. Undaunted, Rossini took matters into his own hands: he first attempted to raise a subscription fund to create an annual income for Beethoven; and, when this failed, he then tried to raise enough money to buy Beethoven a decent place to live. However, this idea too foundered for lack of support.[41] For many Germans, it must have been all too much to bear: the Italian 'musical millionaire', as the *Allgemeine Musikalische Zeitung* had dubbed him, offering to raise a hardship fund for the neglected hero of musical Germany. It was certainly a sequence of events which later German historians preferred to pass over in silence.

Such was the impact of the Rossini season on the German musical world that it led to the revival of Beethoven's *Fidelio* at the Kärntnertortheater in November 1822, in a production which ran for a paltry six performances. Another outcome was that for his second (1823) season at the Kärntnertor, Barbaja, sensing the annoyance of his German critics, had taken care to commission operas from Weber and Schubert. For Weber, the new work, *Euryanthe*, was a second opportunity to advance the theatrical principles which he held dear. The new work attracted a great deal of support: Max von Weber reports that the better part of the Viennese press craved 'for a powerful experience in a truly great German work'; and that Beethoven too wished Weber luck with the observation that there was a 'space on the shelf for a great German opera'.[42]

However, *Euryanthe* was a flop. Its first run ended in humiliation after only twenty performances, with the partisans of Italian opera dubbing the new work, 'Ennuyante'. It was a disaster from which Weber's reputation never recovered in his lifetime. Schubert, the reception of whose opera *Fierrabras* relied heavily on the senior composer's success, was downcast and wrote to his friend, Franz von Schober: 'Weber's *Euryanthe* turned out badly; its poor reception was in my opinion quite justified. [There is...] scarcely any hope for my opera'.[43] He was proved right, and *Fierrabras* was cancelled in rehearsal. Schubert's anger turned on the champion of German opera with venom and declared of *Euryanthe*: 'This is no music. There is no finale, no concerted piece according to the rules of art. It is all striving after effect. And he [Weber] finds fault with Rossini! It is utterly dry and dismal.'⁴⁴ So far from striking a blow for the cause, therefore, *Euryanthe* proved a self-inflicted wound. It drove Schubert's opera off the stage. For fifteen months, Weber himself ceased composition and eventually left Germany to seek financial rewards in England. Not only was Weber's career unhinged, but his operatic ideals were compromised: of his last opera, *Oberon*, written in English, Weber admitted that it was 'foreign' to his operatic 'ideas and maxims' and did not even deserve the title of 'opera'.⁴⁵ In this light, it might be argued that Weber died of nothing other than 'Rossini Fever'.

After the failure of *Euryanthe*, Beethoven seemed to be Germany's only hope. After all, the master had taken a stand against the use of Italian musical terms, preferring the use of German equivalents. Beethoven was an acknowledged German patriot, who celebrated a French defeat in 1813 with his *Wellingtons Sieg*. In the aftermath of the *Rossinifest* in Vienna, an atmosphere of crisis prevailed. Some evidence points to a desperate attempt to bring Beethoven into the fray. As Schindler, Beethoven's archivist and biographer, later recalled:

> The violence of the current carried everyone away with it. No one asked in which direction he was borne, for all were enchanted, intoxicated, with the roulades of the Rossini school. Few, indeed, were they who could resist the force of such a stream and preserve in all its purity their taste for the truly beautiful and ideal in art.⁴⁶

The situation was so grave that an approach was made, in the form of a 'Memorial' signed by the great and the good of Viennese cultural life, for Beethoven to write a new opera. Dispatched to the composer in February 1824, the document powerfully expressed the Rossini 'panic' which was gripping Vienna's musical establishment:

> our German soil has been invaded by the footsteps of foreign art – the seat of the German muse usurped – and German works have become but the echo of those of strangers; threatening a second childhood of taste to succeed its golden age? You alone are able to secure activity to the efforts of the best among us. You alone can bestow new life on national art and on the German opera.⁴⁷

Only Beethoven, it seemed, could save German music. The outcome of the 'Memorial' was a proposal that Beethoven work on a libretto on the subject of Melusine by Franz Grillparzer. Although no opera materialized what did emerge from this new awareness of Beethoven's importance was the grand première in Vienna (May 1824) of the *Ninth Symphony* and parts of *Missa Solemnis*. This occasion was a financial failure despite its prestigious backing. Even more alarming – for some – was that by this time even Beethoven was 'taking a more commercial view of his position than usual'.[48] Could it be that, with Rossini's music sweeping all before it, 'Rossini values' – focusing on the financial rewards of music – were also threatening the very sanctuary of German music with pollution?

Meanwhile other German composers rushed to meet the Rossini challenge and stem the tide of disaster. Louis Spohr wrote several operas, the most successful being *Jessonda*, premièred in Cassel in 1823. In order to strengthen the impact of *Jessonda*, Spohr addressed a strident *Call to German Composers (Aufruf an deutsche Komponisten)* which set out his ideas on the future of German opera along Weberian lines. Mendelssohn too was drawn into the fray with *Die Hochzeit des Camacho,* his only completed opera given its only performance in Berlin in 1827. Overall, however, the cause of national German music remained parlous. Italian operatic hegemony had not been broken though some comfort lay in the success of many leading German courts and civic authorities in curtailing the scope and scale of Italian competition. By the end of the decade, moreover, German music had been cast into the greatest gloom with the deaths of Weber (1826), Beethoven (1827) and Schubert (1828).

In contrast, the star of Rossini seemed ever in the ascendant. The first biography of the composer – by the French writer Stendhal – appeared in 1824, being published simultaneously in Paris, London and Leipzig. Stendhal's *Vie de Rossini* seems to have been a conscious response to the onslaught from Germany. It championed Italian music in general, and Rossini in particular. Worse still, Stendhal announced that the German obsession with 'the black night of harmony' led to an impasse where music was reduced to 'scientific knowledge' and where art would become the preserve of the 'musical physicist'. Rossini was the champion of melody, who stood at the forefront of a revolution in music – after which the dominance of Italian opera in France would be assured.[49] Right on cue, Rossini was invited to Paris to continue his career in close association with the restored Bourbon court, as we have seen, his contract specifically directed him to undertake the musical direction of the Théatre-Italien where he was expected to initiate radical reforms and produce his own works. The one new opera to emerge was *Il viaggio a Reims*, performed specifically for the coronation of Charles X, in 1825. Rossini was never closer to the Restoration system than in this work, with its multinational group of stranded travellers singing the praises of the last Bourbon autocrat. In 1826, Rossini was formally brought into royal service: with a large salary, he became Premier Compositeur du Roi and Inspecteur Général du Chant en France. His task was to compose operas set in French for the Paris Opera, and over the following years, he re-fashioned French opera, in particular with two new works, *Le Comte Ory* (1828) and *Guillaume Tell* (1829). As H. Sutherland Edwards commented in the first English biography of Rossini: 'During the Restoration and until the Revolution of 1830, it was a sign of a good royalist to praise Rossini's music, and a sign of liberalism to condemn it.'[50] Yet throughout his life, Rossini insisted that his art and life were untouched by politics:

> I have never meddled in politics. I was a musician, and it did not enter my head to be anything else, though I take the greatest interest in everything that goes on, especially in the fate of my native country.[51]

'Der Lucifer in der Musik'

> For Weber, Rossini was the Lucifer of Music, originally the most beautiful of the angels, but also the one who fell the furthest: 'He can do everything, even the good, but the Devil in him just does not want to'.[52]

Where the nation's composers had failed in the 1820s, German critics would take up the fight for the high ideals of musical Germany. The site of struggle switched from the opera house to the printed page. The leadership of this new phase of the contest was assumed by Robert Schumann (1810–56). Schumann sought radically to alter the tastes of the musical public, under the sway, as he pictured them, of 'philistines', antagonistic to 'true' art. The critic for Schumann was an artist, a musical poet and a high-priest of a new religion. As co-founder and editor of *Neue Zeitschrift für Musik* (1834–45), Schumann championed the values of his *Davidsbund*, a fictional group dedicated to fighting musical barbarism, that is, those 'philistines' who mistook virtuosity for genius and technical elan for profundity. He proclaimed Beethoven as the great German artist – a hero of the nation who had taught his people 'patriotism and greatness of heart' in his music.[53] From the desk of the *Neue Zeitschrift*, Schumann campaigned ceaselessly for a monument to this 'eagle' of music:

> to build in his name an academy for German music, where music, his word, may be taught ... a school of poets, a school of music in the Grecian sense, to be opened by the hands of a pure priesthood to the chosen ones only.[54]

Schumann was a polemicist and mobilizer of opinion, a critic who re-defined the parameters of musical journalism. More importantly he was also a German patriot who regarded his journal as an instrument of artistic progress in his country. Schumann viewed the artist-critic as reformer, even to the point of direct intervention in the socio-political process as in his support of the 1848 Dresden Revolt. Looking back at the condition of musical Germany in the 1830s, and the task that then lay ahead of him as musician and critic, Schumann later reflected:

> The state of music at that time can hardly be said to have offered any grounds for rejoicing. Rossini still reigned supreme in the theatre ... And yet only a few years had passed since Beethoven, Carl Maria von Weber and Schubert had dwelt among us![55]

As these words suggest, Schumann saw Rossini – or perhaps 'Rossini' – as the major obstacle to musical reform. He thought of the Italian composer as mercenary and cynic, an accomplice in the tyranny of the 'philistines' – above all, therefore, as a threat to Germany's musical future:

> It would be one-sided of us to condemn Rossini, but that the encouragement he meets with is great, out of all proportion with that bestowed upon German efforts. Rossini is an admirable scene-painter; but take away the critically managed light, and the alluring stage distance, and see what remains! ... When I hear so much foolish

twaddle about him as saviour and consoler, I thrill to anger to my very finger-tips.[56]

Schumann loathed the Italian's servility to the social order of the Restoration: 'Rossini and his *confrères* always closed [a work ...] with "Your most humble servant"!'[57] In later years a convention was to emerge in German musicological circles that the meeting (dealt with above) between Beethoven and Rossini had never taken place. Schumann may have been adumbrating this tendency when he writes, in a contemptuous metaphor, that 'The butterfly flew in the way of the eagle; he moved aside lest he might have crushed the insect with the beating of his wings'.[58] This image is not only expressive of the desired relations between German and Italian music, but eloquent testimony to the national view of Rossini as superficially attractive, fragile, colourful and impermanent. In another of his 'Aphorisms' – this time specifically comparing Italian and German styles – Schumann again took up the butterfly metaphor:

> See the lovely floating butterfly! yet brush away his coloured dust, and he becomes a miserable, unregarded creature; but after the flight of centuries, the skeletons of gigantic creations exist, to the astonishment and admiration of posterity.[59]

If Schumann had pointed the way, others soon followed the signs. In the case of Franz Liszt, this was part of an almost Pauline conversion to 'German' sensibilities. Although his initial fame was as a travelling prodigy-virtuoso, by the 1830s Liszt had acquired a certain shame about such a career. He evolved into a political radical, German patriot, and a supporter of the 1830 revolutions.[60] Liszt despised Rossini and his influence. After their first meeting in 1837, he referred to Rossini as 'rich, idle and illustrious'.[61] Although they met and corresponded occasionally, there is no evidence that Liszt changed his opinion – even after he had himself become rich and illustrious.

Liszt's musical ideology was expressed in his work for the Parisian journal *La Revue et Gazette Musicale* in the period 1835–40.[62] Like Schumann, Liszt regarded Beethoven as central and immutable, and Germany as the only site of genuine musical progress.[63] As for Italy, Liszt saw only stagnation, a land where musicians were not prepared to guide public taste in the appreciation of serious music.[64] In Liszt's extended polemic *Considérations sur la situation des artistes* (1835), he lamented the subjugation of art to the forces of the market, which led to moral anarchy and a deadly isolation. The answer – notably close to that of his admirer Schumann – was a mobilization of those who wanted to save music from spiritual collapse.[65]

Perhaps more important in terms of opinion-formation than either of these composers, however, was the music-historian, Anton Schindler (1796–1864). Schindler's authority stemmed mainly from his personal contact with Beethoven, and his custody of the master's papers. More than any other figure, he created the Beethoven cult which dominated European music after 1840. The originality of Schindler's *Biographie* lies in its celebration of Beethoven as 'Romantic Hero': great yet human, humble yet noble, classical yet Romantic, German yet universal. Schindler's Beethoven was a martyr to his art, a composer for whom artistic freedom went hand-in-hand with political freedom.[66] As for the arch-monarchist Rossini – quite literally, Schindler denied him any houseroom. After Ferdinand Hiller published an essay on Rossini (1856) in which the Beethoven–Rossini meeting of 1822 was mentioned, Schindler vehemently denied that this encounter ever took place:

> As for refusing visitors, only one instance is noteworthy. Twice Rossini tried to gain access to Beethoven [and] Beethoven always made some excuse ... We should not fail to mention that Rossini's desire to pay homage to the German master became acute ...[67]

Rossini was, of course, aware of these politically-inspired claims and felt he had to set the record straight in exchanges with eminent German musicians including Wagner and the critic Hanslick. The latter duly reported the composer's detailed recollections of his meeting with Beethoven, and was so incensed by Schindler's dishonesty that he openly criticized 'those musical Jacobins who had glorified the brutal German virtue of denying admittance to Rossini'.[68] But the damage had already been done and Schindler's version of events became the preferred orthodoxy of musical history. It was as though the door to Beethoven's lodgings, remaining firmly closed against Rossini, became a striking trope of the rejection of the Italian composer's aspiration to belong to the priesthood of music. This exclusion also seems like a kind of divine judgement on Rossini who, like Weber's 'Lucifer', was thereby cast into exterior darkness by the 'God', Beethoven.

Worst of all for Rossini's reputation was the entry into the lists of Wagner, Germany's emerging opera champion, and Rossini's most powerful adversary in the 1840s. During his stay in Paris during 1839–42, Wagner kept starvation at bay by writing music reviews. One of the more significant of these was a notice of the première of Rossini's *Stabat Mater* in 1842. This was one of the rare occasions when a German critic had the opportunity of covering a major Rossini première. Schumann published this piece as a leading article in his *Neue Zeitschrift*, placing a featured quotation (from Rückert) to underline editorial support for Wagner's views:

> Of all our evils 'tis the sorriest token
> How wide the spurious has spread its rule,
> That e'en the genuine with false shame is spoken.[69]

What followed was a bitter attack on the new work and its composer, excoriating Rossini's enduring power to excite the musical world. France, erstwhile enemy of 1812 and a nation for which Wagner already had a deep loathing, was also a target: 'Rossini is pious – all the world is pious, and the Parisian salons have been turned into praying-cells. It is extraordinary! So long as this man lives, he'll always be the mode!' Subliminally as well as consciously, Wagner's words encapsulate the German case against Rossini: envy, sexual innuendo, the suspicion of religiosity and rage at Rossini's 'perversion' of the true purpose of music. Present too is contempt for a composer who had abandoned the celestial art for indulgence, idleness and worship of the material: 'Rossini had let nothing be heard of him for ten long years: he sat in Bologna, ate pastry, and made wills'. The near-starving Wagner conjured up the scene when Rossini, in Spain on a holiday, first had the idea for the *Stabat Mater*:

> It was on a journey which he [Rossini] was making with his good friend the Paris banker, Herr Aguado; – they were sitting at ease in a well-appointed chariot, and admiring the beauties of Nature, – Herr

Aguado was nibbling chocolate, Rossini eating pastry. Then it suddenly occurred to Herr Aguado that he really had robbed his compatriots more than was proper, and, smitten with remorse, he drew the chocolate from his mouth; – not to be behind such a beautiful example, Rossini gave his teeth a rest, and confessed that all through life he had devoted too much time to pastry.

According to Wagner, Rossini's penance for pastry was the *Stabat Mater*. The sheer rage of these passages amuses and repels; Wagner presents the work under review (which he had not yet heard!) as no more than another Rossini confidence-trick, beguiling a bourgeois public into feeling itself to be in touch with the profundities of Art-Music. Wagner, whose own work had yet to find a publisher, ended with a hyperbolical vision of Europe going to war over the publishing rights of the new work: 'Spain, France, Germany, all fall to blows around this Stabat: Action! Fight! Tumult! Revolution! Horror!' The bellicose language was both deliberate and appropriate.

Wagner already saw himself as predestined to succeed where Weber and others had failed, and to win through to the grail of a triumphant German opera. The decisive breakthrough occurred with the première of *Lohengrin*, under Liszt's direction in Weimar in 1850. This occasion was designed to affirm Germany's musical tradition in the wake of the failed revolutions of 1848–9 and to confirm Wagner's position as the new hero of German Music.[70] At the time, faithful to the Beethoven–Weber martyrological tradition, Wagner himself was in political exile in Switzerland, a fact that accentuated the intensely political nature of the première. In *Lohengrin* Wagner took up Weber's sword, and made German opera into a contemporary force with truly international appeal; as Edward Dannreuther recorded in the first edition of Grove's *Dictionary*: 'From that memorable night dates the success of the Wagner movement in Germany'.[71]

But by now the anti-Rossini movement was not restricted to Germany. Hector Berlioz (1803–69) shared to a large degree the aesthetic preoccupations of the German Romantics and himself aspired to write a new kind of opera. Accordingly, he pitched into the critical debates with gusto, declaring his allegiance to the high ideals of Gluckian opera and a concomitant loathing of Rossini's anti-dramatic conventions. In his first foray into musical criticism, Berlioz wrote to the arts daily *Corsaire,* attacking adherents of the Rossinian cult:

> Who would seriously deny that all Rossini's operas put together could not stand comparison with a single line of recitative by Gluck, three bars of melody by Mozart or Spontini, the least chorus by Lesueur![72]

Berlioz's journalism ranged widely both in its themes and in its impact on contemporary opinion and, like Weber and Schumann, he understood the power of criticism. Of his long career as a writer, Berlioz observed: 'in one sense the Press is a more useful weapon than the spear of Achilles'.[73] Moreover, for all his enthusiasm for the beauty and romance of Italy (for Berlioz was also a follower of the 'cult of the south'), his opinions on the condition of Italian music were severe:

> Music for the Italians is a sensual pleasure and nothing more. For this noble expression of the mind they have hardly more respect than for the art of cooking. They want a score that, like a plate of macaroni, can be assimilated without their having to think about it or even pay any attention to it.[74]

Indeed, some of Rossini's own compatriots were prepared to admit the force of these criticisms. His aesthetic came under attack in Italy from a very influential quarter: Giuseppe Mazzini (1805–72), republican and revolutionary, founder of the 'Young Italy' movement. In 1833, Mazzini published his tract *Philosophy of Music* (*Filosofica della musica*), which condemned the condition of Italian music, declaring that instead of being the 'harmonious voice of creation' it had become a 'mere amusement' to counter the boredom of 'an idle, sensual and corrupt generation'. Mazzini believed that the construction of the new Italy demanded a music that would, in tandem with poetry, inform 'national and religious education': music – in other words – which would reach out to a social idea. Mazzini saw Rossini as part of Italy's 'problem' to the solution of which he devoted a life's work.

> More powerful in fancy and imagination than profound in thought or sentiment ... lacking that constancy and nobility of soul ... he [Rossini] sought fame instead of true glory, sacrificed the God to the idol and worshipped the effect not the aim.

Mazzini was also in no doubt that music had to express an idea of its own times, play its part in the nation's history, and free itself of the corrupting values of materialism and individualism. Therefore,

> the first thing to be done is to emancipate ourselves from the Rossinian school of Music, and from the spirit of the epoch of which he is the representative ... If music is to be regenerated, it must be spiritualised ...[75]

The 'music of the future' (as Mazzini intriguingly expressed it) lay in the reintegration of music with poetry and in the synthesis of Italian melody and German harmony. Although several of Rossini's operas held their place in the European repertoire – and his heritage briefly flourished in the work of Bellini and Donizetti – the initiative in opera, even in Italy, had passed to the Germans.[76]

Return of Heroes

When Weber lay dying in his London rooms, his thoughts constantly focused on the bitter fact that he would never see his homeland again. When, over forty years later, Rossini too was facing death, he clearly indicated a desire to be buried among the artistic heroes of France in the Père Lachaise cemetery. Thus is illustrated a profound political distinction – Rossini's innate inter- (or non-) national *persona*, on the one hand, Weber's intense identification with his nation, on the other. The response to these testimonies of their family and admirers adds weight to the antiphony. In 1844, eighteen years after his death, and with the acclamation of all concerned, the remains of Carl Maria von Weber were transported with cost, pomp and ceremony to be buried in the Fatherland. For many years Rossini's widow firmly resisted all suggestions – including a proposal, conveyed by Giuseppe Verdi, from the new Italian state – that the composer's embalmed corpse be repatriated to his native land. Eventually, she relented to the extent of permitting such a transposition after her own demise. In 1887 this event was finally organized, and Rossini was laid to rest in the Santa Croce church in Florence – which had now become in effect Italy's national pantheon – with all the circumstantial obsequies of a state funeral.

Carl Maria von Weber, Germany's hero of the 'battle of the operas', returned home from the cold earth of London in 1844. In life, Weber had never fulfilled his own aspirations, and in truth was less than a great success as either composer or critic. Now, in the sanctification of death, he achieved precisely that triumph which had eluded him – though less formally, this also amounted to a 'state funeral'. His self-appointed heir, Wagner, was the S*chauspieldirektor* of this ritual drama of repatriation. The costs and organization of the event were considerable. Amidst a notable stir of interest in Germany, Weber's remains were exhumed from Finsbury, transported by rail, ship, and then by a special 'funeral train' – a journey of nearly 1000 miles – to be re-buried with great solemnity, in the family vault at Friedrichstadt Catholic Cemetery, Dresden. Wagner composed the chorus *An Webers Grabe* for the occasion, as well as the *Trauermusik* based on themes from Weber's ill-fated *Euryanthe*. Notably enough, the former contained material which directly anticipated Siegfried's Funeral Music (from *Götterdämmerung*): apt enough tribute to a German *Held*. The peroration of Wagner's graveside elegy ran thus:

> And lo! the Briton may yield thee justice, the Frenchman admiration; but the German alone can love thee ... From out the world, which thou bedazzledst, we lead thee back into thy country, the bosom of thy family! Ask the hero who went out to victory, what most rejoiced him after glorious days upon the field of honour? For sure the threshold of the father-house, where wife and child await him.[77]

A quarter of a century later Wagner was to reflect on the triumph of German music over adversity in his biography of Beethoven published in the latter's centenary year (1870). This work, written from the august perspective of Germany's musical conquests, stressed that the salvation of music itself was at stake in the battles which Beethoven, Weber, and Wagner himself, had fought: 'The German spirit ... stood up against an artificially constructed corruption of the spirit of European peoples, and saved it'.[78]

In the years between these two events, the site of struggle explored in this chapter had undergone subtle – and in some respects unexpected – topographical alterations. Once *Lohengrin* (1850) had secured the high-ground for German opera, Rossini's reputation took a turn for the better. There were two reasons: the Germans had won and could afford to be magnanimous in victory; secondly, the victory itself had been so complete, occupying so much territory, that division over the spoils was almost inevitable. In this 'civil war', the anti-Wagnerians ironically reached for Rossini as a model. They put forward his work as embodying an older operatic ideal which could be used to counter the alarmingly radical forces unleashed by the Wagnerian aesthetic. Not surprisingly, a leading protagonist of this reaction was Wagner's greatest adversary, Eduard Hanslick, music critic of the *Neue freie Presse* and a committed supporter of the 'classical' spirit in German music. Hanslick's *Vom Musikalisch-Schönen* (1854) polarized German opinion for the remainder of the century.[79] He propounded the hypothesis that music could not 'represent anything' beyond itself and composers (like Wagner) who thought otherwise only pedalled 'vision-promoting medicine'.[80] In this central aesthetic context, Hanslick expressed an admiration for Rossini, whom he considered could 'only think and work in sound', and whose operas he regarded as 'pure music'. Hanslick visited Rossini twice (1860 and 1867) at the composer's Parisian retreat, the 'Villa Rossini' located in the exclusive Parisian suburb of Passy, upon whose gates hung a golden lyre when the maestro was in residence. Hanslick not only thought Rossini to be 'precious and dear', but also saw him as an ally against the *philosophie-komponist*.[81]

Max Maria von Weber also made the pilgrimage to Passy in the 1860s. Now that his father's place in musical history was assured, his account of his father's relationship with Rossini displayed a spirit of reconciliation. Yet it presents a truly Napoleonic vista; here the operatic landscape is filled with the carnage of battle, wherein victorious marshals pick their way between the mounds of slaughtered warriors. Here is the discourse of musical campaigns, of heroism, of victories secured and defeats endured. The bellicose metaphor pervades Weber's memoir, as when describing Rossini's impact on Vienna in 1822: 'surrounded on his victory campaign, and what first-class troops formed the front of his brilliant phalanx so that all his battles were turned into triumphs'.[82]

But surely the most unexpected visitor to the villa of the golden lyre was the ultimate *Heldenkomponist*, Richard Wagner himself. Wagner's motive for visiting Rossini partly stemmed from curiosity over the psychology of a musician who, despite prodigious talent, could simply walk away from music into total retirement. But in addition, some process of reconsideration – even of reconciliation – was present in the German composer's own psyche. Their conversation did not avoid thorny issues – Rossini had evidently not forgotten his rough treatment by Weber in the musical press, and we know that Wagner had his host's celebrated jibe about his music-dramas being akin to 'a serving of turbot without sauce' much in mind.[83] Essentially, however, the discussion concerned differing concepts of opera: Rossini's melodic priorities pitted against Wagner's fully integrated dramatic imperatives. The upshot of the encounter was an acceptance of Rossini which, although highly qualified, was perhaps surprising in the contexts of Wagner's character and the course of German musical history: 'What might he have not produced if he had received a forceful and complete education? Especially if, less Italian and less sceptical, he had felt within him the religion of his art?'[84] According to Wagner's own account, during the meeting the Italian composer was good-humouredly prepared to concur with many of his observations. At Rossini's death in 1868, Wagner's tribute, published in the *Allgemeine Zeitung*, was fulsome:

> Rossini will never be judged aright, until someone attempts an intelligent history of the Culture of our current century ... Were this character of our age correctly drawn, it would then be possible to allot to Rossini also his true and fitting station in it ... for with the same title as Palestrina, Bach, Mozart, belonged to their age, belongs Rossini to his.[85]

In winning their struggle against Rossini the Germans had won far more than just a 'battle of the operas'. They had triumphed in a war of ideas, and thus the right to assume the musical leadership of Europe. 'Art-Music', its aesthetics, its philosophy, its forms, its reception, were all dictated by German experience and Germanic norms. In Italy, which had long exported its tastes and styles to other European centres, complaints were made about the 'de-Italianizing of Italian music', a situation of which the eclectic Verdi was only too aware.[86] Rossini himself had doubts whether his countrymen could prove wrong Metternich's dismissal of Italy as being merely a 'geographical expression'. Italian to the core, he remained to the end of his life a stubborn 'European'. In 1862, the composer had remarked: 'the only benefit that I can foresee from national unification is that of a new intellectual awakening among Italians; for the rest, I have small faith.'[87] Indeed it was paradoxical that, as Italy lost its centuries-old leadership in the most international of the arts, it at last achieved political unity and independence. The new Italian state chose to overlook Rossini's apatriotic conservatism, preferring instead to regard him as a national asset. In the composer's last year, Victor Emanuel II offered to make him a Grand Knight of the Order of the Crown of Italy – Rossini accepted. Already he seemed content that his reputation should be established on the basis of 'national music'. More than this, he seems to have come to know his place in the history of music. In the dedication of the *Petite Messe* addressing the Almighty, Rossini may have written his own epitaph: 'I was born for opera buffa, as well Thou knowest'.[88] Already by his death, remarkably few of his works still held the international stage; apart from *Il barbiere di Siviglia*, it was only in Italy that his legacy was truly appreciated. From the perspective of a full century later, we can see that Beethoven had indeed sounded the keynote of posterity's estimation of Gioacchino Rossini: 'Above all, make a lot of Barbers'.

Notes

1 Quoted in H. Weinstock, *Rossini: A Biography* (New York, 1968, repr. 1987), 122. Beethoven thus exhorted Rossini at their meeting in Vienna in 1822.
2 Henri Beyle (Stendhal), *Life of Rossini* (Paris, 1824, repr. London, 1985), 3.
3 H. Sutherland Edwards, *The Life of Rossini* (London, 1869), 274.
4 G. Chouquet on Rossini in G. Grove (ed.), *Dictionary of Music and Musicians* (4 vols., London, 1879–89) 3, 175.
5 Chouquet, loc. cit.
6 F. Toye, *Rossini: A Study in Tragi-Comedy* (London, 1934), xi.
7 Toye, op. cit., xvii.
8 Rossini, quoted in F. Hiller, 'Conversations with Rossini (1856)', *Once a Week* 58 No. 3 (6 February 1869), 82.
9 *Der Freischütz* was performed in over twenty German theatres within eighteen months of its première. By the mid-1820s, the opera had travelled to England, Russia and the United States; J. Warrack, 'Giving Germany an Operatic Identity: Weber's Der Freischütz' liner-note, Philips CD 426 319-2, 1990.
10 J. Benedict, *Weber* (London, 1881), 23. This biography was largely

based on the composer's diary.
11 M. M. von Weber, 'Ein Name, besser als eine Hausnummer: Erinnerungen an K. M. von Weber und Rossini', *Deutsche Rundschau* 5 (1875), 260. This item was kindly translated by my friend and colleague, Phyllys Greenhead. For a recent analysis throwing light on how Weber and other German composers made a special acquisition of the Romantic project, see J. Daverio, *Nineteenth-Century Music and the German Music Ideology* (New York, 1993), esp. ch. 4.
12 M. M. von Weber, op. cit., 261.
13 Rossini, quoted by F. Hiller, 'Conversations', 83.
14 The composer recalled Weber's visits in a conversation with Richard Wagner in 1860; Weinstock, *Rossini*, 150.
15 P. Spitta on Weber in Grove's *Dictionary*, 4, 409.
16 J. Stone, 'Creative Malice: Il barbiere revisited', *Musical Times* 133 (Feb. 1992), 63–5.
17 Rossini on his invitation to attend the Congress of Verona, quoted in F. Hiller, 'Conversations', 83.
18 In the 1790s, Cherubini (1760–1842) set the pace in the 'rescue opera' genre, notably with *Lodoiska* (1791). Later, Spontini (1774–1851) edified the Napoleonic court with operas depicting heroic grandeur, the most famous being *La Vestale* (1807).
19 N. Till, *Mozart and the Enlightenment* (London, 1992), 48.
20 The competition was the Emperor Joseph II's idea. Two short operas were staged, one Italian, one German, in order that the court could sample the rival styles of *opera buffa* and *Singspiel*. Salieri's *Prima la Musica e poi le parole* was pitted against Mozart's *Der Schauspieldirektor*. Both works were on the subject of opera and the setting up of an opera company. For Joseph's support for a *Nazionalsingspiel* as a means of promoting German language and culture in the Habsburg lands, see E. Manning, 'The Politics of Culture: Joseph II's German Opera', *History Today* (January 1993), 15–21.
21 R. Engländer, 'The Struggle between German and Italian Opera at the Time of Weber', *Musical Quarterly* 31 (1945), 479–91.
22 Rossini's international reputation gathered pace with the première of *L'Italiana in Algeri* in Germany (1816) and France (1817): C. Osborne, *The Bel Canto Operas of Rossini, Donizetti and Bellini* (London, 1994), 35.
23 Domenico Barbaja (1775–1841) was a hugely successful businessman who dominated the operatic life of Naples for over thirty years. He was close to the Bourbon court, and received a licence to operate gaming tables in the city's opera-houses. Barbaja also had excellent Austrian contacts, having financial interests in the Kärntnertortheater and the Theater an der Wien during the 1820s. Rossini became Barbaja's 'house' composer both in Naples and in Vienna. See Weinstock, *Rossini*, 47–8.

24 C. de Grunwald, *Metternich* (London, 1953), 150.
25 R. M. Schafer, *E. T. A. Hoffmann and Music* (Toronto, 1975), 142.
26 P. Spitta, 'Weber', loc. cit., 402.
27 J. Warrack, *Carl Maria von Weber* (London, 1968), 198.
28 Weber quoted by Spitta, 'Weber', loc. cit., 402.
29 *Tonkunstlers Leben* (1817), quoted in J. Warrack (ed.), *Carl Maria von Weber: Writings on Music* (Cambridge, 1981), 338.
30 M. M. von Weber, 'Eine Name', loc. cit., 258.
31 Perhaps the most influential musical periodical in Germany was the *Allgemeine Musikalische Zeitung*, founded by J. F. Rochlitz in 1798. Weber and Rochlitz were friends and allies in the struggle for German opera.
32 Weber quoted by Spitta, 'Weber', loc. cit., 395.
33 Ibid., 426.
34 Weber quoted, ibid., 405.
35 M. M. von Weber, 'Eine Name', loc. cit., 225–6.
36 Schubert quoted by Benedict, *Weber*, 99.
37 Weinstock, *Rossini*, 114.
38 Ibid., 116.
39 Hegel, quoted in ibid, 118.
40 Ibid., 121.
41 Ibid., 122–3.
42 M. M. von Weber, 'Eine Name', loc. cit., 259.
43 Schubert to Schober, 30 Nov 1823, quoted in J. Reed, *Schubert* (London, 1987), 108.
44 Schubert quoted in Benedict, *Weber*, op. cit., 99.
45 Weber to J. R. Planché, 19 Feb 1825, quoted in Spitta, 'Weber', loc. cit., 420.
46 A. Schindler, *Life of Beethoven* (London, 1841) 2, 3.
47 Quoted by Schindler, op. cit., 9.
48 G. Grove on Beethoven in the *Dictionary*, 1, 197.
49 Stendhal, *Rossini*, 128 and 200.
50 H. Sutherland Edwards, *Life of Rossini* (London, 1869), 274.
51 Rossini in 1854, quoted in Hiller, 'Conversations', loc. cit., 83–4.
52 Weber quoted by M. M. von Weber, 'Eine Name', loc. cit., 258.
53 R. Schumann, 'A Monument to Beethoven' (1836) in *Music and Musicians: Essays and Criticisms* (London, 1877), 22–3.
54 Loc. cit.
55 R. Schumann quoted in H. Pleasants (ed.), *Schumann on Music* (Mineola, 1988), 13. See also Daverio, *Nineteenth-Century Music*, ch. 2.
56 R. Schumann, 'Rossini', in *Music and Musicians*, 61–2.
57 R. Schumann, 'Chopin's Sonata' (1841), in Pleasants, op. cit., 174.
58 R. Schumann, 'Rossini's Visit to Beethoven', in *Music and Musicians*, 62.

59 R. Schumann, 'Italian and German', ibid, 62. Schumann was one of the few German intellectuals of his day who was resistant to the lure of the south.
60 P. Merrick, *Music and Revolution in the Music of Liszt* (Cambridge, 1987), 5.
61 Liszt quoted in R. Osborne, *Rossini* (London, 1986), 91.
62 Liszt's music journalism for *La Revue et Gazette Musicale* was collected in *Pages Romantiques* (Paris, 1912), with an introduction by J. Chantavoine.
63 Ibid., 265.
64 Ibid., 269–70.
65 Although Liszt generally had no time for Rossini, he did acknowledge Rossini's musicianship in pieces such as his piano transcriptions of the *Soirées Musicales* (1837). In these works (perhaps) Liszt managed to ignore his artistic reservations in favour of commercial considerations.
66 A. Schindler, *Life of Beethoven*, 1, 89.
67 A. Schindler, ed. D. W. McArdle, *Beethoven As I Knew Him* (London, 1966), 376. This memoir was first published in Germany in 1860.
68 *Neue Freie Presse* (18 July 1867), quoted in Weinstock, *Rossini*, 347–50.
69 *Neue Zeitschrift für Musik* (28 Dec. 1841) in W. Ashton-Ellis (tr. and ed.), *Richard Wagner's Prose Works* (London, 1892–9), vol. 7, 142–9. The references to Wagner's opinions here are to these pages.
70 J. Deathridge, 'Wagner's "Alter Ego"', liner-note on *Lohengrin*, Deutsche Grammophon DGG 437-808-2, 1994.
71 E. Dannreuther, 'Wagner', Grove's *Dictionary*, 4, 358.
72 From a letter published in *Corsaire* (12 Aug 1823), quoted in D. Cairns, *Berlioz: The Making of an Artist (1803–32)* (London, 1990), 132.
73 D. Cairns (ed.), *The Memoirs of Berlioz* (London, 1970), 288.
74 Ibid., 251.
75 *Life and Writings of Joseph Mazzini* (London, 1864–70) vol. 4, 9, 14, 27–8, 35–6.
76 In 1849, Verdi bade farewell to Rossinian bel canto with the opera *Luisa Miller*.
77 R. Wagner, 'Speech at Weber's Last Resting-Place', W. Ashton-Ellis, *Prose Works*, 7, 235–7.
78 R. Wagner, *Beethoven* (London, 1880), 41.
79 E. Hanslick, *The Beautiful in Music* (London, 1891).
80 Ibid., 13.
81 For a full account of the 1860 encounter between Rossini and Hanslick, see Weinstock, *Rossini*, 300–3.
82 M. M. von Weber, 'Eine Name', loc. cit., 258.

83 Edmond Michotte records Wagner's touchiness at Rossini's witticisms about his music then circulating in Paris; Weinstock, *Rossini*, 302–3.
84 Wagner to Michotte after his meeting with Rossini, ibid, 297.
85 R. Wagner, 'A Remembrance of Rossini', W. Ashton-Ellis, *Prose Works*, 4, 273. Despite this fulsome tribute, in *Die Meistersinger*, premièred that same year, Wagner could not resist parodying the cavatina 'i tanti palpiti' from *Tancredi* in his tailors' chorus.
86 J. Rosselli, *Music and Musicians in Nineteenth-Century Italy* (London, 1991), 102–3.
87 Rossini to G. de Sanctis in 1862, quoted in Weinstock, *Rossini*, 319.
88 I am grateful to Nick Till for suggesting the valedictory nature of this quotation. I would also like to thank Robert Stradling for all his encouragement and advice in the preparation of this chapter.

~3~
Administering the Constitutional Pill: Britain, Italy and the Italian Policy of Lord Malmesbury

NICK CARTER

I

British policy in Italy was well established when Lord Malmesbury became foreign secretary in February 1858. Since the 1830s it had consisted of supporting moderate constitutional government where it existed (for example, in Piedmont after 1848), and pressing for progressive political improvement where it did not (British efforts concentrated on the autocratic regimes in the Papal States and the kingdom of Naples). 'Peaceful progress from above rather than violent revolution from below' was the intention.[1]

Successive British governments were anxious to prevent revolution in Italy for two reasons. Firstly, revolution *per se* was abhorrent to a British ruling class conditioned by the experience of the French revolutionary wars and possessed with a 'horror of revolutionary excesses and democratic extremes'.[2] Mazzini's vision of a democratic Italian republic, created through spontaneous popular revolt, was anathema to the British political establishment. The ideas of democracy and republicanism were still closely associated with the French 'terror' of 1793–4. Secondly, revolution in Italy appeared to carry with it the seeds of a European war. Austria, which since 1815 had ruled Lombardy-Venetia directly and exerted great influence over much of the rest of Italy, had intervened militarily to crush revolutions in Naples and Piedmont in 1821, in central Italy in 1831–2, and in northern and central Italy in 1848–9. France, too, sent troops into Italy in 1832 and again in 1849. A French garrison was established at Ancona in 1832 and only removed in 1838. French troops were permanently stationed in Rome after 1849.

The presence of rival French and Austrian armies on Italian soil was seen at Westminster as a recipe for further unrest in Italy and conflict between two of the 'Great Powers'. This in turn could upset the continental balance of power.[3] The maintenance of peace and of the political status quo in Europe were fundamental to British foreign policy. British interests and power lay outside of Europe. British governments had not the time, the resources, nor the inclination, to become materially involved in European affairs. What British governments feared most was the revival of French power on the continent. A French victory over Austria in Italy would make France the dominant power there. Defeat for Austria could threaten the internal stability of the multinational Habsburg Empire, which France might also try to exploit. Palmerston summed up British concerns in February 1848:

> Upon Metternich's decision in regard to the affairs of Italy depends the question of peace or war in Europe ... If he takes upon himself the task of regulating by force of arms the internal affairs of the Italian states there will infallibly be war ... which, beginning in Italy, will spread over all Europe ... the principal champions contending against each other would be Austria and France ... We set too great a value upon the maintenance of Austria as the pivot of the balance of power in Europe to be able to see without the deepest concern any course of action begun by her Government which would produce fatal consequences to her ...[4]

Traditional British francophobia was accentuated after 1848 with the rise to power in France of Louis Napoleon, the nephew of Napoleon Bonaparte. It was widely feared in Britain that Louis Napoleon – who in 1852 proclaimed himself Emperor Napoleon III – sought to emulate the achievements of the first Napoleon.

The rationale, then, behind British policy in Italy was simple: promote political reform to prevent revolution; prevent revolution to preclude European war. Constitutional government in Italy was thought to be a goal worth pursuing for its own sake, it was considered to be of advantage to Italy ('as laying a solid foundation for the regeneration of Italy'), and it was seen to be in the wider interests of both Britain and Europe. As Derek Beales has commented, it was Britain's 'usual attitude to the troubles of other countries. Their recipe for the cure of all the world's political ills, and a good part of any other ills.'[5]

The question of Italian independence was less clear-cut. Many in the British political establishment felt a strong romantic attachment to Italy based primarily on an admiration for its classical and renaissance past, and reinforced by first-hand experience of its people, countryside, and climate. Italy's former glories contrasted sharply with present reality. Italians had 'twice civilized the world' but now 'the soul and body of poor Italia was bound in fetters'.[6] Gladstone wondered 'whether anywhere in Christendom there be an instance corresponding with the Austrian power in Italy; an instance where a people glaringly inferior in refinement rule ... over a race much more advanced.'[7] Not unnaturally then, although Mazzini's brand of revolutionary nationalism 'won virtually no support among the [British] upper classes', the efforts of the moderate liberal-nationalist movement in Italy (led after 1848 by Piedmont) to secure independence attracted considerable sympathy. Some, like Palmerston, argued that Austria would actually benefit from a retreat to the north of the Alps, 'her natural barrier and her best defence', arguing that Austria's presence in Italy merely encouraged unrest and weakened the Habsburg Empire. What Palmerston hoped to see was the creation of a northern Italian kingdom, 'conducive to the peace of Europe, by interposing between France and Austria a neutral State strong enough to make itself respected, and sympathising in its habits and character neither with France or Austria'.[8]

Yet, as far as British foreign policy was concerned, Italian independence was only desirable if it could be secured by peaceful means and without upsetting the European balance of power. Austria had to be persuaded to leave Italy of its own free will, and with its integrity intact. The use of force to expel Austria was not an option. Piedmont, as the focus of Italian liberal-nationalist aspirations, was reminded not to forget 'the rules of prudence and reserve' and not to launch itself 'on a dangerous slope in listening to the counsels of anyone who would advise her to depart from that road.'[9] As Lord Minto told Massimo d'Azeglio, the prime minister of Piedmont, in 1851:

> You know how entirely I agree with you in regarding the independence and well being of Italy as an object of European, and more especially of British interest; in the actual position of affairs, however, it is difficult to see what means are open to us for its present attainment ... England as well as Italy must bide its time ...[10]

Although Britain was far more sympathetic than any of the other Great Powers towards the moderate liberal-nationalist cause in Italy, in practice this counted for little. Constitutional reform was put forward as the remedy for the cycle of reaction and revolution which afflicted Italian states, and which threatened European conflict. British governments, though, had no intention of actively intervening to enforce such reforms. In principle, Italian independence was acceptable to Britain. In reality, however, it was not, since Austria had no intention of voluntarily surrendering her Italian possessions. Lord Clarendon inadvertently summed up the contradictions in British policy when, in 1862, he looked back on his years as foreign secretary (1855–8), and recalled meetings with Cavour at the Paris Peace Congress in 1856:

> I gave him [repeated assurances] that our invariable principle was to maintain out treaty engagements and to be guided by the principles of international law. At the same time, I did not disguise from him, what he knew and what everybody else knew, that our object at that time was to free Italy from foreign occupation, and to reform the Papal and Neapolitan governments, and that toward that end the moral support of England would always be forthcoming.[11]

The Paris Peace Congress was a watershed in Anglo-Piedmontese relations. After 1849, Piedmont, as the only constitutional and truly independent state in Italy, had been the particular object of British goodwill in the peninsula. Palmerston in the House of Commons described Piedmont as 'a model of the success of parliamentary government.'[12] Cavour, the prime minister of Piedmont from 1852, endeared himself to the British political classes because of the liberal economic, political and religious (anti-papal) policies he pursued. His decision in 1855 to commit 18,000 Piedmontese troops to the Anglo-French alliance in the Crimea was especially well received in Britain. On Piedmont's accession to the Treaty of Alliance, Clarendon wrote to Hudson, the British minister at Turin,

> the Treaty has been discussed in all the large towns, I would almost say in the villages, to an extent he [Cavour] can hardly imagine, among a people who generally take little interest in foreign affairs. There is, however, throughout England such an admiration for the wisdom and courage of which Sardinia [i.e. Piedmont] has given proof in difficult

circumstances, and such sympathy with the successful efforts made to secure national [i.e. Piedmontese] liberty, that any measure which binds the two Countries more closely together is hailed here with a feeling little short of enthusiasm.[13]

When the war finished, Piedmont's place in British affections seemed unshakeable. Clarendon secured full representative status for Piedmont at the Paris Congress. Palmerston, the British prime minister, was 'ready to forget that the belligerents had decided on no annexations, or at least was willing for Piedmont to be the sole exception and acquire Parma or even Lombardy'.[14] At Paris, Clarendon told Cavour he did not 'mind taking the initiative in the conference about the state of Italy, which was a scandal to Europe and which a European congress was bound to consider'.[15] This Clarendon did on 8 April 1856, criticizing the papal government in central Italy and Bourbon rule in the kingdom of Naples. Britain and France subsequently broke off diplomatic relations with Naples.

Relations between Britain and Piedmont, however, soon began to deteriorate. Clarendon expected Piedmont to follow the British line in all European matters, claiming that 'the position which Sardinia is now occupying as a sort of first rate Power is due exclusively to England'.[16] Cavour, though, was not prepared to do this. Having failed to secure any tangible compensation for the political, economic, and military cost of the Crimean campaign (Piedmont, despite Palmerston's wishes, gained no territory from the Paris Congress) Cavour was anxious to reassert his own domestic political position, and wanted to make the most of Piedmont's new international status as the 'representative' of Italy. Consequently, Cavour began to push the issue of Italian independence ever more insistently.

For Cavour (and the wider Italian liberal-national movement) political and economic progress in Italy was dependent upon the removal of illiberal Austrian influence (political and economic; direct and indirect). Since Austria had no intention of withdrawing from Italy, independence would only be achieved by military means. Events in 1848-9, however, had shown that Piedmont by itself could not defeat Austria. Foreign military assistance was required. Frustrated by Britain's refusal to commit itself unconditionally to the cause of Italian independence (a position which was made quite plain to him when he visited London after the Paris Congress) Cavour began to look elsewhere for such support. He looked to imperial France. 'Italy was going to be made not peaceably, but by war; not by evolution, but by revolution; not by non-intervention, but by French arms.'[17]

Cavour's decision to turn to Louis Napoleon for military assistance increased his isolation from Britain. British fears that Louis Napoleon meant to use the Italian question as a first stepping stone to French domination of Europe caused even the most ardent British supporters of Italian independence to balk at supporting Cavour's strategy.

II

Malmesbury's Italian policy in 1858–9 bore many similarities to that of his recent predecessors at the Foreign Office and displayed the limitations of 'traditional' British policy in Italy, which in 1858–9 were to be cruelly exposed. His remedy for Italy's ills was constitutional reform. He showed the common British (Protestant) hostility toward papal government. He offered British 'moral' support to the Italian liberal cause. His aim, when confronted with a deepening international crisis with its roots in Italy, was to try and preserve the European peace and the balance of power. He vigorously opposed the use of force to expel Austria from Italy.

In many ways, however, Malmesbury's views on and approach to the Italian question were unusual. Although Malmesbury regarded himself as 'Italianissimo' (in 1858 he talked of 'those romantic feelings which the former history and the present degradation of Italy may naturally inspire even at a more advanced time of life') he considered absurd the idea of an Italian 'nation'. To Malmesbury, Italy was a 'mosaic of nationalities'. 'Leave Italy to govern herself,' he wrote to Lord Cowley, the British ambassador to Paris, '[and she] will become a 2nd Mexico ... the prejudices and even dislike of the various provinces to one another is ingrained by centuries.' Malmesbury considered it 'sound policy' to leave Austria 'in quiet possession of her Italian dominions'.

Malmesbury also believed it to be 'sound honesty' to allow Austria to maintain her Italian territories. Malmesbury regarded the territorial arrangements agreed to at Vienna in 1815 as inviolable (although by 1858 they already had been violated, for example, in the creation of Belgium). According to Malmesbury, Austrian rule in Italy was as legitimate as British rule in Ireland and India because 'Lombardy belongs to Austria by European treaties confirming ancient rights'. As important for Malmesbury was the fact that forty years of European peace between the Great Powers, from Waterloo until the Crimean War, had followed the Vienna settlement. In Malmesbury's view, European peace in the future was dependent upon the maintenance of the 1815 treaties. Palmerston's talk of the creation of a northern Italian kingdom 'conducive to the peace of Europe', was completely alien to Malmesbury's way of thinking.[18]

Malmesbury was not alone in holding these opinions. Many Tories were sceptical of Italian nationalism. Queen Victoria regarded Italian independence as 'a mere theory' and was consistently legitimist and pro-Austrian in her attitude to Italian affairs.[19] Nevertheless, as Mack Smith notes, such views were 'those of a minority' in the British political establishment.[20]

Given Malmesbury's views it is not surprising that he had little time for Cavour, or for that matter, any of the other (mainly Piedmontese) leaders of the moderate liberal-nationalist movement in Italy. Cavour's insistence on the need to expel Austria from Italy, and his apparent willingness to 'set Europe ablaze' in order to achieve this, obviously conflicted with Malmesbury's own desire to maintain a European peace based upon the territorial arrangements of the 1815 treaties. Moreover, because Malmesbury had no concept of Italian nationhood, he regarded the whole idea of war in Italy against Austria merely as an exercise in Piedmontese aggrandisement. Malmesbury expressed his 'utter repulsion' at the thought of acting with Cavour:

> I can muster no patience towards that little conceited mischievous State now called Sardinia ... That Europe should be deluged with blood for the personal ambition of an Italian attorney and a tambour major like Cavour and his master is intolerable.[21]

Again, Malmesbury was not alone in holding such views. Not only Tories but also some Whigs 'looked upon Cavour as a man moved not so much by the desire to liberate Italy as to enlarge his own region of Piedmont at the expense of other states in the peninsula.'[22] No one wished to see Europe 'deluged with blood'.

What really set Malmesbury apart from his peers was his attitude and policy toward Louis Napoleon and France. Malmesbury's Italian policy did not reflect the 'fear of French ambitions' that had characterized previous British Italian policy (and which shaped it subsequently) and which exercised such a strong hold over the public mind.²³

Throughout 1858, Malmesbury refused to believe that Louis Napoleon was considering war in Italy. In December, for example, Malmesbury told Queen Victoria that no war 'is at present contemplated by the emperor Napoleon (who has just contradicted the report officially) ... no warlike preparations are making in France, such as must precede such a plan as an Italian war'.²⁴ Yet, it was Louis Napoleon who, in July 1858, had invited Cavour to Plombières to discuss a possible military alliance against Austria; who in September 1858 had begun negotiations with Tsar Alexander II for Russian neutrality in the event of war in Italy; and who in November 1858 had even talked to Palmerston and Clarendon of the possibility of a French alliance with Piedmont and war in Lombardy against Austria.²⁵ In the first months of 1859, although French military preparations eventually forced him to accept that France was, after all, readying itself for war, Malmesbury was convinced that Louis Napoleon would have peace if he could. Louis Napoleon was simply the unwilling – and unwitting – 'victim of Cavour and of his "entourage"'. As Malmesbury told Prince Albert in February 1859:

> Count Cavour is the moving spirit in this conspiracy against Austria ... it was at Plombières that he first divulged it to the Emperor who was then alone there. He has made Napoleon believe that last summer Italy was on the point of rising, which is not true, and that Austria meant to attack Piedmont, which is equally false ... the Emperor ... must be surrounded by a clique who are bounded to deceive him.²⁶

Such a view was a nonsense. 'Plombières was an exercise in the diplomacy of *Realpolitik*. Napoleon was the true master of the art, Cavour a mere amateur by comparison'.²⁷ The alliance between France and Piedmont was controlled throughout by Louis Napoleon, not Cavour. Malmesbury, however, persisted in this illusion almost until the outbreak of war, claiming in mid March that Louis Napoleon 'would give anything to undo the work of the last four months into which he has been betrayed by Cavour'.[28] During these months, it was not at Paris, but at Vienna (through negotiation), and at Turin (through verbal intimidation), that Malmesbury sought to resolve the Italian crisis and avert European conflict.

Two factors seem to have led Malmesbury to adopt such an unusually lenient attitude toward Louis Napoleon. The first was the singular personal bond that existed between Malmesbury and Louis Napoleon. The second (which served to reinforce Malmesbury's own convictions) was the influential opinion of the British ambassador to Paris, Lord Cowley.

Malmesbury and Louis Napoleon had been friends ever since they first met in 1829, in Italy. Such was the strength of their friendship that, in 1845, Malmesbury visited Louis Napoleon while the latter was in prison in the castle of Ham, on the Somme, for conspiring against the king of France, Louis Philippe. Malmesbury 'returned to London deeply impressed with the calm resolution, or rather, philosophy' of the prisoner. In 1852, Louis Napoleon, by then the French president, sent a personal letter of congratulations to Malmesbury on his becoming foreign secretary in the first Derby administration. In October 1852, Malmesbury defended Louis Napoleon to Derby, amid widespread concern at the possibility of a French attack on Britain. In this defence, Malmesbury acknowledged his peculiar position:

> the feeling of apprehension is universal ... [but] this general terror of what is to come is a *presentiment*, for none can give any reasons founded on facts to show the sinister feelings and intentions of Louis Napoleon. I believe I stand alone, therefore, in disbelieving them.[29]

Hearder suggests that the Derby government's swift recognition of the Second Empire under Louis Napoleon was largely due to Malmesbury.[30]

Malmesbury's feelings of admiration and respect for Louis Napoleon are best summed up in his recollection of a meeting they had in 1871, after the collapse of the Second Empire, and following Louis Napoleon's exile to England:

> he shook me heartily by the hand. I confess that I never was more moved. His quiet and calm dignity and absence of all nervousness and

irritability were the grandest examples of human moral courage that the severest Stoic could have imagined.
I felt overpowered by the position. All the past rushed to my memory: our youth together at Rome in 1829, his dreams of power at that time, his subsequent desperate attempts to obtain it; his prison, where I found him still sanguine and unchanged; his wonderful escape from Ham, and his residence in London, where, in the riots of 1848, he acted the special constable like any Englishman. His election as President by millions in France in 1850; his further one by millions to the Imperial Crown; the part I had myself acted as an English Minister in that event, which had realised all his early dreams; the glory of his reign of twenty years over France, which he had enriched beyond belief, and adorned beyond all other countries and capitals; his liberation of Italy – all these memories crowded upon me as the man stood before me whose race had been so successful and romantic, now without a crown ...
I must have shown, for I could not conceal, what I felt, as, again shaking my hand, he said: 'A la guerre, comme à la guerre. C'est bien bon de venir me voir'.[31]

Malmesbury's long friendship with Louis Napoleon helped Anglo-French relations to survive the grave diplomatic crisis which followed Orsini's attempt on the life of the emperor in January 1858.[32] However, it also blinded Malmesbury to the reality of French imperial policy in Italy. Even at the end of March 1859, as France stalled progress on arrangements for a European congress on the Italian question (the idea of her Russian ally, devised in part to wreck British peace efforts at Vienna), Malmesbury's sympathies remained with Louis Napoleon. 'We appear to be moving in a vicious circle', he observed to Cowley on 28 March, 'and the friend we want to save is like a millstone around our necks'.[33]

Cowley's own views on the Italian crisis of 1858–9 served to reinforce Malmesbury's convictions. Like Malmesbury, Cowley could not believe Louis Napoleon would ever commit 'such an act of insanity' as to make war with Austria over Italy. He denied the existence of a Franco-Piedmontese military alliance (signed in January 1859) until French troops entered Piedmont in late April. Like Malmesbury, Cowley held Cavour ('the Sardinian agitator') responsible for the deteriorating international situation. 'I should like to know who but Sardinia is the cause of any agitation that may exist in Italy', Cowley stated in February 1859. 'His [Cavour's] conduct, in my humble opinion, is little less than infamous.' Commenting on the recent marriage between Princess Clothilde, the fifteen-year-old daughter of Victor Emanuel, and Prince Jerome Napoleon, the thirty-five-year-old rakish cousin of Louis Napoleon, Cowley wrote:

> when one sees this Child, sacrificed, for it is nothing else, to the ambition of her father, and Cavour, what can one think of such men? It is positively horrible to see that poor little frail creature by the side of the brute (I can call him nothing less) to whom she has been immolated.[34]

Cowley omitted to mention (or did not know) that the marriage was the idea of Louis Napoleon.

Not surprisingly, Cowley became Malmesbury's 'chief adviser and informant and his most trusted envoy'. Malmesbury even sent Cowley's observations to Turin, to 'correct' Hudson's despatches which portrayed Cavour as the dupe of Louis Napoleon. Such was Cowley's influence on Malmesbury that, when Malmesbury published the Blue Book on Italian affairs, he described Cowley as its co-author.[35]

Cowley's support also helped Malmesbury to convince his cabinet colleagues of the propriety of his approach to the Italian question. As ambassador to Paris, Cowley was the occupant of one of the two most important British diplomatic posts in Europe. In 1859, only Paris and Constantinople were accredited with Embassy status. Though associated in domestic politics with the Whigs (he was especially close to Clarendon), Cowley had been retained in 1858 as ambassador by Malmesbury, at Queen Victoria's expressed wish, because of his intimacy with Louis Napoleon. Cowley's belief in Louis Napoleon's pacific intentions, and the government's faith in Cowley's convictions and ability, prompted Malmesbury to give Cowley the task of implementing the first British peace initiative of the Italian crisis. The peace effort was not directed at France, but at Austria. Cowley was instructed to go to Vienna in late February 1859, to secure Austrian concessions over Italy. Such was the trust that the British government placed in him that Cowley was given rein to conduct the mission as he saw fit. The venture, however, was not a success. Buol, the Austrian foreign minister (and chancellor), refused to credit the mission with full diplomatic status (partly because Malmesbury had declared the mission was unofficial) and the whole project was ambushed in mid March by the Russian proposal for a European congress on the Italian question. Nevertheless, the importance of Cowley to British foreign policy was clear.[36]

Cowley's mission to Vienna had been with the objective of gaining Austrian agreement on what Malmesbury regarded as the four major issues at stake in Italy: the evacuation of French and Austrian troops from the Papal States; the reform of the Papal States; the security of Piedmont; and the repeal or modification of Austria's 1847 treaties with the minor Italian States. Although the Cowley mission failed, Malmesbury persisted with the four-point plan, arguing that it should form the basis of the proposed congress. Malmesbury's intention was to preserve the treaties of 1815, while at the same time resolving the main sources of discontent in Italy, so to starve Cavour and Piedmont of a cause or an excuse for war against Austria.[37]

It was only when Malmesbury attempted to turn the congress proposal into a reality that he ran out of patience with Louis Napoleon. At the beginning of April, Cowley reported from Paris that Louis Napoleon, having earlier given his word that he would ask Piedmont to disarm, had changed his mind and was now denying having given any such pledge. The issue of Piedmontese disarmament was one of the major stumbling-blocks to be overcome if a congress was ever to sit to consider the Italian question. Malmesbury had placed all his hopes for peace on such a meeting. Consequently, the emperor's latest prevarication proved to be the last straw for the British foreign secretary. 'You and I must stand clear before the public of the rascality going on at Paris', Malmesbury told Cowley, 'I want to put on record that Austria is justified and that we have been deceived by France'. Malmesbury now considered that Louis Napoleon had, 'from the first meant an Italian war'.[38]

Malmesbury's comments have often been taken to indicate a general anti-French stance in his approach to the Italian question. Instead, they were the bitter recriminations of a man who had only just realized that his friend Louis Napoleon had been deliberately playing false toward Britain over Italy. They were also a last-ditch attempt to encourage Austria to make concessions.

'State that ... France has now put herself quite in the wrong by breaking her promise to Cowley to make Sardinia disarm but that Austria may take advantage of this and claim every merit', Malmesbury instructed Loftus (British minister at Vienna) on 5 April. 'Conclude by stating that I consider the only sound reason Austria could have for refusing [to withdraw troops five leagues from her Italian borders] would be her intention to attack at once and forestall her enemies. This I do not believe'.[39]

Once again, Malmesbury was mistaken. Austrian impatience with Piedmont, combined with her fears of isolation at congress and the immense cost of maintaining the Imperial army on a war footing, prompted Vienna, in mid April, to send an ultimatum to Piedmont to disarm. If Piedmont refused to do so, Austria stated it would use force to restore peace in Italy. The ultimatum fulfilled Cavour's long search for a *casus belli* which he required to invoke the French alliance. Cavour formally rejected the Austrian demand on 26 April 1859. By then the first French troops had already arrived on Italian soil.

The fact that Austria appeared as the aggressor in the conflict which followed meant that Cavour and Piedmont regained the sympathy and support of much of the British parliament and public – to Malmesbury's disgust:

> the nation is *Italian* on this question, and Parliament is made up of ... [those] who understand nothing of Foreign Policy and its great ramifications and only comprehend what is familiar to their minds, namely the stupid [illegible] of Austrian Rule in Italy and at home. Had not the hated French interfered an English Government would have been obliged *openly to defend Sardinia*.[40]

III

It has been argued that Malmesbury, although unsuccessful in his efforts to find a peaceful solution to the Italian crisis, nevertheless maintained a strong policy for peace, and retained the diplomatic initiative up to the outbreak of war. Certainly, Malmesbury had a policy for peace (the four points), and he could take credit for initiating the peace process via the Cowley mission to Vienna, and for sustaining that process by laying down the four points as the basis for the proposed congress. While recognizing that 'everybody has been so dishonest in all their transactions', and threatening that 'England cannot go on ... like an old aunt trying to make up family squabbles', Malmesbury never gave up trying to bring the potential combatants to the negotiating table. Even after the Austrian ultimatum had been sent, Malmesbury attempted to get Cavour to agree to mediation. Only on 29 April 1859 did Malmesbury admit that he had 'abandoned all hope of preventing war by the imposition of our good offices'.[41]

Malmesbury's peace efforts, however, were hampered by a number of factors. In his defence, it should be noted that he was serving in a minority government which, by the spring of 1859, was widely expected to fall. Malmesbury suspected that both France and Piedmont sought to delay the peace process in the hope that an incoming Whig administration would be more readily disposed towards the Italian cause – and to an Italian war – than was the Derby government. Yet many of Malmesbury's problems were self-inflicted. His approach underlined the limitations of 'traditional' British policy in Italy. Although Malmesbury claimed that his 'private sympathies were with Italian regeneration', 'moral support' for Piedmont and the promotion of political reform ('the famous Constitutional Pill which is to be administered as usual to people who don't want it', as Hudson described it), was no longer sufficient in Italy. However, Malmesbury's opposition to any territorial change in Italy meant he could not satisfy the ambitions of Cavour, Piedmont and the Italian national movement. Malmesbury, in fact, did not even understand the national question ('Geographically speaking I know what they [the Italians] are but when I come to a *policy*, an *army* and a *navy* I don't see them', he once wrote). Consequently, he could only watch and 'see Piémont throw herself into the arms of France in order to avoid what to her is worse than France, namely Austria and the pope'.[42]

Malmesbury's efforts for peace were further undermined by his almost exclusive reliance upon Cowley at Paris for information and opinion, much of which was misleading, some of which was false. Reports from Lord Loftus, appointed by Malmesbury to the mission at Vienna in 1858 – and described by Disraeli as 'a pompous nincompoop, and of all Lord Malmesbury's appointments the worst, and that is saying a good deal'[43] – were, perhaps not surprisingly, given little attention. However, reports from

Hudson at Turin, who was one of the more perceptive British diplomats, that Louis Napoleon rather than Cavour was the *agent provocateur* in the Italian crisis, were also ignored by the foreign secretary. Malmesbury's friendship with Louis Napoleon and his confidence in Cowley's judgement had much to do with this. Consequently, little pressure was put on France to reverse its war policy – and France was the key to peace in 1859.

Notes

1 K. Bourne, *The Foreign Policy of Victorian England, 1830–1902* (Oxford, 1970), 33.
2 Lord Minto to Massimo d'Azeglio, 4 April 1852, Museo centrale del Risorgimento, Rome (MCRR), busta 563.
3 'Her Majesty's government ... cannot hesitate to declare their opinion that the occupation of the Papal territory by foreign troops constitutes an irregular state of things which disturbs the equilibrium and may endanger the peace of Europe, and that by indirectly affording sanction to misgovernment, it promotes discontent and a tendency to revolution among the people.' Clarendon to Hudson (British minister at Turin), 26 May 1856, in F. Curato (ed.), *Le Relazioni diplomatiche fra la Gran Bretagna e il regno di Sardegna* (Rome, 1969), V, 279–80.
4 Palmerston to Ponsonby, 11 February 1848, quoted in Bourne, *The Foreign Policy of Victorian England*, 289–91.
5 D. Beales, *England and Italy 1859–60* (London, 1961), 28.
6 Hudson to unknown correspondent, 3 January 1861, Biblioteca Municipale 'Antonio Panizzi', Reggio Emilia, Mss.regg E.212/12; Hudson to Palmerston, 10 October 1851, Southampton University Library, Papers of Lord Palmerston, GC/HU/39.
7 Quoted in Beales, *England and Italy*, 21.
8 Ibid., 31; Bourne, *The Foreign Policy of Victorian England*, 294–5.
9 Lord John Russell, quoted by E. d'Azeglio to Dabormida, 26 January 1854, Archivio di Stato, Turin, (AST), Lettere ministri Gran Bretagna 1854–1855, cass.127.
10 Minto to M. d'Azeglio, 10 October 1851, MCRR, b.34(9).
11 Speech by Clarendon to the House of Lords, 17 February 1862, in D. Mack Smith, *The Making of Italy 1796–1866* (2nd edn., London, 1988), 206.
12 Palmerston, quoted by E. d'Azeglio to M. d'Azeglio, 22 May 1852, AST, Lettere ministri Gran Bretagna 1852, cass.122.
13 Clarendon to Hudson, 31 January 1855, in Curato, *Le Relazioni diplomatiche*, V, 53.
14 D. Mack Smith, *Victor Emanuel, Cavour, and the Risorgimento* (London, 1971), 80.

15 Clarendon to Palmerston, 13 March 1856, in Curato, *Le Relazioni diplomatiche*, V, 246.
16 Clarendon to Hudson, 17 October 1856, ibid, 352.
17 Mack Smith, *Victor Emanuel, Cavour, and the Risorgimento*, 90.
18 Malmesbury to Queen Victoria, 7 March 1858, Hampshire Record Office (HRO), Malmesbury Papers (MP), 9M73/52; Malmesbury to Hudson, 1 July 1858, HRO, MP, 9M73/54; Malmesbury to Cowley, 7 December 1858, HRO, MP, 9M73/53; Malmesbury to Bloomfield, 28 December 1858, HRO, MP, 9M73/54.
19 H. Hearder, 'Politica e opinione pubblica inglese verso l'Italia dal luglio 1859 al marzo 1860', extract from *Atti del XLII Congresso di Storia del Risorgimento Italiano* (Ravenna, 2–5 October 1965), 10.
20 Mack Smith, *Victor Emanuel, Cavour, and the Risorgimento*, 154.
21 Malmesbury to Cowley, 13 January 1859, HRO, MP, 9M73/53.
22 Mack Smith, *Victor Emanuel, Cavour, and the Risorgimento*, 154.
23 Cf. Bourne: 'it was fear of French ambitions alone which determined his [Malmesbury's] attitude and policy': Bourne, *The Foreign Policy of Victorian England*, 100. For the extent of British francophobia see: D. Beales, 'Simpatie e incomprensioni dell'Inghilterra vittoriana', *Osservatore politico letterario*, No.6 (June 1959).
24 Malmesbury to Queen Victoria, 10 December 1858, HRO, MP, 9M73/52.
25 F. Coppa, *The Origins of the Italian Wars of Independence* (London, 1992), 80; A. Blumberg, *A Carefully Planned Accident: The Italian war of 1859* (London and Toronto, 1990), 42–52.
26 Malmesbury to Prince Albert, 17 February 1859, HRO, MP, 9M73/52.
27 J. F. McMillan, *Napoleon III* (Longman, 1991), 84.
28 Malmesbury to Bloomfield, 16 March 1859, HRO, MP, 9M73/55.
29 Malmesbury, *Memoirs*, 272.
30 H. Hearder, 'La politica di Lord Malmesbury verso l'Italia nella primavera del 1859', *Rassegna Storica del Risorgimento*, XLIII (January–March 1956), 36.
31 Malmesbury, *Memoirs*, 666–7.
32 See: H. Hearder, 'The foreign policy of Lord Malmesbury, 1858–9' (unpublished Ph.D. thesis, University of London, 1954); H. Hearder, 'Napoleon III's threat to break off diplomatic relations with England during the crisis over the Orsini attempt in 1858', *English Historical Review* (July 1957), 474–81.
33 Malmesbury to Cowley, 28 March 1859, HRO, MP, 9M73/53.
34 Cowley to Malmesbury, 1 January 1859, HRO, MP, 9M73/8, and to Hudson, 3 February 1859, Public Record Office (PRO), Cowley Papers (CP), FO 519/225; Hearder, 'The Foreign Policy of Lord Malmesbury', 274; Cowley to Malmesbury, 8 February 1859, PRO, CP, FO 519/225; Cowley to Hudson, 13 February 1859, PRO, CP,

FO 519/225; Cowley to Malmesbury, 6 February 1859, PRO, CP, FO 519/225.
35 Beales, *England and Italy*, 45–6.
36 Blumberg, *A Carefully Planned Accident*, 78–83; Hearder, 'The Foreign Policy of Lord Malmesbury', 306-10.
37 Blumberg, *A Carefully Planned Accident*, 92. Malmesbury expressed the hope that Cavour would be without 'a leg left to stand upon'. Malmesbury to Bloomfield, 9 March 1859, HRO, MP, 9M73/55.
38 Malmesbury to Cowley, 4 and 9 April 1859, HRO, MP, 9M73/53.
39 Malmesbury to Loftus, 5 April 1859, HRO, MP, 9M73/57.
40 Malmesbury to Loftus, 1 June 1859, HRO, MP, 9M73/56.
41 Malmesbury to Cowley, 11 and 13 April 1859, HRO, MP, 9M73/53; Malmesbury to Hudson, 29 April 1859, HRO, MP, 9M73/58.
42 Malmesbury to Giuseppe Massari, 14 December 1873, MCRR, busta 47(1); Hudson to Cowley, 30 April 1859, PRO, CP, FO 519/194; Malmesbury to Hudson, 19 May 1859, HRO, MP, 9M73/55; Hudson to Malmesbury, 30 March 1858, HRO, MP, 9M73/13.
43 Hearder, 'The Foreign Policy of Lord Malmesbury', 400.

~4~
Europe's Quest for International Peace, 1870–1914

MATTHEW ANDERSON

The dream of lasting international peace, of some mechanism or form of organization which would end war between the states of Europe, or at least make it much less likely, was by the 1870s one with a long ancestry. In the 1460s the scheme conventionally associated with George Podiebrad, king of Bohemia, had envisaged a union of princes which would produce peace between them and strengthen Christendom against the threatening onrush of Turkish conquest. More than a century and a half later another and better known such plan, that attributed to the duc de Sully, the chief minister of Henry IV of France, had proposed something roughly similar, while in the early eighteenth century the best known of all early schemes of this kind, that of the Abbé de Saint-Pierre, had made its appearance. From a quite different and essentially traditional standpoint many of the humanists of the early sixteenth century, notably Erasmus himself, had denounced conflict as the product of the sinfulness of men and in particular of the pride, greed and anger of princes. Writers of this stamp had therefore called, with the highest intentions and a complete absence of realism, for war to be ended by a moral transformation of rulers; and in this they were followed in the seventeenth century by the Czech educational pioneer Comenius and several Quaker writers. The eighteenth century saw a marked rise in the number of schemes of different kinds meant to secure lasting international peace; and this growth in the volume of discussion, though from an increasingly wide range of viewpoints, continued in the first two-thirds of the nineteenth century.

The Europe which in the decades after 1870 had to confront the challenges of a new age – most immediately that of a great united Germany, and looming behind it the unprecedented possibilities of Russia and the United States – was therefore no stranger to such writing. But the outpouring of hopes and proposals of this kind reached during these two generations a level never before approached. In 1914 their lack of substance and powerlessness to influence events was to be thrown into abrupt and tragic relief. None the less they have an interest of their own and even, as illustrations of differing attitudes to the problem of war and as foreshadowings of the far greater institutionalized efforts after 1918 and 1945, a certain significance.[1]

During the decades between Sedan and Sarajevo the strength of the peace movement in all its aspects, and the activity with which the problem of ending international conflict was discussed, varied markedly between different European states. In Britain activity of this kind had for long been marked. The first British Peace Society, the expression of an essentially religious brand of pacifism, had come into existence in 1816 and become at once a vocal propagandist force. To this type of internationalism, sincere but often emotional and blind to realities, was added by the middle of the century a new and powerful element. This stemmed from the internationalism inherent in the free-trading movement which had now established its intellectual hegemony in Britain. The peoples of the world, it could be argued, were destined to be bound together more and more closely, not merely by trade and economic links but by a complex but natural system of free contacts of all kinds from which all benefited. It followed that war became not merely immoral but criminally irrational, a gross waste of energy and resources. Great armed forces and the material loss and sacrifice they demanded were a stupid and unnecessary burden, a mere gratification of the vanity and aggressiveness of rulers and aristocracies. In Britain, then, by 1870 the demand for measures to strengthen and perpetuate international peace had already deep roots of more than one kind.

In France there were equally vociferous forces at work, though their inspiration was often very different. There free trade never achieved the intellectual ascendancy and almost unquestioned acceptance as an orthodoxy which it did in Britain. But in France as well as across the Channel there were publicists in the 1850s and 1860s, inspired by a kind of high-minded materialism, who attacked war largely because of its enormous cost in wasted resources and misplaced effort. Thus the Ligue de la Paix set up in Paris in 1867 had among its leading members liberal and internationally-minded economists such as Michel Chevalier, Frédéric Passy and Paul Leroy-Beaulieu. Moreover, there was by the middle of the nineteenth century a well-marked French radical tradition, sometimes with distinct utopian socialist overtones, of a kind which was much weaker in Britain. This insisted that the achievement of international peace must depend on sweeping political and social change within each of the states of Europe. In its more uncompromising forms it asserted, as no significant body of British opinion ever did, that nations could be permanently at peace only if they were governed in a particular way. To end war they must become republics, democratic and constitutional. More vocally than all but a small minority of British commentators such writers called for the influence of aristocracies and military leaders, and often also of established churches, contaminated by their close association with existing political regimes, to be banished from national life.[2] Many French propagandists in the cause of peace, as a recent writer has noted, 'defined their work as the refinement of the human rights legacy of the French Revolution'.[3]

In the two great west European states, therefore, the agitation for peace between nations, though it might take different forms and have very limited practical effect, was alive, vocal and probably growing in the popular support it could command. In the other major powers the position was very different. A small peace movement developed in the Habsburg Empire in the 1870s and 1880s; but it had very shallow roots. It was in the main the product of foreign (largely British) influences and attracted only a small following among the well-to-do middle class and a few liberal aristocrats.[4] In Russia also the idea of lasting peace as a realistic goal had only the most limited impact. Most important of all, the new united Germany, the most powerful state in Europe and in the generation after 1870 in many ways the most successful, proved very stony ground for the growth of any significant peace movement. Throughout this period what German support there was for efforts of this kind remained disproportionately concentrated in the south-west, where there was a relatively strong liberal and democratic tradition: in 1913 a quarter of the total membership of the existing German peace societies could be found in the small state of Württemberg alone. In Prussia, completely dominant in the empire, the peace movement in any form, by contrast, was exceptionally weak; and everywhere official disapproval and discouragement were marked. The German peace movement was vocal far beyond its real strength, and this helped to give many foreign observers a quite inflated idea of its practical possibilities. In its case, however, the gap between high aspirations and depressing reality, something from which every propagandist group of this kind suffered, was wider than anywhere else in Europe.[5]

Everywhere agitation and assertion, however vocal, were in the event a pathetically flimsy barrier against the outbreak of devastating international conflict. All the talking and writing, all the speeches, the congresses, the pamphlets, the optimistic reports of growing support and increasing activity, all the genuine goodwill and lofty aspirations which inspired such activity, counted in the last analysis for nothing. This was to be shown with brutal clarity in 1914. Yet for a generation or more before the collapse of that year it was possible for many intelligent men to believe that Europe was now in the grip of a whole series of developments which were strengthening the prospect of international peace and which were irreversible. Practical and constructive cooperation between states seemed to be growing rapidly. An increasing use of quasi-legal methods to settle peacefully disputes between them seemed now well established. Even the forces making for a reduction in armaments seemed to be gaining ground.

More and more by the 1870s states were working together on a widening range of practical issues. Sometimes they were being forced to do so by the quickening pace of economic change and technological development. It was easy, therefore, to see in this good grounds for optimism. It appeared that history was moving inexorably towards a future in which such interdependence must progressively increase and possibilities of conflict correspondingly lessen. The striking growth of international communications seemed the clearest of all indicators that this better future must come. The International Telegraphic Union of 1865 was followed by the International Postal Union of 1874, the most successful and lasting creation of this kind. 'The great ideal of international freedom and union', wrote one enthusiast at the end of the century,

> is to be found in the post office. Wherever you see the red pillar-box, there you see the dumb prophet of the Millennium ... The

International Postal Union is the avant-courrier, or John the Baptist, of the Kingdom of Heaven, in which all frontiers would disappear and all mankind would be made free of the planet in which they dwell.

Another, a few years earlier, had been equally confident that 'The victories of Alexander and Napoleon are cast into the shade by the triumphal procession of the tiny postage-stamp around the world'.[6] International cooperation in the cause of public health, one of the most obviously necessary developments of this kind, was slower to develop. But there too, after a series of international conferences in the early 1890s, a body of internationally-agreed rules for the control of epidemic diseases had been established by 1903.

War itself, it seemed, might be not merely limited and humanized by international consensus, in the Geneva Convention of 1864 and that signed in Brussels ten years later. It might eventually be ended by the irresistible civilizing and moralizing tendency of material progress and the growing co-operation between states which it demanded. The 'technical regularity of warfare' which these agreements fostered, hoped an English lawyer in 1880, 'may be silently nurturing the very moral sentiments which, in time, will become the direct agency for the abolition of war itself.'[7] Some sorts of international co-operation failed notably to develop as their supporters had hoped. Trade unionism, still often faced by powerful social and governmental opposition in many states, was never able, from the creation of the International Miners' Federation in 1890 onwards, to become an effective supranational force. The most radical effort to ease communication between nations, the development of new synthetic languages – such as Volapuk, Esperanto and Ido – remained the preserve merely of small groups of enthusiasts. Nevertheless, enough was achieved to make credible, especially to those who already wished to believe, the assertion that Europe was now treading a path which led inevitably to a great strengthening of all the forces which made for peace.

Improvements in international communications or health precautions were usually quite readily accepted by governments. Even international rules governing the treatment of prisoners of war or banning the use of particular weapons they might, with more hesitation, be willing to agree to. But the greatly increased use of legal or quasi-legal methods of settling international disputes, the strengthening and codification of international law, still more the creation of new and efficient international institutions which might even have the power to coerce national governments, inevitably aroused much more opposition.

That law had a role of fundamental importance to play in fostering peace no internationalist disputed. However, hopes of this kind were actively encouraged by the growing use from the 1870s onwards of arbitration, an at least quasi-legal technique, in the settlement of disputes between states. Frequently used during the middle ages,[8] this method of adjusting differences had fallen into progressive and almost complete disuse during the seventeenth and eighteenth centuries. During the decades after 1815 it began, for reasons which are not altogether clear, to revive: according to one calculation, the mere eight such arbitrations of the years 1821–40 were followed by twenty in the period 1841–60.[9] But the disputes which were settled in this way were all relatively minor ones. There seemed even before the 1870s some ground for hope that the future might see an increased use of arbitration;[10] but it still played only a minor role in discussion of the problems of international peace. In 1871, however, the situation was suddenly changed by the settlement by an arbitral commission of the American claims against Great Britain in the *Alabama* case.[11] For the first time in centuries a truly serious dispute between two major states, one which had aroused strong feelings on both sides, had been peacefully ended in this way. The effects were considerable. The judgement and its successful application seemed to one enthusiastic observer 'probably ... one of the finest moments of our century', and to show that the movement in favour of international arbitration was now gaining ground and must soon become irresistible.[12] Later commentators had equally little doubt that the judgement marked a decisive change in the political and intellectual climate.[13] The veteran Passy claimed triumphantly in the 1890s that 'upon the slightest disturbance appeal is made to arbitration as an unfailing resource', while another Frenchman claimed with equal exaggeration that 'the idea of a Tribunal of International Arbitration has become universal'.[14] The events of the generation after 1871 seemed to give considerable support to this optimistic view. The number of international arbitrations grew sharply, especially from the 1890s onwards. A number of proposals for the creation of some permanent machinery to replace merely ad hoc arbitral arrangements, and thus root arbitration firmly in the structure of international relations, were put forward.[15]

Observers willing to look a little under the surface saw less ground for optimism. They could hardly fail to notice that it was the English-speaking countries, moulded by a powerful common-law tradition, which were much more willing than any others to make use of legalistic expedients such as this. Of all the successful international arbitrations of 1870–1914 Great Britain was a party to about half and the United States to about a third. Though the British House of Commons passed in 1873 a resolution calling for some permanent system of international arbitration, and similar ones were adopted in the following years in Sweden, the Netherlands and Belgium, no major continental country (apart from Italy, if she could be considered such) followed their example. The great states of continental Europe, with no Channel to protect them against invasion and with quite different histories, were inevitably less receptive than Britain to such methods. In Germany, in particular, official hostility to international arbitration was marked, perhaps most of all because such a method of settling disputes between states, it was correctly suspected there, must inevitably tend to strengthen democratic forces and parliamentary influences over foreign policy.[16] Moreover the propagandists who advocated arbitration so enthusiastically seldom faced its real problems. How could states be persuaded to accept the decision of some foreign body on issues which they regarded as of fundamental importance, those of national safety or honour? How could such a decision be enforced if one of the parties in dispute were unwilling to accept it? Such questions were too often glossed over.[17]

Nevertheless the belief that the relations between states could and should be regulated by law, and thus made less arbitrary and dangerous, gained many adherents in these decades. It seemed to many idealists that Europe must now advance from the ad hoc and relatively informal method of arbitration to others which were founded on permanent institutions. A standing international court must be created to administer a clear and universally accepted code of international law. This would establish finally and irrevocably the primacy of legal norms and procedures in the relations between states and rescue them for ever from the aggressiveness and arbitrary use of force which had disfigured them for so long. Clear rules of law effectively applied would have the great advantage of preventing dangerous disputes arising in the first place, or at least nipping them in the bud, whereas arbitration, however effective in its own sphere, could merely attempt to settle them after they had arisen.

The idea of some kind of international court as an essential foundation of lasting peace was far from new. Several eighteenth-century theorists, notably Jeremy Bentham, had stressed the need for one, though Bentham explicitly insisted that the body he envisaged should have no power to coerce any state which refused to accept its judgement. The great international congresses of delegates from different peace societies which met in 1850 and 1851 in Frankfurt and London had called for a codification of international law as an essential step towards the ending of war. But the last decades of the nineteenth century, and particularly perhaps the 1870s, saw interest in such issues reach an unprecedented level. Liberal idealism, now at its apogee, provided a fertile soil in which such projects could take root and grow. In the United States the National Association for the Advancement of Social Science set up a commission in 1866 to codify international law, the most serious and large-scale effort of this kind hitherto made anywhere. Six years later, it produced an ambitious draft code in 700 articles.[18] An Association for the Reform and Codification of the Law of Nations and an Institute of International Law both appeared in 1873.

As to the court which was to interpret and apply such a code there was wide scope for disagreement. How far should such a body be more than a permanent and formalized arbitral tribunal? How should its members be appointed? Should each European state have the right, through its parliament or otherwise, to nominate a member or members? (All these schemes were preoccupied more or less exclusively with peace in Europe, still for most practical purposes the only continent which mattered in terms of international relations.) Should the great powers be entitled to more members than the smaller states? Most important of all, what power should the court have to enforce its decisions? Should it be able, if necessary, to coerce in some way a refractory state? To this last crucial question the answers given by most of the writers willing to confront such a thorny subject were remarkably optimistic. Just as Bentham a century earlier had believed that publicity and public opinion would be powerful enough to force any government to obey such a judicial decision, so it was now often believed that these pressures, backed perhaps by some form of non-violent sanctions, would be sufficient. Democracy in some shape, parliamentary government and the free expression of ideas and opinions, were certain, in the eyes of liberal idealists, to gain ground everywhere. They were the wave of the future; and they would make it impossible for any government to ignore such condemnation of its actions. Publicity, the moral effect of widespread international disapproval, perhaps the severing by other states of normal relations with the recalcitrant one, would exert so much pressure that no government could for long withstand it. This optimism was not universal. One or two writers on the subject envisaged the need to enforce the decisions of any international court by sterner measures, even perhaps by armed force. Nevertheless the 1870s and early 1880s were by no means only the age of Bismarck. They were also years in which it seemed to many intelligent men, at least in the liberal states of western Europe, reasonable to look forward to the achievement in the not too distant future of a new status for law and legal institutions in the relations between states.[19]

The most fundamental condemnation of war during these decades was that based on moral and humanitarian considerations. Yet pragmatic or ostensibly pragmatic ones were also freely deployed on occasion. This is most clearly seen in the pressure for disarmament, or at least for some check to the menacing growth of armed forces, which became increasingly vocal as time went on. Until the 1860s disarmament had played a very minor role in discussion of the peace problem. Bentham in the later 1780s had called for a sharp reduction in armed forces. Immanuel Kant, in his *Perpetual Peace* of 1795, had envisaged the progressive abolition of standing armies throughout Europe. The peace societies which sprang up after 1815 in Great Britain and across the Atlantic in New England had incessantly urged governments to reduce their armies and navies. But the issue had been one which seemed in general rather secondary; and what significant agitation in favour of disarmament there was had been essentially religious in inspiration. By the middle of the nineteenth century this situation was clearly changing. The call to halt and even reverse the growth of armies and navies was now becoming notably louder and more insistent. Richard Cobden's moving in the House of Commons in 1851 of the first resolution in favour of their reduction to be put forward in any parliament was merely one indication, though a notable one, of a changing intellectual and emotional climate. The issue was now being discussed more and more in pragmatic, even materialistic, terms. Armies and navies, it was argued, devoured resources which could be used constructively in other ways, in public works, education or the fostering of industry. By unnecessarily raising taxation they depressed living standards and in this way again impeded economic progress. By coercing hundreds of thousands of young men into unproductive conscript military service they inflicted massive loss on the societies concerned, and also fostered a militaristic psychology which was potentially very dangerous. The world was moving inexorably towards greater economic and intellectual unity. It was destined to be bound together more and more closely by bonds of free trade and free movement of ideas. Great and costly armed forces therefore were no more than an irrational and ultimately futile attempt to obstruct this inevitable movement.

This materialism and pragmatism was far from being the only basis on which the condemnation of great armed forces was founded. They were still attacked, above all in the English-speaking world, on religious grounds, as unchristian and immoral. Radicals, most of all in France, feared and disliked them, as they had for long done, as an instrument which autocratic monarchies and traditional aristocracies might use to buttress their own power. One aspect of this was the demand, voiced by several writers on the subject, for state constitutions which would strip rulers of their power to declare war and place it instead firmly in the much safer hands of elected parliaments.[20] But the pragmatic and materialist argument had now added a new and vocal element to the growing pressure for some measure of disarmament. It does much to explain the new prominence of the issue from the 1860s or 1870s onwards.

The unprecedented prominence, and even to some extent and in some countries popular appeal, which the disarmament issue had achieved by the end of the nineteenth century, is most clearly seen in the enthusiasm with which a wide variety of idealists – pacifists, free-trading liberals, republican and utopian radicals, believers in some form of world government – greeted the initiative of Tsar Nicholas II which led to the first Hague Peace Conference of 1899. The practical achievements of the conference were very modest. Its main constructive result, the creation of a Permanent Court of Arbitration, was a gesture as much as anything of much practical value. German opposition meant that the court was weakened by the abandonment of a British proposal that recourse to it be made compulsory in certain relatively minor types of dispute. The dismissive verdict of a leading international lawyer immediately after the conference ended that 'the substantive provisions contained in the Arbitration Convention amount really to nothing'[21] was quite justified. Disarmament stimulated rather more discussion: but again the practical results were slight – the prohibition of the use of dumdum bullets, of poison gas and the launching of projectiles 'from balloons or by similar methods'. Yet these meagre achievements did not significantly damp the high hopes which the Tsar's rescript of August 1898 calling for the meeting of such a conference had evoked in every strand of the European peace movement. The enthusiast who believed that the conference would not only establish arbitration firmly as the method of settling international disputes but also be the first step towards the creation of a united federal Europe spoke for many besides himself.[22] Even in Germany there was a flicker of popular interest. The spring of 1899 was the only moment during these years when the peace societies there, normally so pathetically weak, managed to hold public meetings in several large cities; and the most persistent German pamphleteer in the cause of peace even claimed that the conference had the same historical significance as the discovery of America or the invention of gunpowder.[23]

The diplomats and experts who met in The Hague in 1899 were, virtually without exception, completely cynical about the possibility of achieving anything effective. The head of the American delegation thought that 'probably, since the world began, never did so large a body come together in a spirit of more hopeless scepticism as to any good result', while one of the German delegates published in that very year a pamphlet which denounced the hopes and ambitions of the peace movement as not merely impractical but positively undesirable.[24] Yet this official pessimism and even ridicule did nothing to check the flush of hope, however misplaced and exaggerated, which the conference had aroused. The same contrast between hard-headed official attitudes and inflated idealist hopes can be seen again in 1907, when the Second Hague Conference met. So far as disarmament was concerned it achieved even less than its predecessor. Even before it met, Prince Bülow, the Imperial Chancellor, proclaimed publicly that Germany would have nothing to do with the disarmament question, while a French observer complained that at The Hague 'words fall like a fine rain and veil the distant contours of reality'.[25] Yet again the same exaggerated hopes of lasting peace, that the conference might lay the foundations of new and effective international institutions, were aroused. It is easy to understand why the head of the American delegation complained that 'the merely eloquent pacifists write as though it were only necessary for the conference to decree that there should be eternal peace and that then eternal peace there would be'.[26]

The two Hague conferences aroused such a response in the ranks of the peace movement largely because they seemed (with the wish of course very much father to the thought) an essential step towards the creation of international institutions which worked and the achievement of meaningful international government. Arbitration, the codification of international law, a permanent international judicial tribunal and disarmament – all could be seen as leading to this ultimate goal; and in the two or three decades before 1914 proposals for some kind of government which transcended national boundaries became unprecedentedly numerous. The most obvious and popular form for them to take was that of a European federation; and for this there was an obvious, and to many writers attractive, model in the United States. The advocates of such a federation were predominantly convinced supporters of free trade: this meant that the immediate practical advantages of European unity bulked large in their arguments. A united Europe would no longer waste its energies in maintaining national armies and navies, each anxiously watching and competing with those of neighbour-states. This meant that the peoples of Europe would be not merely richer but happier because more secure. Such a Europe (though this was an argument less frequently used and one with little appeal to liberals) would also be better able to influence and even dominate the outside world. In particular it might control more effectively the great areas of European imperial expansion in Africa and Asia.[27]

But whatever the gains it brought and however its powers were used, how was a united Europe to be created? Should it begin in a relatively unambitious way, perhaps as a federation of one or two of the more advanced states of western Europe which might later be joined by others when they were ready to do so?[28] Or ought it rather to aim high from the beginning? Should it be controlled by a fully-fledged international government, equipped with armed forces more powerful than those of any member-state or combination of states, and with supervisory powers which ensured that none of these covertly increased its power to make war?[29] There was therefore plenty of scope for disagreement about the powers and functions of any international régime. This was one reason, though by no means the most important one, for the complete failure of these schemes to have any practical effect or even, in most cases, to attract much attention outside a narrow circle of the converted. Even the most balanced and workmanlike proposal of all, that put forward in the 1880s by the Scottish international lawyer James Lorimer, a professor at Edinburgh, shared this fate (though it aroused a certain amount of interest in academic circles). Lorimer's suggestions – a European legislature of two houses whose members would be elected by a rather rough system of proportional representation, an international government under a president chosen by itself, an international court of justice, and an international army made up of contingents from national ones and financed by a system of international taxation – was highly ambitious. Yet at the same time he showed a grasp of realities not common in schemes of this kind, particularly in his insistence that any supranational union must depend for its success on the support of a small number of great powers.[30] Nevertheless his proposals had no more practical effect than the wildest suggestions of the most visionary idealist.

The cause of international government, and indeed the whole peace movement, had so little practical success above all because much of the intellectual and emotional atmosphere which surrounded them was overwhelmingly hostile. International arbitration, a strengthened and codified international law, disarmament, effective international institutions; all these were out of tune with many of the currents of thought and even more of feeling which ran strongly during the half-century before the First World War. Everywhere there was still, as for centuries past, a pervasive assumption that conflict between states and nations, however costly and destructive, could not in the end be avoided. Everywhere men looked back to a history pervaded by inter-state rivalries and forward, whether with pleasurable anticipation or pessimistic resignation, to a future in which they would still play a dominant role. Anyone who sought lasting peace therefore had constantly to struggle against a deadening assumption that he was trying to achieve the impossible.

In any case, was such a peace, even if achievable, really desirable? Was not struggle, conflict, the resulting victory of the stronger, the braver, the more intelligent, the vehicle of progress and of the whole forward movement of humanity? Did not the test of war force a state to become more efficient, more productive, and thus more able to survive and flourish? If this were so, war could have a value as a creative stimulus which far outweighed its cost, especially if it were a short and decisive struggle like those of 1864, 1866 and 1870–1 which had created a united Germany. There in particular a long line of economists, many of them of great ability, beginning in the 1840s with Friedrich List, the most important prophet of economic nationalism, argued along these lines.[31] At a deeper level it could be contended that war evoked and strengthened the finest aspects of the human character. It called forth courage, discipline and self-sacrifice. Endless peace, on the other hand, would allow mankind to degenerate in an atmosphere of selfish materialism and corroding self-indulgence.

This line of argument made war an engine of moral regeneration and raised it almost to the level of a spiritual force, even to one divinely ordained for the improvement of mankind. Conflict of this kind, claimed an anonymous English pamphleteer in 1871, was 'appointed by a Higher Power as one of the means of education and discipline for the human race'.[32] A decade later Helmuth von Moltke, as chief of the General Staff the greatest architect of German military success, produced the best-known and one of the most forcible statements of this attitude: 'Perpetual peace is a dream and not even a beautiful dream. War is an element of the divine order of the world. In it are developed the noblest virtues of man: courage and self-denial, fidelity to duty and the spirit of self-sacrifice, soldiers give their lives. Without war the world would stagnate and lose itself in materialism'.³³ Such attitudes had a long history. For centuries it had been a convention to assert that prolonged peace led inevitably to a moral flabbiness which could be cured only when war roused men once more to effort and sacrifice. Indeed even among the strongest protagonists of the idea of international peace most were willing to admit that war was sometimes necessary in defence of some higher ideal of right and liberty, that as one French pacifist argued in 1909 'No one has the right to allow justice to be destroyed because of fear of struggle'.³⁴

By the 1870s a popularized and over-simplified form of Darwinian evolutionary theory, the 'social Darwinism' of the later nineteenth century, was adding a new element to such claims and giving them apparent scientific backing. This made it easy to believe, with complete sincerity, that without struggle between states and nations those which merited only decline and death would have their lives prolonged artificially and undeservedly. This could not be for the long-term good of humanity as a whole. The protection of the weak would inhibit the growth, which nature demanded, of the more vigorous and energetic; and it was on these that the future of the human race depended. Perhaps, on a rather less uncompromising view, it might be possible to retain this essential element of conflict without recourse to outright war. A competitive growth of armies and navies might perform the same function at much smaller human cost, since in an arms race the more enduring and determined of the competitors, the vehicle of future progress, would be the victor. The American Admiral Mahan, in many ways a typical exponent of this whole strain of thinking, believed this might be possible since 'armament represents the aggregate of the natural forces inherent in any community'.³⁵ But struggle, real struggle, in some form there must be. Faced by assumptions so widespread and deeply rooted, the peace movement in the decades before war overwhelmed Europe in 1914 was fighting an uphill struggle. The extent of its propaganda, at least in one or two states, the outpouring of pamphlets, the meetings and resolutions, the schemes and plans, the sincerity of its hopes, might do something to conceal this fact but could do little to alter it.

It is easy to dismiss the strivings of late nineteenth- and early twentieth-century Europe towards an end to war for their ineffectiveness and naïve optimism. Those who championed the cause of peace in these years were to be justified only too well in their stressing of the unprecedented cost and destructiveness of any future war; but they were quite unrealistic in the great majority of cases in their expectations of the ease with which it might be prevented. Yet the hopes and plans of these years were more widespread and vocal than ever before. More than ever in the past it was now beginning to be felt that the problem of safeguarding peace was one of fundamental importance, and even one which was soluble. The great outpouring, at least in Britain and France, of discussion of such issues, which began very soon after the outbreak of the war of 1914 and grew as it progressed,[36] therefore rested on substantial foundations which had been laid years before. It is not too fanciful to discern in the hopes and strivings of these pre-war decades, some of the outlines of the world which emerged after 1918.

Notes

1 A general discussion of all aspects of the peace movement in the years 1870–1914 can be found in M. S. Anderson, *The Rise of Modern Diplomacy, 1450–1919* (London, 1993), 248–79, on which this essay is largely based.
2 C. Lemonnier, *Les Etats-Unis d'Europe* (Paris, 1872), is a good example of a radical proposal of this sort and of the attitudes which underlay it. The author insisted that all the members of the European federation he advocated must be republics, and denounced monarchical and clerical influences as the greatest of all obstacles to international peace.
3 Sandi S. Cooper, 'Pacifism in France, 1889–1914: International Peace as a Human Right', *French Historical Studies* 17 (1991–2), 360.
4 R. R. Laurence, 'The Peace Movement in Austria, 1867–1914', in S. Wank (ed.), *Doves and Diplomats: Foreign Offices and Peace Movements in Europe and America* (Westport, Conn. and London, 1978), 24–7.
5 The weakness of the peace movement in Germany is illustrated in detail in R. Chickering, *Imperial Germany and a World without War* (Princeton, 1975), especially 47, 59–60, 66–7, 197.
6 W. T. Stead, *The United States of Europe on the Eve of the Parliament of Peace* (London, 1899), 14; K. P. Arnoldson, *Pax Mundi* (London, 1892), 139.

7   S. Amos, *Political and Legal Remedies for War* (London, 1880), 336. For a similar hope in Germany, see H. Hetzel, *Die Humanisierung der Krieges in den letzten Hundert Jahren* (Frankfurt, 1891).
8   See the long list of medieval arbitrations printed in M. Novacovitch, *Les Compromis et les arbitrages internationaux du XIIe au XVe siècle* (Paris, 1905), 100–59.
9   J. B. Scott, *The Hague Peace Conferences of 1899 and 1907* (Baltimore, 1909), 226.
10 For example, M. Bernard, *Four Lectures on Subjects connected with Diplomacy* (London, 1866), 226.
11 The *Alabama* dispute arose from the failure on the part of the British government to prevent the departure of a newly-commissioned Confederate warship of that name from Merseyside. The ship went on to take a severe toll of Northern shipping during the American Civil War, as a result of which the USA later sought compensation from Great Britain.
12 E. de Lavelaye, *Des Causes actuelles de guerre en Europe et de l'arbitrage* (Brussels and Paris, 1873), 191–2.
13 Comte L. Komarovsky, *Le Tribunal international* (Paris, 1887), 264–5; F. Dreyfus, *L'Arbitrage international* (Paris, 1892), 205; M. Revon, *L'Arbitrage international; son passé – son présent – son avenir* (Paris, 1892), 327–9.
14 F. Passy, 'Peace Movement in Europe', *American Journal of Sociology* ii (1896), 6; C. Richet, *Peace and War* (London, 1906; French original, 1899), 76.
15 P. Lacombe, 'Mémoire sur l'établissement d'un tribunal international', in A. de Marcoartù, *Internationalism* (London, 1876), 143ff.; Lavelaye, *Des Causes actuelles*, pt. iii; N. Notovich, *La Pacification de l'Europe et Nicholas II* (2nd edn., Paris, 1899), 176–83.
16 Chickering, *Imperial Germany*, 220–5.
17 For some discussion of difficulties of this kind, however, see E. Rouard de Card, *L'Arbitrage international dans le passé, le présent et l'avenir* (Paris, 1877), 111–18, and the same author's *Les destinées de l'arbitrage international depuis la sentence rendue par le tribunal de Genève* (Paris, 1892), 206–8; E. von Holtzendorff-Vietsmannsdorff, *Die Idee des ewigen Völkerfriedens* (Berlin, 1882), 41–3.
18 Dudley Field, *Draft Outlines of an International Code* (New York, 1872).
19 Contemporary discussion of this aspect of the problem of peace is summarized in Anderson, *The Rise of Modern Diplomacy*, 258–9.
20 See, for example, Marcoartù, *Internationalism*, chap. ii; A. P. Sprague, *The Codification of Public International Law* (printed as an appendix to Marcoartù's book); Rouard de Card, *L'Arbitrage international*, 145–6.

21 T. E. Holland, 'Some Lessons of the Peace Conference', *Fortnightly Review* 72 (1899), 957.
22 J. Novicow (Novikov), *La Fédération de l'Europe* (Paris, 1901), 761–7, 771–2.
23 A. H. Fried, *Die Haager Conferenz, ihre Bedeutung und ihre Ergebnisse* (Berlin, 1900), Introduction, viii.
24 C. de A. Davis, *The United States and the Second Hague Peace Conference* (Durham, NC, 1975), 25; K. von Stengel, *Der ewige Friede* (Munich, 1899).
25 G. Hanotaux, *La Politique de l'équilibre* (Paris, 1912), 22.
26 Quoted in Davis, *The United States and the Second Hague Peace Conference*, 194.
27 For arguments of this more aggressive and expansionist kind, see, for example, (M. Adler), *Der Krieg, der Congressidee und die allgemeine Wehrpflicht* (Prague, 1866), summarized in Komarovsky, *Le Tribunal international*, 381–3; and the idiosyncratic and untypical *Mission actuelle des souverains. Par l'un d'eux* (Paris, 1882), chap. xii.
28 As proposed by e.g. E. Goblet, Comte d'Alviella, *Désarmer ou déchoir. Essai sur les relations internationales* (Brussels and Paris, 1872), 210.
29 As proposed by R. de la Grasserie, *Des Moyens pratiques pour parvenir à la suppression de la paix armée et de la guerre* (Paris, 1894), 57–64, 88–99.
30 The details can be found in Lorimer's *Institutes of the Law of Nations* (Edinburgh and London, 1883–4), ii, chap. xiv.
31 E. Silberner, *The Problem of War in Nineteenth-Century Economic Thought* (Princeton, 1946), 149–50.
32 *War, its Causes and Consequences and How it May be Averted* (London, 1871), 6–7.
33 Quoted in G. Best, *Humanity in Warfare: The Modern History of the International Law of Armed Conflict* (London, 1980), 145.
34 Cooper, 'Pacifism in France', 381.
35 A. T. Mahan, *Armaments and Arbitration, or, The Place of Force in the International Relations of States* (New York and London, 1912), 11.
36 Some aspects of this are discussed briefly in Anderson, *The Rise of Modern Diplomacy*, 279–90.

~5~
Joseph Chamberlain and Tariff Reform: British Radicalism, Modernization and Nationalism

SCOTT NEWTON

The accepted view of Joseph Chamberlain is that he was an early radical who turned Conservative with advancing years, a political odyssey described by Winston Churchill as being characterized by passage from 'fiery red' to 'true blue'.[1] This essay challenges the orthodox line, arguing that Chamberlain never lost his radicalism, but that for this to be understood 'Radical Joe's' career has to be seen against the background of a state divided into producing and non-producing interests. Everything Chamberlain did or tried to achieve was undertaken out of a belief that the producing interests needed to take over the British state, for reasons to do with democracy and with economic efficiency. The Tariff Reform campaign was a direct descendant of the radical protests against 'those who toil not, neither do they spin', of the 1880s – the means had shifted in the search for parliamentary and political support; the ends had not.

The Political Economy of Victorian Britain

Joseph Chamberlain was born in 1836. His political consciousness was therefore shaped during the early Victorian epoch. Conventional wisdom still depicts this period as one in which the old agrarian order bowed to the economic power of manufacturing industry. The crucial dates in this view of British development are 1832 (the Reform Act) and 1846 (the repeal of the Corn Laws). By the first an aristocrat-dominated Parliament changed the electoral system and the distribution of seats in the House of Commons to secure greater representation for the provincial middle class whose welfare was bound up with industry. With the second agricultural protection was brought to a conclusion, inaugurating an era of cheap food for the masses, low wage costs for the employers, and free trade in commerce with the rest of the world.[2]

Yet in recent years persuasive arguments have been produced, calling into question the accuracy of this picture. The outlines of an alternative approach to British development were initially sketched by Perry Anderson and Tom Nairn in articles written for *New Left Review*.[3] Anderson and Nairn have held their ground and their position has been supported by the researches of Geoffrey Ingham, W. D. Rubinstein, John Scott, Martin Wiener and, most recently, P. J. Cain and A. G. Hopkins.[4]

According to these revisionists the influence of manufacturers over British society was 'relatively limited, even in the early twentieth century.'[5] Industry failed to expand beyond its provincial citadels in Leeds, Manchester and Birmingham, while the south of England remained green and pleasant, decorated with old churches, old villages, country houses and public schools. This uneven landscape reflected a process of uneven development, carried out within an environment dominated by an aristocratic establishment which since the Glorious Revolution of 1688 had based its wealth on high finance and high farming. The key to the prosperity of this landowning élite was the City of London, which had expanded dramatically with the formation of the national debt and the creation of the Bank of England after 1690. Making common cause with a mercantile oligarchy sustained by the activities of great companies such as the East India Company and the Hudson's Bay Company, the aristocracy pursued an aggressive strategy of commercial expansion. The 'first British Empire' was founded on the achievement of monopoly over the trade of India and north America, a position won after long and costly wars with the French.

It was the City of London which first mobilized the credit for these conflicts, expanding the national debt in the process, and then provided the banking, shipping and insurance facilities for the British traders who, by the end of the Napoleonic Wars, dominated world commerce and returned their wealth to the great landed estates. Between 1748 and 1815 the national debt grew from £78 m to £700 m; interest payments on the debt absorbed 50 per cent of all public spending in peacetime, equivalent, according to one estimate, to half the value of all Britain's exports throughout the whole of the eighteenth century.⁶ Taxation became steadily more regressive: the consumer paid the price of aggressive commercial expansion in customs and excise duties while the contribution of land tax to the government's revenue diminished. English taxation was as a rule higher, both on a *per capita* basis and as a share of national income, than French after 1700. As the century progressed, the discrepancy became more pronounced.⁷

It is of course true that many of the trappings of mercantilism were stripped away after 1815. Yet the process was initiated within the Tory banking and landowning élite which dominated the City. By the end of the Napoleonic Wars the level of accumulated debt and the taxation needed to finance it were generating concern. Almost 80 per cent of the public revenues were by now devoted to financing the national debt. The worries were most concisely expressed by the Tory radical David Ricardo, who published his *Principles of Political Economy and Taxation* in 1817. The main concern was to reassure investors and property holders that the debt could be redeemed without on the one hand resorting for the foreseeable future to a level of taxation destructive of enterprise or on the other inflating the currency and destroying confidence in the financial system.⁸

Accordingly the aftermath of the Napoleonic Wars saw a return to the gold standard and massive reductions in public expenditure, followed in the 1820s with tariff reductions and the shrinkage of State intervention in the economy. The ultimate objective was the replacement of 'Old Corruption' by a 'Nightwatchman State' committed to low taxes and a currency whose value was guaranteed by convertibility to gold at a fixed rate of exchange. Against such a background the repeal of the Corn Laws no longer appears as the triumph of the manufacturing over the landowning interest, but as the accommodation of the former by the latter – by now itself thoroughly committed to market values and commercial practices. Certainly it was appreciated that free imports of corn would guarantee food supplies for a domestic population whose growth was threatening to outstrip local agricultural resources. It was also understood that the abolition of duties would assist manufacturers, both with labour costs and with exports to countries possessing the means to buy them as a result of their access to the British market. Reciprocal reductions in foreign tariffs were confidently expected, creating in the process a virtuous spiral of international trade. But free trade was also in the interests of the City. By the 1840s the City was well-established as the world's clearing-house, and free trade, by widening world trade, would generate wealth from the financial services London was so well-placed to provide.[9]

On the basis of free trade, therefore, an alliance was formed between the City and the manufacturers of commodities such as cotton textiles, coal, and semi-finished manufactures, notably pig-iron, which provided 'inputs for industrialization' for overseas economies. At the same time British shipbuilders grew prosperous on the basis of their near-monopoly of the world's carrying trade. After 1850 these exports increasingly made their way to the recently settled food and raw material producing areas of the world economy, in the Americas, India, South Africa and Australasia. In turn these regions became the heaviest recipients of British investment, flowing to construct the infrastructures, composed of railway networks, ports and harbours, which tied the primary producers to the metropolitan economy.[10]

The accommodations of 1832 and 1846 may have averted a revolution in Britain. Far from uniting with the working-class leadership behind the cause of Chartism, manufacturers and the middle class joined with the financial aristocracy thereafter in a coalition cemented by a common interest in free trade and in the defence of order and property. In 1851 the Great Exhibition at Crystal Palace had celebrated Britain's international industrial supremacy and the cosmopolitan philosophy which seemed to underpin it. But the alliance was not one of equal partners, as events were to demonstrate.

In the period after 1850 Britain gradually lost its domination of world trade in manufactured goods. Between 1880 and 1913 Britain's share of total world manufacturing output slipped from 22.9 per cent to 13.6 per cent while the shares of the United States and Germany grew from 14.7 per cent to 32 per cent and from 8.5 per cent to 14.8 per cent respectively.[11] Some manufacturers, particularly those in the metal-bashing industries centred in the Midlands, responded to this new situation by calling for protection. They established the National Fair Trade League, and during the 1880s and 1890s its members called for tariffs as a bargaining weapon to reduce German and American trade barriers. It was a modest demand. Yet its implementation was rejected and Britain remained committed to free trade even if this meant that local trades were to be put out of business by German goods being dumped on the home market at prices with which no British manufacturer could compete. The experience of relative economic decline provoked no change of economic philosophy.

Stout resistance to the protectionist lobby came from the City since it was able to increase its revenue from servicing the growing volume of world commerce. Free trade guaranteed multiplying opportunities for foreign investment and accumulating profits for banks and insurance companies, from, respectively, the short-term financing of international trade and mounting premiums derived from overseas. This wealth was then reinvested abroad, where returns were as a rule higher than they were at home, especially after 1870 when the recurring speculative booms associated with the era of 'railway mania' were becoming rare. It followed that the experience of relative decline was not repeated in the City. Visible exports grew from £187.8 million in 1865–70 to £488.9 million in 1911–13, a factor of 2.6, while over the same period invisible income expanded from £98.7 million to £340 million, a factor of 3.4. The ratio of invisible to visible income narrowed during these years from 0.53:1 to 0.70:1. Britain's accumulating balance of capital overseas rose from an annual average of £1065 million in 1871–5 to £3990 million in 1911–12.

There is, therefore, ample evidence to suggest that there was no necessary compatibility between the interests of British manufacturers and those of the financial sector, a disjunction which became increasingly clear with the expansion of overseas investment. Given the volume of investment abroad it is not surprising that City institutions were more interested in overseas economic developments than they were in those in Britain. Even the liberal *Economist* remarked that, 'London is often more concerned with the course of events in Mexico than what happens in the Midlands and is more upset by a strike on the Canadian Pacific than by one in the Cambrian Collieries'.[13] The relationship between City institutions and British manufacturers was not close during this period. In 1905–6 no more than 600 of the 5000 securities quoted on the London Stock Exchange were 'home industrials'. At the end of the Victorian era all but five of the City's leading wealthholders owed their fortunes to commercial rather than to industrial activity.[14]

The disjunction between finance and industry was reflected in the regional picture of late nineteenth-century Britain. The fastest growing region of the British economy in the second half of the nineteenth century was the south-east. By 1911 25 per cent of the British people lived there, earning the income which generated the world's first mass consumer society, along with the development of suburbs and seaside holiday resorts such as Southend and Margate. The region had become, as C. H. Lee has noted, 'the focal point of an affluent society enjoying conspicuous consumption and giving employment to a wide range of labour-intensive services'. These services were both professional, embracing medicine, education and the law, and domestic, providing work for butlers, nannies, maids and cooks. Demand was stimulated for consumer and light industry, such as the fashion and luxury clothing trades, furniture manufacturing, and for printing and publishing, as well as for retailing and distributive services and for transport.[15] The prosperity of the south-east and of the City were mutually reinforcing: the savings generated by the service sector were ploughed into 'rentier home and foreign stocks'.[16]

Between 1870 and 1914 the sociological and political map of Britain reproduced the two worlds of an increasingly sophisticated and prosperous financial system and service sector on the one hand and on the other an industrial base in relative decline. It was a development noted by perceptive contemporaries; the radical economist J. A. Hobson argued that voting in the 1910 general elections derived from the existence of two Englands, one dominated by the consumer, the other, deemed by him to be more politically progressive and enlightened, by the producer. Producer's England was rooted in the industrial centres of the Midlands, northern England, south Wales and southern Scotland. It was characterized by nonconformism in religion and the political hegemony of new liberalism and organized labour. Consumer's England, centred on the Home Counties and on the cathedral and university towns, was mainly Anglican and Conservative. At its apex was the network of families whose fortunes had originally been made in agriculture but who were now sustained by commerce.[17]

This was a culture and society which reproduced itself via an educational system whose career path took pupils through the public schools and Oxbridge. Here young men were trained in the 'gentlemanly' values of an establishment which regarded the world of the provincial manufacturer as vulgar and materialistic. The possession of property and rentier incomes meant that the gentleman would not be dependent on full-time work. If he needed money it was to be made in a form of occupation far removed from the world of the factory. Suitable careers were to be found in the City, the liberal professions, the arts, the Church, in political leadership at home and in the colonies. It follows that the characteristic products of such a background were not industrialists but administrators, financiers, merchants and Conservative MPs. Down to 1914, for example, more than twice as many pupils from Winchester went into commerce as into manufacturing. The proportion of permanent secretaries from public schools reached two-thirds between 1900 and 1918.[18]

By 1900 the pattern of British socio-economic development clearly reflected the hegemony of Consumer's England. The nation's political leadership shared the culture of the City and identified with its economic internationalism. It was this liberal order which the Tariff Reform Campaign challenged, so that industrial capitalism and not commercial, cosmopolitan capitalism became the dominating force in British society. The Tariff Reformers hoped to reach their objective through 'imperial preference' – which meant providing tariff protection for domestic producers, with duties lower on Empire-made than on foreign-made goods.

Tariff Reformers have frequently been dismissed as conservatives keen to insulate industrialists and farmers from the consequences of their own inefficiency. The criticism is not without foundation: but there was another side to the Tariff Reform campaign. It was amongst other things a radical movement whose success might have transformed the balance of power in favour of Producer's England, elevating the issue of industrial modernization, to meet the German and American challenges, to the top of the political agenda.

The Radical Tradition

The radical side of the Tariff Reform Campaign has not generally been appreciated by historians. Yet in leading this crusade from

1903 until partially crippled by a stroke in 1906 Joseph Chamberlain was articulating many of the traditional themes of a peculiarly British radical tradition which was at least a century old.

During the eighteenth and the first decades of the nineteenth centuries radicals had maintained that Britain was a nation divided into two societies, one 'natural' and the other 'unnatural'. The 'natural society' was composed of small-scale capitalist producers; the 'unnatural society' embraced the establishment and was dominated by the City and the landowning aristocracy. It was this establishment which expropriated the wealth of the producer by penal taxation, raised to fund the national debt and to finance an adventurist foreign policy.[19]

The discourse of radicalism was not limited to a socio-economic critique of the establishment. To this was added moral contempt. Thus John Wade, in his *Extraordinary Black Book* of 1831 and William Cobbett, both in *Rural Rides* and in the *Political Register*, pointed to the distinction between the productive and the unproductive groups in society. 'Productive' groups included capitalists, farmers, workers and agricultural labourers. The 'unproductive groups' were, in Cobbett's words, made up of

> twenty thousand parsons; more than twenty thousand stock brokers and stockjobbers perhaps; forty or fifty thousand tax gatherers; thousands upon thousands of military and naval officers in full pay; in addition to all these, here are thousands upon thousands of this Dead Weight, all busily engaged in breeding gentlemen and ladies ... all receiving *a premium for breeding*.[20]

Richard Cobden, leader of the provincial manufacturers in their crusade to abolish the last remnants of a system designed to protect the wealth of the landed aristocracy, was part of this tradition. Yet after the repeal of the Corn Laws Cobden became a disillusioned man and came to believe that he had failed: the old order had survived, its values still hegemonic, because it had made a judicious concession to the manufacturing interest. He came to identify the City of London and its 'bankers and money mongers' as part of a system which obstructed the development of industry[21] and lamented the political feebleness of the middle class:

... feudalism is every day more and more in the ascendant in political and social life. So great is its power and prestige that it draws to it the support and homage of even those who are the natural leaders of the newer and better civilization. Manufacturers and merchants as a rule seem only to desire riches that they may be enabled to prostrate themselves at the feet of feudalism.[22]

By the end of his life Cobden had come to the conclusion that the power of the establishment could only be broken by universal (manhood) suffrage and by the break-up of the large landed estates.

Chamberlain, the Empire and Tariff Reform

Joseph Chamberlain was Cobden's successor as the archetypal bourgeois radical. During the 1880s, when compared by Lord Salisbury to a 'Sicilian bandit', by others to Dick Turpin or Jack Cade, he employed the radical rhetoric of attacks on unproductive wealth. The aristocracy and the Lords were people 'who toil not, neither do they spin'. But Chamberlain's radicalism contained a new ingredient: confronted by widespread poverty he abandoned the *laissez-faire* of Cobdenism and came to advocate using the resources of the community, at the levels both of the municipality and the State, to improve the living standards of the working class. As mayor of Birmingham he had organized the municipal takeover of the gas and water industries, on the grounds that 'all regulated monopolies should be controlled by representatives of the people and not left in the hands of private speculators'.[23] He brought the case for activism into the heart of government as a member of Gladstone's Cabinet after 1880, and at Warrington in September 1885 argued that

> The great problem of our civilization is still unsolved. We have to account for and to grapple with the mass of misery and destitution in our midst, co-existent as it is with the evidence of abundant wealth and teeming prosperity. It is a problem which some men would put aside by reference to the eternal laws of supply and demand, to the necessity of freedom of contract and to the sanctity of every private right of property. But, gentlemen, these phrases are the convenient cant of selfish wealth.[24]

In place of the old Liberal agenda of non-interventionism Chamberlain offered a new platform, published under the title of the 'Unauthorised Programme'. Here, he called in the short term for free education, 'three acres and a cow' for rural labourers, the introduction both of land taxation and of a graduated tax on property, and for local housing and slum clearance initiatives funded through the rates. These were short-term objectives, the proposals on taxation justified by reference to the need for property to pay a 'ransom' for 'the security it enjoys'; in the long term the Programme advocated manhood suffrage, the establishment of County Councils, and the disestablishment of the Church of England.[25]

Chamberlain's uneasy relationship with Gladstonian Lib-eralism finally broke down beyond repair in 1886, over the issue of Home Rule for Ireland. Thereafter he became leader of the Liberal Unionists, and the exigencies of parliamentary politics led to an increasing degree of co-operation with the Conservatives. Yet the commitment to interventionism remained: Chamberlain stuck by the central demands of his 1885 programme, adding to it calls for state old age pensions, an eight-hour day for miners, industrial arbitration, compensation for injury at work, cheap rail travel for workers, municipal mortgages and immigration control.[26]

All this made Chamberlain potentially as explosive an ally of Conservatism as he had been for old-fashioned Liberalism, and throughout the Tariff Reform campaign he sought to remain Radical Joe, the spokesman of the provinces at loggerheads with the provincial élite. A free trader himself for many years, he increasingly became convinced that if industry were not to wither away in Britain, then cosmopolitan capitalism itself would have to be jettisoned. Given Chamberlain's background this espousal of economic heresy is unsurprising. His political base was Birmingham. Birmingham and Black Country manufacturers had become increasingly vocal advocates of protectionism in the 1880s. Chamberlain himself had been a partner in Nettlefold and Chamberlain, a successful Birmingham screw manufacturing business, and was therefore precisely located, both politically and sociologically, to reflect the discontent of the provincial industrialist.

The first steps on Chamberlain's journey to leadership of the Tariff Reform Campaign were taken during the 1880s, when several of his speeches focused on the economic importance to Britain of its Empire. This assertion flew in the face of orthodox Liberal opinion, which held that the Empire was at best an irrelevance to the growth of national prosperity and at worst a drain on it. It explains his hostility to Irish Home Rule, a proposal whose implementation would, he believed, ultimately precipitate the disintegration of the Empire. In 1888 Chamberlain argued that 'half at least of our populace would be starved' were such an eventuality to occur. He took the view that the Empire would absorb an increasing share of British goods which could be paid for by exports of food and raw materials. By the turn of the century the Empire was taking about 33 per cent of all British exports. If, as Chamberlain believed, the rest of the world was to turn protectionist while the populations of the white colonies were expanding, this proportion was likely to grow. In the circumstances of mounting international rivalry, therefore, trade with the Empire offered guaranteed markets to British producers as well as access to plentiful and secure supplies of primary goods. From this would follow job security, good wages and higher living standards.[27]

As colonial secretary in the Conservative–Liberal Unionist Coalition led by Lord Salisbury after 1895, Chamberlain sought to promote the cause of Imperial economic unity. First of all, he favoured the use of public funds to develop tropical territories. In particular he wanted to build railways and encourage agricultural development in West Africa and in the West Indies. But this 'constructive imperialism' was greeted with hostility in the Treasury, the City and the Conservative party, where there was common ground on the importance of keeping government budgets low and balanced.[28] Secondly, in 1896 he proposed the establishment of a free trade Empire protected against the outside world by a common tariff – a *Zollverein* on the model of contemporary Germany. The idea was, however, doomed from the start because of fears in the white colonies that its realization would frustrate all attempts to nurture local economic development. They wanted *preferences* so that they would be protected against British as well as foreign-made goods. All the same the *Zollverein* remained Chamberlain's ideal, even if the tactics of achieving Imperial unity might have to change.[29]

The shift in tactics came with Chamberlain's call for a tariff which would finance social reform and safeguard British manufacturing by promoting Imperial unity through the provision of fiscal remissions, or preferences, to the colonies. He made the case for a 10 per cent tariff on imports of foreign manufactured goods, 5 per cent on foreign meat and dairy produce and two shillings a quarter on foreign grain and flour. By contrast colonial producers would be allowed free access to the home market. In 1903, having failed to gain Cabinet backing for this proposal, he resigned from Arthur Balfour's government and began his public campaign to persuade Britons to 'think imperially'. It was an act of dramatic political dissidence and reflected a growing conviction, reinforced by the battles with the Treasury and his colleagues over colonial development schemes, that the contemporary Conservative party was no more responsive to the needs of provincial industrialists than the Liberal party.[30] In taking his views outside the Cabinet Chamberlain was attempting to change the agenda of British politics and economic policy – indeed to *give* Britain an economic policy in place of a system in which the government's only significant economic function was to be a tax collector.

Chamberlain's actions split the Unionists between 'free fooders', who opposed tariffs, and his supporters, who established the Tariff Reform League. The League now became a vehicle for the mobilization of popular opinion behind an attack on what Chamberlain called the 'outdated shibboleths' of free trade, seen as responsible for industrial decline, future weakness and permanent mass poverty. It set off a bitter struggle within the Conservative–Liberal Unionist alliance, waging war at constituency party level against the free traders who stood in the way of Chamberlain's attempt to purge Unionism of the gentlemanly ethos and recreate it as a political force which explicitly represented the interests of the domestic manufacturer.[31]

Chamberlain's assault on free trade and cosmopolitanism reflected a belief that there was a structural bias against production. He drew a connection between flourishing overseas investments and growing domestic weakness. In 1904 he warned that the continued export of capital from Britain implied the neglect of industry and agriculture at home. If no action was taken to staunch the haemorrhage Britain would become

> a nation – there are several such – where manufacturing and productive industry is at a low ebb, where the people are all either men of leisure or hawkers, or distributors of goods, or occupying some one or other of the professions which are not productive. You may become a

nation of that kind. But in that case how are you going to provide for your ever-increasing population? The amount of money in the banks may increase. The investments abroad are increasing every day. They bring interest to the people who are fortunate enough to make these investments, but they bring no work for the working man.[32]

On another occasion he pointed out that finance, distribution and domestic service rather than manufacturing were providing employment for a growing share of the population. Continuation of this trend would lead to the creation of a society dominated by rentiers, living off income from abroad, engaged at home in leisure and service-sector activities at the expense of an ill-paid and under-employed workforce: 'more wealth but ... less welfare'. The future of Britain would be that of Holland writ large: diminishing industrial power would be reflected not only in growing social inequalities but in the disappearance of great power status.[33]

The thrust of Chamberlain's strategy for reversing British decline was unlikely to appeal to the City although he did not set out to antagonize it. He argued that it should support a policy of tariffs and imperial economic consolidation for the sake of industry because 'banking is not the creator of our prosperity, but the creation of it'. London could never have become the world's clearing-house unless Britain had first become its workshop, and if industrial enterprise were to fall into decay then 'finance, and all that finance means, will follow trade to the countries which are more successful than ourselves'.[34] Yet, limited support notwithstanding, the idea that finance and industry were interdependent was not likely to appeal to the majority who earned their living in the Square Mile. This was not only because the overall consensus favoured cosmopolitanism on the grounds that free trade generated more business and hence more revenue. It was also a function of Chamberlain's assumption, central both to his position at the head of the campaign for Tariff Reform and to the radicalism which inspired him throughout his active political career, that manufacturing industry was the foundation of national welfare and strength. From within the financial establishment and the higher reaches of the Conservative party, heartland of gentlemanly capitalism, such a perspective on national development was regarded as 'utterly sordid'.[35]

A Movement for the Modernization of Britain?

Britain's final repudiation of protection in 1846 had been motivated by a liberal political economy which associated free trade between nations with gains in efficiency and welfare. It was an argument which had first been made by Adam Smith before being developed by Ricardo, and in the mid-nineteenth century, by John Stuart Mill. Mill had argued that 'foreign commerce' not only enabled countries to obtain commodities which they could not produce at all:

> its advantage consists in a more efficient employment of the productive forces of the world. If two countries which trade together attempted, as far as was physically possible, to produce for themselves what they now import from each other, the labour and capital of the two countries would not be so productive, the two together would not obtain from their industry so great a quantity of commodities, as when each employs itself in producing, both for itself and for the other, the things in which its labour is more efficient.[36]

According to this orthodoxy the protection of native industry against foreign competition naturally involved the support of inefficiency. Mill argued that, infant industries excepted, it was a waste of resources to impose duties on a particular import in order to protect domestic production of the same commodity. The artificial preservation of a domestic trade in this manner prevented the movement of factors of production to the manufacturing of other goods, where local advantages existed in the costs of labour and capital, which could pay for the import in question.[37]

It was exactly this discourse which Chamberlain challenged when he suggested that far from enhancing the welfare of the community, unrestricted international competition could undermine it:

> Your once great trade in sugar refining is gone; all right, try jam. Your iron trade is going; never mind, you can make mousetraps. The cotton trade is threatened; well, what does that matter to you? Suppose you try doll's eyes.... But how long is this to go on? Why on earth are you to suppose that the same process which ruined the sugar refining will not in the course of time be applied to jam? And when jam is gone? Then you have to find something else. And believe me, that although the industries of this country are very various, you cannot go on for

ever. You cannot go on watching with indifference the disappearance of your principal industries.³⁸

Taking his stand in the discourse of national political economy which had been so influential in the development of contemporary Germany, Chamberlain argued that it was the duty of the State to nurture domestic industry.

Critics, steeped in the liberal tradition, accused the Tariff Reformers of seeking to protect waste and inefficiency. They argued that the introduction of import duties would penalize the consumer and bring an end to the era of cheap food which had started with the repeal of the Corn Laws. In general economists and historians during and since the Tariff Reform controversy have taken sides with Chamberlain's opponents, citing the worn-out metal-bashing and agricultural producers who jumped onto the protectionist bandwagon as soon as it had started to roll.³⁹

Yet Chamberlain did not set out on his crusade with the object of protecting sunset industries. His initial ambition was, as the sympathetic economist W. A. S. Hewins put it, 'the deliberate adoption of the Empire, as distinct from the United Kingdom, as the basis of public policy'.⁴⁰ Enthusiasm for such a revolution was motivated not simply by the conviction that Empire markets were those of the future but in addition stemmed from the belief, reinforced by the examples provided by Bismarckian Germany and the United States, that small states would lack the labour, capital and markets to prosper in the new century. This was a policy for the long term which would entail sacrifices for the domestic consumer, whose support was to be gained by the promise of 'work for all' and social reform (including the introduction of old age pensions) to stifle class confrontation. At the same time it was envisaged that a Tariff Reform government would not provide indiscriminate protection. Another of Chamberlain's academic advisers, W. J. Ashley, first professor of Commerce at the new University of Birmingham, envisaged the tariff as a facilitator of reorganization and efficiency. Duties would be varied, both to ensure trades would still receive the stimulus of foreign competition and to permit the abandonment of some industries, dogged by 'genuine natural disadvantage'.⁴¹

Chamberlain's agenda appealed to many constructive imperialists. His concern with relative decline was widely shared in the early twentieth century. The triumphalism of the 1897 Diamond Jubilee had soon given way to national anxiety and soul-searching. The loss of confidence had been brought to a head finally by the Boer War. It had been, in the words of Kipling, 'no end of a lesson' which revealed not simply weaknesses in military training and organization but in Britain's social fabric. Many volunteers had been turned away by army recruiters because medical examination had revealed them to be unfit for service, their infirmities a function of widespread bad housing and malnutrition. In consequence interest across parties developed in the idea of 'national efficiency', whose political spearhead was the Liberal peer and ex-prime minister, Lord Rosebery. Early Fabians such as the Webbs and George Bernard Shaw were attracted, as were W. A. S. Hewins and Chamberlain, by a programme of social and educational reform designed to build a society whose people were physically and mentally fit enough to compete successfully in a world where British pre-eminence was under threat from Germany and the United States.[42] But although this modernized Britain was to be the centre of an imperial federation, Rosebery's project, which endorsed the commitment to free trade, was insufficiently radical for Chamberlain. Why should the colonies remain in the Empire if there was no incentive for them to do so and how would the social reforms be financed? Tariff Reform answered both of these questions.

Chamberlain's problem was, however, that the modernizing impulse behind Tariff Reform became diluted during the political struggle to mobilize popular support and powerful industrial interests behind it. Chamberlain's objective was the creation of a 'producers' alliance', embracing workers and industrialists. But although the Tariff Reform League was reasonably successful in attracting cross-class support, not all those who rallied to the cause were forward-looking radicals. It is true that support came from new industries, such as electrical goods and chemicals, which were facing tough competition from German and American rivals. Backing could be found as well in well-established trades, notably iron and steel, heavy engineering, glass, and building materials. At the same time, however, the campaign naturally drew in those who saw in tariffs not an incentive to reorganization and growth but merely a weapon which would guarantee their survival in unchanged form into the indefinite future against all competition, however efficient and cheap.[43] Into this category fell many arable farmers unable to compete with American grain imports and a cluster of metal-based Midland industries which included manufacturers of tin and brass, many of whom had been struggling for the best part of twenty years. This was an unwieldy coalition: both Chamberlain and the Tariff Reform League found that it was held together by propaganda which stressed the merits of unconditional protection 'all round'. It was a far cry from the discriminating State interventionism advocated by Ashley and Hewins. The Tariff Commission, established in 1903 with Hewins as secretary to make the case for a 'scientific tariff', was increasingly drawn into special pleading.[44]

Yet the negative aspects of Tariff Reform should not be exaggerated. Recent research has tended to provide some support for the claims made by Chamberlain and his supporters that domestic industry was starved of funds as a result of the City's enthusiasm for foreign investment. In both Germany and the United States after 1870 about 12 per cent of national income was invested annually; in Britain the figure was 7 per cent, another 5 per cent making its way overseas.[45] About 6 per cent of all the finance raised in London between 1865 and 1914 went into manufacturing whereas 25 per cent went into railway companies, whether in the Empire or in foreign countries.[46] This bias might have been corrected by protection, which in raising the rate of profit within capital-intensive sectors such as the iron and steel industry might have stimulated higher levels of domestic investment. Certainly producers of pig iron had a point when they argued that under free trade there was no incentive to reorganize along American lines given the small size and profitability of their existing markets.[47]

Of course it does not follow from this that a Tariff Reform government would have succeeded in reversing British industrial decline. Yet during the twentieth century the behaviour of the economy has conformed to the most pessimistic projections of the Tariff Reformers. It is arguable that the failure to 'put domestic industry, rather overseas economic interests, at the forefront of policy', has undermined British industrial power, with grim consequences for employment, welfare and national influence. That the day of reckoning came later than Chamberlain and his supporters expected was perhaps only a function of the necessity to reverse traditional priorities and replace economic liberalism with *dirigisme* in two world wars.[48]

The Failure of Tariff Reform

Chamberlain and his supporters attempted to mobilize mass support by populist appeals, both for social reform and to nationalist, even jingoistic sentiment. The Tariff Reform League embraced campaigning techniques familiar in America, such as doorstep canvassing, a prodigious output of leaflets and pamphlets, music hall songs and records which took Chamberlain's personal message that workers could only afford their food bills if jobs were secure into scores of homes and meeting houses.[49] The Tariff Reformers were fond of using the image of John Bull, embodying all the virtues of the British working man – bluff, beef-eating, chauvinist, muscular, in danger of being tricked by domestic traitors and unscrupulous foreigners. The discourse and rhetoric of Tariff Reform was consistent with an attempt, to be repeated by third-world modernizers such as Mossadegh and Nasser half a century later, to shock into existence a popular alliance committed to the replacement of *laissez-faire* and cosmopolitanism by a managed, nationalized form of capitalism, through the depiction of an outside world dominated by hostile and predatory powers.[50]

The third-world radicals were often successful in winning popular support for economic as well as political nationalism because what they said about the greed and power of foreign banks and multinational corporations squared with the day-to-day experience of their populations. British nationalists found life more difficult, for three reasons. First of all it became clear in the 1906 General Election that the electorate would need a lot of persuasion before accepting the end of cheap food. There were still many memories of the 'hungry forties'.[51] Secondly the Tariff Reformers were unlucky with the timing of their campaign. At the turn of the century, after a period of stagnation, British exports began to grow. Foreign trade grew by 36 per cent between 1900 and 1910, exports rising by 47 per cent over this period.[52] The expansion was particularly notable in the export industries rather than those which produced mainly for the home market, with textile mills, coalmines and shipbuilding yards all prospering. Nevertheless the figures appeared to give the lie to the dire predictions of the Tariff Reform League and instead reinforced confidence in free trade. The third cause of failure was the popular strength of cosmopolitan capitalism. In 1910 the Liberal party, committed to free trade and social reform through redistributive taxation, won its strongest support from the industrialists and workers most closely integrated into the world economy.[53]

It was this third cause of failure which was most serious for the Tariff Reformers. The third world modernizers were able to build coalitions capable of uniting around a platform of economic nationalism because collaborators with international economic interests were comparatively small in number and in general limited to sections of the bourgeoisie. In Britain, however, the political environment was far less friendly to those attempting the construction of a mass movement committed to the rejection of cosmopolitanism. The course of British development had created not just two middle classes but a fractured working-class movement, whose own political party, rooted in the great export trades, was for many years a standard-bearer for free trade. Thus the City had its own internal collaborators in the shape of a popular alliance whose number ran into millions.[54] Although this alliance did not share the City's faith in the free market at home, its ability to transform the status quo was limited by its international Cobdenism. It followed that the achievements of the Labour party in its two periods of power (1924 and 1929–31) before the Second World War were modest; having rejected Oswald Mosley's alternative strategy in favour of free trade and the gold standard in 1930 it could only attack a mounting external financial crisis through the employment of stringent public expenditure cuts to reduce demand.[55]

In 1930 Mosley's manifesto was based on a combination of proto-Keynesian measures to reflate the domestic economy, insulating it from international shocks via import controls and a developmental approach to the Empire designed to guarantee markets for British industrialists. Categorized by one critic of the time as 'Birminghamism rampant', it was a programme which evoked the spirit of Joseph Chamberlain. Like his predecessor, Mosley called for the adoption of economic nationalism in place of a cosmopolitanism which penalized the producer and protected the rentier by allowing capital to flood out of the country. Just as the Tariff Reformers had wrapped themselves in the Union Jack so Mosley, with inadequate support both inside and outside the Labour party, attempted to generate popular enthusiasm for his strategy by recourse to an extreme form of nationalism which took him all the way to Fascism: John Bull with a blackshirt.

The difficulty which has always faced industrial modernizers in modern Britain is the absence of a popular nationalist tradition able to understand that national sovereignty is an economic as well as a political concept. This was a function of the developmental path which had led to the integration of the British with the international economy after the Napoleonic Wars. It followed that the hegemony of cosmopolitanism collapsed only when the international economy disintegrated as a result either of slump or of war. The disappearance of export markets and threats to national security from aggressive foreign states created a political as well as an economic imperative behind the prioritization of production for the home market. Thus protection became politically acceptable in the 1930s just as 'war socialism' had been between 1916–18 and was to be again after 1940. Chamberlain would not have been surprised to learn that during these periods the growth rate of the British economy regularly exceeded 3 per cent per annum, a considerable improvement on the twentieth-century average of between 2 and 2.5 per cent.[56]

Notes

1 Quoted in Scott Newton and Dilwyn Porter, *Joseph Chamberlain 1836–1914: A Bibliography* (Westport, 1994), 109.
2 A classic statement of this view, written for popular consumption, can be found in F. E. Halliday, *A Concise History of England* (London, 1980), chs. 14 and 15. Most recently, B. Porter, *Britannia's Burden: The Political Evolution of Modern Britain 1851–1990* (London, 1994), founds his argument on similar if qualified assumptions.
3 See for example, P. Anderson, 'Origins of the Present Crisis', *New Left Review*, 36 (1964); T. Nairn, 'Britain: Fateful Meridian', *New Left Review*, 60 (1970).
4 See for example, W. D. Rubinstein, 'The Victorian Middle Classes: Wealth, Occupation, and Geography', *Economic History Review* 2nd ser., XXX (1977), idem, 'Wealth, Elites and the Class Structure of Modern Britain', *Past and Present* 76 (1977), idem, 'Entrepreneurial Effort and Entrepreneurial Success: Peak Wealth-Holding in Three Societies, 1850–1930', *Business History* XXV (1983), and 'Gentlemen, Capitalism and British Industry, 1820–1914', *Past and Present* 132 (1991); T. Nairn, *The Break-Up*

of Britain (2nd edn., London, 1981); M. Wiener, *English Culture and the Decline of the Industrial Spirit* (London, 1981); J. Scott, *The Upper Classes: Property and Privilege in Britain* (London, 1982); G. Ingham, *Capitalism Divided? The City and Industry in British Social Development* (London, 1984); P. Anderson, 'The Figures of Descent', *New Left Review*, 161 (1987); and P. J. Cain and A. G. Hopkins, *British Imperialism I: Innovation and Expansion 1688–1914* (London, 1993), and *British Imperialism II: Crisis and Deconstruction 1914–1990* (London, 1993).

5 Cain and Hopkins, *Innovation and Expansion*, 41.
6 See Cain and Hopkins, *Innovation and Expansion*, 74; P. Mathias, *The First Industrial Nation: An Economic History of Britain 1700–1914* (London, 1983), 38.
7 Cain and Hopkins, *Innovation and Expansion*, 74.
8 See B. Hilton, *Corn, Cash and Commerce: The Economic Policies of Tory Governments 1815–1830* (Oxford, 1977), ch.1. Ricardo was born into a stockbroking family and himself made a fortune on the Stock Exchange, retiring in 1815 at the age of 43 to become a country gentleman and Tory MP. His views on the national debt can be found in D. Ricardo, *The Principles of Political Economy and Taxation* (London, 1973 edn.), 160–4.
9 See Cain and Hopkins, *Innovation and Expansion*, 80–2.
10 R. Davis, *The Industrial Revolution and British Overseas Trade* (Leicester, 1979), 34; Cain and Hopkins, *Innovation and Expansion*, 162.
11 P. Kennedy, *The Rise and Fall of Great Powers: Economic Change and Military Conflict from 1500 to 2000* (London, 1988).
12 Derived from P. Mathias, *The First Industrial Nation*, Table IX, 279.
13 See S. Newton and D. Porter, *Modernization Frustrated: the Politics of Industrial Decline in Britain since 1900* (London, 1988).
14 Newton and Porter, *Modernization Frustrated*, 8; Rubinstein, 'The Victorian Middle Classes', 602–3.
15 C. H. Lee, 'Regional Growth and Structural Change in Victorian Britain', *Economic History Review*, 2nd ser., XXXIV (1981), 438–52.
16 P. J. Cain, 'J. A. Hobson, Financial Capitalism and Imperialism in Late Victorian and Edwardian England', in A. N. Porter and R. F. Holland, (eds.), *Money, Finance and Empire 1790–1960* (London, 1985), 15.
17 J. A. Hobson, 'The General Election: A Sociological Interpretation', *Sociological Review*, 3 (1910), 112–13.
18 Scott, *The Upper Classes*, 158–9.
19 This argument is developed in P. J. Cain, 'Hobson, Wilshire and the Capitalist Theory of Capitalist Imperialism', *History of Political Economy* 17 (1985), 455–60.
20 Quoted in R. Williams, *Cobbett* (Oxford, 1983).

21 See P. J. Cain, 'Hobson, Wilshire and the Capitalist Theory of Capitalist Imperialism', *History of Political Economy* 17 (1985), 455–60.
22 Letter to Mr Houghton, 18 April 1863, quoted in J. Morley, *Richard Cobden*, 946.
23 Quoted in Newton and Porter, *Joseph Chamberlain 1836–1914*, 8.
24 Quoted in D. Judd, *Radical Joe* (Cardiff, 1993), 122.
25 See J. Chamberlain, *The Radical Platform* (Edinburgh and London, 1885); and idem et al., *The Radical Programme* (London, 1885).
26 Judd, *Radical Joe*, 178–9.
27 See Porter, *Britannia's Burden*, 123–5.
28 R. E. Dumett, 'Joseph Chamberlain, Imperial Finance and Railway Policy in British West Africa in the Late Nineteenth Century', *English Historical Review* 90 (1975), 287–321; and R. Kubicek, 'Joseph Chamberlain, the Treasury and Imperial Development 1895–1903', *Canadian Historical Association Annual Report* (1965), 105–16.
29 Chamberlain's increasing conviction that the Empire was crucial to the future of Britain is traced in J. Amery, *The Life of Joseph Chamberlain IV: at the Height of his Power* (London, 1951) and in J. L. Garvin's *The Life of Joseph Chamberlain III: Empire and World Policy* (London, 1934), as well as in P. Fraser, *Joseph Chamberlain: Radicalism and Empire* (London, 1966), chs.10–12.
30 See Newton and Porter, *Modernization Frustrated*, 21; Cain and Hopkins, *Innovation and Expansion*, 213–14.
31 See P. Fraser, 'Unionism and Tariff Reform and the Crisis of 1906', *Historical Journal* 5 (1962), 149–66; N. Blewett, 'Free Fooders, Balfourites, Whole Hoggers: Factionalism within the Unionist Party, 1906–10', *Historical Journal* 11 (1968), 95–124; A. Sykes, *Tariff Reform in British Politics 1903–1913* (Oxford, 1979).
32 Quoted in J. Tomlinson, *Problems in British Economic Policy, 1870–1945* (London, 1981), 54. A representative collection of speeches covering all phases of Chamberlain's political career can be found in C. W. Boyd, *Mr Chamberlain's Speeches* (London, 1914).
33 See W. J. Ashley, *The Tariff Problem* (London, 1903), 111–13.
34 This speech is discussed in Newton and Porter, *Modernization Frustrated*, 21, and in Cain and Hopkins, *Innovation and Expansion*, 216–17.
35 Robert Cecil quoted by D. Judd, *Balfour and the Empire: A Study in Imperial Evolution 1874–1932* (London, 1968).
36 J. S. Mill, *Principles of Political Economy* (London, 1848), 394.
37 Ibid., 590.
38 Quoted in Judd, *Radical Joe*, 253.
39 A review of the pamphlet literature concerning the tariff issue can be found in Newton and Porter, *Joseph Chamberlain 1836–1914*,

116–20. See also A. J. Marrison, 'British Businessmen and the "Scientific" Tariff: A Study of Joseph Chamberlain's Tariff Commission, 1903-21' (University of Hull Ph.D. dissertation, 1970).
40 W. A. S. Hewins, *Apologia of an Imperialist* (London, 1929), 50–61.
41 See Ashley, *The Tariff Problem*, 133–4.
42 See G. R. Searle, *The Quest for National Efficiency: British Politics and Political Thought 1899–1914* (Oxford, 1971); and R. J. Scally, *The Origins of the Lloyd George Coalition: The Politics of Social Imperialism* (Princeton, 1975).
43 The composition of the Tariff Reform League is discussed in D. Porter, 'The Unionist Tariff Reformers 1903–1914' (University of Manchester Ph.D. dissertation, 1976).
44 Marrison, 'British Businessmen and the "Scientific" Tariff', and 'The Tariff Commission, Agricultural Protection and Food Taxes, 1903–13', *Agricultural History Review* 34 (1986), 171–87; Newton and Porter, *Modernization Frustrated*, 22.
45 S. Pollard, 'Capital Exports 1870–1914: Harmful or Beneficial?', *Economic History Review*, 2nd ser., XXXVIII (1985), 495–8.
46 The nature of British investment overseas is discussed in W. P. Kennedy, 'Foreign Investment, Trade and Growth in the United Kingdom, 1870–1913', *Explorations in Economic History* II (1974), 425–39.
47 See Cain and Hopkins, *Innovation and Expansion*, 191, 221; Newton and Porter, *Modernization Frustrated*, 20.
48 Cain, 'J. A. Hobson, Financial Capitalism and Imperialism', 20; Newton and Porter, *Modernization Frustrated*, ch. 7.
49 See Judd, *Radical Joe*, 251.
50 See E. H. H. Green, 'Radical Conservatism in Britain, 1899–1903' (University of Cambridge Ph.D. dissertation, 1986), and 'Radical Conservatism: the Electoral Genesis of Tariff Reform', *Historical Journal* 28 (1985), 667–92. The question is also discussed at length in B. Semmel, *Imperialism and Social Reform: English Social-Imperial Thought 1895–1914* (London, 1960).
51 Judd, *Radical Joe*, 243.
52 B. R. Mitchell and P. Deane, *Abstract of British Historical Statistics* (Cambridge, 1962), 334, 283–4.
53 Cain and Hopkins, *Innovation and Expansion*, 219–20.
54 The free trade views of the Labour party during the first decades of its history are discussed in R. W. D. Boyce, *British Capitalism at the Crossroads: A Study in Politics, Economics and International Relations* (Cambridge, 1987).
55 See the discussion in Newton and Porter, *Modernization Frustrated*, 65–76. R. Skidelsky, *Politicians and the Slump* (London, 1967), is still worth reading.
56 See A. H. Halsey (ed.), *British Social Trends since 1900* (London, 1989), Table 3.4.

~6~
Democracy and Nationalism in Wales: The Lib-Lab Enigma

CHRIS WILLIAMS

'Now consigned to the dustbin of history, Lib-Labism still awaits its academic champion ...' claimed David Howell in his *British Workers and the Independent Labour Party*.[1] It is the contention of this essay that the neglect of the Lib-Labs in the histories of the development of the British Labour movement, and of working-class politics more generally, is to be regretted, not least because Lib-Labism was an important and powerful force in the making of both.[2] The focus of this study will be upon the Lib-Labs of Wales, and, in particular, those of the south Wales coalfield, for two reasons. First, south Wales is often given as the paradigm case both for the rapid rise of socialist ideas and for the explosion of class conflict in the early decades of the twentieth century. Such developments are conventionally located against the backdrop of an earlier history characterized by the allegedly timid industrial and political strategies of the Lib-Labs. But a clearer understanding of the continuities between Lib-Labism and its inheritors can only emerge if the strategies of the former are subject to investigation rather than the caricature to which it is often subjected. Second, it was in south Wales that the clash of interests between a Welsh-speaking, largely rural, Wales, and an increasingly anglicized, industrial, and urbanized Wales was given clearest form in the political controversy surrounding the rise of the nationalist Cymru Fydd league in the 1890s. The role of prominent Lib-Labs in the odyssey of Cymru Fydd, and the relationship of Lib-Labs to nationalist identifications and aspirations more generally, has been misconstrued, even parodied. Establishing the true nature of these relationships not only assists in revealing the popular weaknesses of the Cymru Fydd programme, but also permits an appreciation of the more enduring and distinctive qualities of Lib-Lab political leadership. The Lib-Labs of south Wales drew strength from their self-understanding as representatives of a democratic polity, and guarded carefully against the distortion of what they saw as that polity's interests by any political programme based upon sectarian principles, even those clothed in the assumed garb of Welsh nationality. In this case-study of Wales's Lib-Lab leaders the dynamic tensions between the principles of democracy and the inspirational powers of nationalism are clearly manifested.

There can be no doubting the significance of Lib-Labism in Welsh public life in the decades before the Great War. With the sole exception of Keir Hardie (MP for Merthyr Boroughs), Wales's four other 'Labour' MPs were Lib-Labs, whether sitting on the Liberal or Labour party benches.[3] Furthermore, the single most important trade union in Wales, the South Wales Miners' Federation (SWMF), was dominated by Lib-Lab leadership, often the same men, from its formation in 1898 through to 1914. William Abraham (generally known by his bardic name, 'Mabon') was both MP for the Rhondda constituency (1885–1920) and president of the SWMF (1898–1912).[4] William Brace served in the House of Commons on behalf of the constituents of South Glamorgan (1906–18) and Abertillery (1918–20) and was successively SWMF vice-president (1898–1912) and president (1912–15). Thomas Richards was the SWMF's general secretary (1898–1931) and MP for West Monmouth (1904–18) and Ebbw Vale (1918–20); and John Williams was advisory agent to the Western District Miners' Association (a district of the SWMF, 1897–1922) and MP for Gower (1906–22). Such a pattern of both industrial and political leadership can be found not only at the highest levels: a 'Labour' local government representative would normally hold a position of responsibility in a local trade union, most frequently the SWMF.[5]

Despite the extent and longevity of the leadership of the Lib-Labs in south Wales many historians of the 'Forward March of Labour' have chosen to minimize their industrial and political contributions. In the industrial relations arena, Lib-Labs have been typified as attempting a syncretism rendered increasingly difficult as the gulf between capital and labour widened. Lib-Labs such as Mabon might preach the mutual dependence of employer and employee, but in the tense circumstances of the new century such pleading appeared irrelevant, particularly as the employers themselves seemed not to share in the gospel. Politically the achievement of building a tradition of working-class representation has been credited largely to the Independent Labour party, advocating as it did the strategy of independence that led eventually to the replacement of the Liberal party by Labour in the early 1920s.[6] Lib-Labism has been portrayed as a deviation from the 'high road' to independent working-class politics, characteristic of an era during which sections of the organized working class were contaminated by Liberal ideas and perspectives, their power and influence emasculated by fruitless negotiations with Liberal associations, and their leaders beguiled by the false praise and patronage characteristic of bourgeois notable politics. Taken together, these interpretations result in Lib-Labism appearing a 'blind alley', a 'no-man's land', a cul-de-sac on Labour's 'Forward March'. Whilst Lib-Labs led, the cause of Labour marked time: only with their demise could real progress be made.[7]

Insofar as the ultimate *telos* of the British Labour movement is seen as being socialist, then such interpretations are not without foundation. Lib-Labs did obstruct the realization of a socialist purpose and orientation within the movement. They were not socialists, and their pragmatism never gave way to speculation as to how to overturn, rather than mitigate, capitalism: 'Mabon's perception of his role as a miners' MP, clearly, was to represent their interests without seeking any underlying socio-economic transformation.'[8] However, to judge the Lib-Labs as socialists manqué is to do them an injustice. For Lib-Labism was not indistinguishable from Liberal politics, nor was it simply a 'firm attachment to the Liberal Party'.[9] Lib-Labism was expressive of greater discontent with the forms and patterns of Liberal party politics than has been appreciated, and, far from being completely divorced from the development of independent working-class politics, made a major contribution to that process.[10]

Recent writing on nineteenth-century British radicalism has been concerned to stress the temperamental and ideological continuities between the movements of the late Victorian era and those of the Chartist and immediate post-Chartist decades. The distinctiveness of any class-conscious Labour socialism has, in the process, been minimized, and instead cross-class, even non-class radicalism with at least one foot in the Liberal party, has been given credit as having a lasting impact upon the Labour party.[11]

Without necessarily accepting the full implications of such work, not least the commitments to ousting 'class' as an analytical and descriptive concept, and to marginalizing 'socialism', both historical and contemporary, this approach can be used to arrive at a more satisfactory understanding of Welsh Lib-Labism.[12]

The Lib-Lab political and industrial vision was characterized by a single principle: democracy. The progressive evolution of a reformed and expanded parliamentary electorate via the Reform Acts of 1867 and 1884, along with the Secret Ballot Act of 1872 and the redistribution of constituencies in 1884–5, was considered to have created something akin to a representative (male) democracy. At local level these developments were paralleled by the election of school boards, by the County Councils Act of 1888, and by the creation of urban and rural district councils in 1894. In the industrial arena, the removal of the most important legal restrictions upon the operation of trade unions in the 1870s was seen as heralding a new law-abiding atmosphere in which mutual respect between employer and organized workforce would replace hostility, suspicion and violence. Taking their places in Parliament, or across the negotiating table, the Lib-Labs could feel confident of their legitimacy as the chosen representatives of a new popular citizenry, to whom they were ultimately responsible. Their understanding of this democratic world was one in which they acted not as automatic delegates of their (industrial or political) constituencies but in which they took responsibility for framing their own understandings of the problems with which they were beset, and, in their eyes, acting as a benevolent, protective barrier around their 'people'. Ultimately, their opponents were to accuse them of diluting the convictions of their constituencies, draining them of energy, twisting their purposes, sometimes for personal gain.[13] Nevertheless, throughout most of their long careers as public figures, the reliance of the Lib-Labs upon the democratic principle facilitated their distinctive contributions to the Labour movement.[14]

The centrality of 'democracy' to the political careers of the Lib-Labs is revealed most clearly in any attempt to define the characteristics of 'Lib-Labbery' as both identity and a practice. Precise definition is elusive, not least because the terms 'Lib-Labs', 'Lib-Labbery' and 'Lib-Labism' have been subjected to many uses, some with the deliberate aim of misleading electorates.[15] 'Lib-Lab' originated as a descriptive label, applied to parliamentary candidates (and subsequent MPs) who not only had firm attachments to specific trade unions, but who were also recognizably 'working men'. Northumberland miners' leader Thomas Burt, who along with fellow miners' leader Alexander McDonald formed the first pair of Lib-Lab MPs, defined this relationship in 1899:

> The House of Commons has itself practically decided the point. Those whom it has accepted as labour members are, without exception, men who worked at their respective trades, and who still maintain a close connection with large associated bodies of workmen, such associations selecting and recognising them as their representatives and spokesmen.[16]

It was this web of institutional, occupational and class connections that justified the 'Lab' in 'Lib-Lab', and which set these 'labour members' apart from their colleagues on the Liberal benches.[17] Lib-Labism signified an individual's identity and loyalties, but did not imply the possession of an ideological creed distinctive from Liberalism itself.[18] As Henry Bowen, Lib-Lab county councillor for Tredegar, claimed in 1909, he 'had never been able to find the distinction between Liberal and Labour.'[19] Welsh Lib-Labs believed in the touchstones of disestablishment (the subject of Mabon's maiden speech in the House of Commons), land reform, free trade, and the freedom of educational practice. However, all of these were upheld by a political discourse expressed most clearly at national level. Adherence to these principles did not necessitate unwavering support for the local manifestations of Welsh Liberalism.

It is this compound of occupational and class identity with political attitudes that best defines Lib-Labism, rather than, as often implied, any electoral pact or organizational alliance. It is significant that all four Welsh Lib-Lab MPs faced considerable opposition from Liberal party organizations before winning their seats. Thus, in Rhondda in 1885, Mabon was twice rejected as candidate by the Liberal Three Hundred in favour first of coalowner Lewis Davis, and then of his son Frederick. Mabon, although quite clearly a Liberal in his political beliefs, and with the support of Liberal figures outside the Rhondda, fought the election as a 'Labour' candidate. Only in 1886, with the absorption of the Rhondda Liberal Association in the Rhondda Labour and Liberal Association (RLLA) were the two sides reconciled.[20] Similarly John Williams defeated the official Liberal candidate in Gower in 1906, standing as a 'Labour' (but not Labour party) candidate.[21] As for Thomas Richards and William Brace, although both eventually gained the official nomination of their local Liberal Associations, this was due to the interventions of the Liberal Chief Whip Herbert Gladstone, who had to force local Liberals to comply with the wishes of the National Liberal party.[22] In Monmouth West the miners had in any case already decided to challenge the sitting Liberal MP before his impending retirement was announced.

Once elected, more consensual arrangements between middle-class Liberals and their Lib-Lab MPs prevailed. But at the level of local elections, recent research indicates that, if anything, Liberal associations were even more reluctant to accept working men candidates. In the Rhondda Valleys miners' candidates, even those of considerable seniority, rarely took up a representative position in local government without a fight against a Liberal opponent, and invariably had to fight further opponents when re-election was due.[23] In many areas formal Liberal party organizations were absent, even obsolete. Middle-class cliques, composed of shopkeepers, solicitors, professional men and nonconformist ministers, dominated local politics, and their petty snobbery and social exclusiveness closed avenues of access to working-class leaders.

In many respects, therefore, there was no Lib-Lab 'alliance', and working-class political representation did not flourish in any measure as a result. This state of affairs generated considerable disenchantment with the channels of orthodox Liberalism. By the early twentieth century, some within the Labour movement were claiming that Labour itself was the true guardian of Liberal principles, which were being corrupted and betrayed by the 'shallow self-seeking place hunters' of the local Liberal cliques:

> Labour measures must of necessity always be progressive, and their tendency uplifting: and so the more Labour makes its power felt, the better for unspecious Liberalism. The floating garbage of political nonentities whose contemptible performances render the name of 'Liberal' nauseous to all men and women who have been accustomed

to identify it with principles which form part of the moral birthright given them by their God will pass out of sight with the incoming of the new and exalted spirit of the true Democracy which is slowly but surely growing in strength and sturdiness in these and other constituencies of the country.[24]

The impetus grew for Labour to act independently of local Liberal bodies, and non-socialist Lib-Labs took the lead in such action from an early stage. The demand for 'Labour' men on political bodies was voiced not just amongst the miners of the Rhondda in the 1880s, but amidst the diverse industries of the Swansea area:

> We know that white collared gentlemen in time of elections are very good at promising and often when in power very poor at performing. I trust that when the time comes not tinplate workers but all classes of working men will unite to secure direct representation on our County Councils.[25]

Even Thomas Richards, an advocate of moderation in the industrial arena, spoke of the need 'to smash up the ostracism of the working classes'.[26] Lib-Labs were not, of course, aiming to replace the Liberal party, much less to subvert their Liberal principles, but they recognized that the Liberal party in south Wales was failing to meet their aspirations. Without any accommodation of their demands, they were forced to fall back upon their own resources, and build organizational machinery that would enable them to make their voice heard at all levels of political representation.

Such machinery varied from area to area: 'Electoral Associations', 'Labour Councils', 'Labour Representation Committees' and 'Miners' Funds' were all established, and were often of short-term duration, at least in the beginning. As the twentieth century opened, in recognition of the increased challenge from socialist bodies, more permanent structures were developed. In the Rhondda Valleys, the 'Labour Representation Fund' was established by the Rhondda No. 1 District in 1904, and although faltering in its early years was responsible for the sponsorship of a slate of candidates at the 1908 elections for the Rhondda Urban District Council. By 1910 the union was supporting sixteen local government representatives, of whom nine were 'Lib-Labs'.

The paradox of Lib-Labism in the south Wales coalfield, was that although ostensibly committed to the programme of the Liberal party, the organizational and electoral realities were such as to foster a tradition of independent working-class politics. When the miners finally affiliated to the Labour party in 1909 they were able to take with them not only a body of public representatives at all levels of government, but also an efficient nominating and electioneering system that was far in advance of any possessed by the local Liberal coteries they had so often opposed.

Such institutional developments were assisted by the elaboration of a separate language of working-class interest, placed at the core of Lib-Labism's democratic identity. 'Labour', the 'working man', the 'working classes' – whichever terms were used – constituted a separate entity from the middle classes. Labour's industrial experience was clearly different, and this generated a belief that Labour had a set of political rights which should not be thwarted, and which demanded, if necessary, autonomous and independent organization. The earliest manifestation of this discourse can be found in the unsuccessful campaign of miners' leader Thomas Halliday, the 'Working Man's' or 'Labour' representative in the Merthyr Boroughs election of 1874.

Halliday first signalled his intention to stand for Parliament at the conference of the Amalgamated Association of Mineworkers (AAM) held in Newport in April 1873, when he 'took occasion to express a hope that working-men would endeavour to secure the return of representatives of their own class, when an opportunity arose for doing so'.[27] With the launch of the Merthyr-based newspaper *The Workman's Advocate* in September 1873 Halliday was given considerable support. The paper proclaimed itself 'devoted, fully, heartily, and exclusively to the true interests and honest claims of the working classes'. In its opening editorial it proclaimed Halliday 'THE FUTURE MP FOR MERTHYR', arguing that 'labour should be represented by the sons of labour' for it was 'both folly and madness for the mice to expect fair play and equity in a Parliament of cats'. Halliday, as a *'bona fide* working man' possessed the necessary credentials to be 'the people's choice' against 'the tradesmen and mercantile interest', and his claim to take one of the two seats available was considered just as '[t]he great majority of the electors are working men, pitmen, ironworkers, &c.'.[28] In a later edition of the *Advocate*, 'Cymro Tawel' encapsulated the argument thus:

> It is full time that the working classes should be properly represented in the House of Commons. The middle and upper classes have held their sway long enough, too long, in fact. And now that the working classes have the voting power, I hope and trust that they will exercise it for their own benefit and their own advantage. Let us send men from amongst ourselves, men of sound common sense, men who can and will sympathise with us and who know our wants, and when this is done the time will soon come when the abominable laws which enable employers to have nearly everything their own way will soon be swept from the statute book and the rich and poor will have equal justice done to them.[29]

Opposition to Halliday's candidature, which came from the Liberal Press and from organized nonconformity, was seen by the *Advocate* as indicating fear of 'The great tide of democracy'.[30] The sitting Liberal MPs were Richard Fothergill (an ironmaster) and Henry Richard, and Halliday set out to distinguish his programme from theirs by his support for the repeal of both the Criminal Law Amendment Act and the Masters and Servant Act, for introducing legislation for 'Workman's Compensation' and for limiting the hours of factory labour to nine. Such policies were considered 'the most important questions of the day for us working men'. That the language of class and of interest was evident throughout the campaign is indicated by the labels attached to the candidates by the *South Wales Daily News*: Halliday was 'the collier's candidate', Fothergill the representative of 'capital', and Richard of 'principle'. The message of Halliday's defeat was not that the framing of such an appeal on class lines was flawed, but that greater organization of 'the working men' was necessary, and in particular the formation of a political association to advance candidatures in future.[31]

The significance of the 1874 campaign ('watched with intenser interest perhaps than any other election in the Kingdom') lies not in the development of any lasting form of working-class organization in the Merthyr constituency, but rather in the clear articulation of the language of class interest, and in the way that language embraced a class-specific sense of democracy resistant to assimilation into a cross-class sense of 'the popular'.[32] This style was to be echoed in the subsequent, and successful, campaigns of other Lib-Labs, such as that of Mabon, who had supported Halliday in 1874.[33] In 1885, before the election for the new Rhondda seat, the Rhondda miners passed a resolution:

> That ... it is not only necessary but imperative that the newly enfranchised working classes should use their political power for the purpose of returning the representatives of their class and by themselves supported, not with the intention of subordinating any other interest, but with a view to placing themselves in a position to help on legislation peculiarly concerned with the working classes, and to shape the House of Commons that it may be the true expression of the opinion of the nation, which cannot be attained except all classes have some practical interest therein.[34]

This belief that only through electing genuine Labour representatives would the democracy function to the satisfaction of all its citizens was reiterated throughout the coalfield over the next quarter-century. This was not hollow rhetoric, for although sharing a faith in all the major Liberal policies of the age, Lib-Lab candidates continued to make space for emphasizing material questions that affected organized workers. Like Halliday in 1874, Mabon in 1885 deviated from Fred Davis's Liberal policies in stressing safety and compensation (in the form of the Mines Inspection Act and the Employers' Liability Act) and in desiring the payment of Labour representatives in the House of Commons. Thomas Richards, in 1904, spoke out against the Taff Vale decision and for the Eight Hours Bill.[35] Once in Parliament, the Lib-Labs took a keen interest in matters including mining royalties, the safety and general welfare of miners, wages, employment, hours of work, liability and compensation, and of course industrial disputes. Outside the chamber, they also made a major contribution to discussions of labour matters through their service on various Royal Commissions.[36]

The contention of this essay thus far has been that the role of the Lib-Labs of south Wales in contributing to the building of the Labour movement, and, equally, in articulating a separate 'language of Labour' demands greater appreciation than it has hitherto received. The importance of the distinctive political perspective generated by the Lib-Labs is further revealed by the part played by Mabon, his supporters, and other Lib-Labs in the Cymru Fydd agitation of the 1890s. Discussion of this episode not only extends our understanding of Lib-Labism, but also questions the adequacy of existing interpretations of the history of Cymru Fydd itself.[37]

Wales's modern history has been burdened with a relentless contradiction between nationalism and democracy. The most pervasive definition of Welsh nationality, if at the same time the most frustrating, has been a linguistic and cultural one, centred upon the Welsh language and, to a lesser extent, nonconformity. As Mabon himself explained in October 1888: 'The Welsh had a language of their own; he was almost going to say that they had a religion of their own, and all this gave them a distinct claim to be recognised as a nation.'[38] Given the pace of anglicization and indeed secularization in the twentieth century, such a definition has appealed to a progressively smaller constituency of the people of Wales with the passing of each year. Framed culturally, nationalism has had little option but to be the creed of the minority, and as such has often stumbled against the democratic imperative. Projects to reconfigure Welsh nationality as a more inclusive category have themselves been hindered by an absence of social or political common ground across Wales as a whole once the cultural definition is removed.

It is arguable that the 1890s represented the last decade during which such a contradiction might have been avoided. According to the 1891 Census Wales may then still have had a bare majority of its citizens who spoke the Welsh language and were thus welcomed by the prevailing definition of nationality. However, Cymru Fydd, the Welsh Home Rule movement that for a while captured the allegiance of some of Wales's greatest Liberal politicians (such as David Lloyd George and Tom Ellis), failed to build a successful national movement, even on the basis of limited autonomy within the framework of the British Imperial state.[39] In explaining the failure of Cymru Fydd, attention has usually been paid to the divisions within Welsh society, caused by the industrialization, urbanization and anglicization of the south Wales coalfield and the ports of the south-east. The common image for the demise of the league has been the 'howling down' of Lloyd George by 'Newport Englishmen' which brought the dream to an end in January 1896 and persuaded Lloyd George that his personal destiny lay in a larger British arena.⁴⁰ This chapter, extending the discussion of democracy outlined above, argues for a rather different understanding. Cymru Fydd's failure to capture the allegiance of south Wales Liberalism was in part due to the interests and priorities of south Wales's Lib-Labs, who perceived in the Home Rule movement an elevation of the principle of national self-government at the expense of the cause of Labour. Temporarily, the Lib-Labs were prepared to join those who were their opponents in so many matters, the coalowners, in thwarting the Cymru Fydd project.

That this dimension of the Cymru Fydd story has been ignored is to some extent due to the ambivalent relationship that existed between the Lib-Labs and the conventional badges of Welsh nationality. All four Lib-Lab MPs were nonconformists and made the right national noises when it suited them. Mabon in particular played the 'Welsh card' in the House of Commons with regularity, breaking into Welsh on occasion.⁴¹ Mabon's use of hymns, even the Welsh national anthem 'Hen Wlad Fy Nhadau', at public meetings is well-known.⁴² Furthermore, the possession of an adequate range of Welsh national credentials was an important qualification for any prospective Lib-Lab candidate. Thomas Halliday, when fighting Merthyr Boroughs in 1874, suffered from his identity as a monoglot Englishman in a constituency where approximately half the population spoke only Welsh. According to the *South Wales Daily News*, '[b]y nationality, by training, and by habit and sympathy Mr. Halliday is out of harmony with the people of Merthyr. He will scarcely be able – a stranger and an Englishman – to realise their stand point, or to appreciate the feelings and sentiments with which they view public questions.'⁴³ Halliday's claim that he was learning Welsh 'and would, before long, be able to address his hearers in their mother tongue' was evidently insufficiently persuasive. In contrast, his opponent Henry Richard could be characterized as 'the selected advocate and exponent of the views of tens of thousands of Welshmen', who 'speaks on the questions specially affecting Wales, with their voice, and endorsed by their authority'.⁴⁴ Even within Halliday's own AAM there was dissension that ran along the lines of linguistically-defined nationality, and that resulted in the 'Red Dragon revolt' later in the year, with an attempt to establish a Welsh-speaking trade union.⁴⁵ Halliday's successors did not encounter this particular difficulty, with Mabon and John Williams in particular offering considerable evidence of their involvement in contemporary Welsh-language culture. However, playing the national card, living up to the national stereotype, even playing a part in creating it (as surely Mabon did) was not the same as placing the national question ahead of all others.⁴⁶ Such was apparent in the reception given to the Cymru Fydd proposals as they relegated their initial cultural and educational objectives beneath the ambition of some form of home rule for Wales.⁴⁷

Mabon might be only too pleased to stress his identity as a Welsh-speaking Welshman at Westminster, where it might be deployed to dramatic effect, but he was concerned to limit the impact that nationalist agitation might have upon the Liberal party in Wales, and in particular upon the 'working people of Wales' who were its bedrock. As their representative he did not feel that he could 'subordinate every other interest to that of their nationality ... although they were Welshmen they were also working men'.⁴⁸ There is no doubt that Mabon's views were complex. He was prepared, in his early years, to support the general notion of self-government, and so were other miners' leaders such as Isaac Evans, David Morgan, and William Brace. However, support in principle could turn into opposition in practice, a point missed by Dewi Rowland Hughes in his attempt to find links between Cymru Fydd and the Welsh Labour movement. Hughes interprets any expression of sympathy for the Cymru Fydd programme at any time as evidence of support throughout the period of agitation.⁴⁹ This is untenable for two reasons.

First, the very nature of the Cymru Fydd agitation changed over time, and was subject to comment for the 'multifarious character of the views and "objects" of its various promoters'. Support given to the movement in 1894 may well have been withdrawn or muted by the crisis at Newport in 1896. Early supporters such as William Brace preferred to stress the need for unity by May 1895, and, in the wake of the Newport meeting, Brace was able to make a public statement in support of Robert Bird, who had drawn so much criticism from the Cymru Fyddites for his part in the defeat of their plans on that occasion.⁵⁰

Even when support was given, this could be qualified by warnings that action was necessary to realize Cymru Fydd's intentions of advancing the claims of the 'labouring classes'. Thus miners' leader Isaac Evans pointed out in August 1894 that although he was in support of the principle of self-government 'the working classes had not been invited to join these [Cymru Fydd] associations'. Throughout 1894 there were frequent references to the lack of attention paid by Cymru Fydd to 'our class', and Lloyd George himself admitted that working men constituted no more than 5 per cent of Liberal association membership across Wales.[51] This is not to suggest that orthodox Liberal organizations were any more representative, merely that statements by Cymru Fydd leaders that they intended to embrace and uphold the working men of Wales should not be accepted as proof of success.

Such ambiguities are less evident in the case of Mabon who, more than any other Lib-Lab leader, was prepared to make his concerns over Cymru Fydd explicit. In October 1888, at the second annual conference of the Welsh National Liberal Council at Newtown, and having a week earlier told the Cardiff Junior Liberal Association that '[t]hey could not afford to subordinate the great industrial questions of the day to nationality' Mabon now warned his fellow Liberals:

> Welshmen were working men first of all. They subsisted by their daily toil, and they could not be expected to given an unqualified allegiance to any party if that party forgot industrial questions. He wanted the Welsh party of Wales to be very careful indeed not to let the working people of Wales for a moment think that, even inadvertently, the Welsh Liberal party were losing sight of the great importance of the labour questions of the day. Such a calamity should be averted.[52]

The great flowering of Cymru Fydd agitation took place in the mid-1890s, with the issue in May 1894 of a new manifesto by the league. This document contained a pledge to improve the conditions of miners and quarrymen, but Mabon remained suspicious of Cymru Fydd and of what he saw as its domination by groups lacking roots in the industrial democracy of south Wales, and hence lacking adequate concern for labour questions. Again he issued a warning:

> Let the friends of Liverpool, Manchester and the North distinctly understand that there must be no further misunderstanding with regard to this matter. If South Wales is to have any part in this new national party, the Labour question, the claims of the wage-earners, must not only be

quietly included in the programme, but they must be made the centre point and the pivot around which all other questions must spin in turn, ... the North may be allowed to follow its inclination after localism, nationalism, and sentimentalism, or any other 'ism' they think proper; but we in the South must look after the bread and cheese of the people, also protecting their lives and limbs in the shape of useful and practical legislation; in which a real Employers' Liability Bill and a bona-fide measure for limiting the hours of labour must be included.[53]

Cymru Fydd's aim was to restructure the organization of the Liberal party in Wales, bringing together the two regional federations (of north and south Wales) in one body, to be known as the Welsh National Federation. During the remainder of 1894 the league made significant advances, but was more successful in north Wales than it was in the south. This diversity in fortunes has been explained by Emyr Williams as reflecting a fundamental difference in the nature of Liberal organizations, whereby Cymru Fydd, led by Lloyd George, represented 'popular democratic reformers', but was resisted by 'undemocratic and unscrupulous conservatives' led by coalowner D. A. Thomas. Williams considers that within 'proletarian South Wales in particular, Liberal constituency associations, where they existed, appear to have been notoriously undemocratic and unrepresentative.'[54] Hughes has gone further still in suggesting that the opposition of the coalowners and capitalists of the south was based upon material self-interest, and particularly upon resistance to the campaign for an Eight Hours Bill. He suggests that by spring 1895: 'roedd [D. A. Thomas] yn benderfynol i geisio rhwystro Cynghrair a allai beryglu buddiannau y Cambrian Collieries.' ['D. A. Thomas was determined to try and hinder the League which could endanger the profits of the Cambrian Collieries.'][55]

Such views are unsatisfactory on three grounds. First, much of Williams's impression of Cymru Fydd success, which he considers led it to a 'political hegemony over Liberalism in Wales' during the summer of 1894, is based upon optimistic and partisan press reporting in *Y Faner* and the *South Wales Daily News*.[56] As Thomas Gee, proprietor and editor of *Y Faner*, was a leading supporter of Cymru Fydd, and as the editor of the journal *Cymru Fydd*, Thomas John Hughes (Adfyfyr) was also sub-editor on the *South Wales Daily News*, these sources have to be treated with some caution.[57]

Second, the contrast between the Liberal associations of the north and south is without any evidential foundation: it is likely that both were equally 'undemocratic' as has already been argued.[58] Following the Newport meeting it was suggested that 'the two best organised counties in North Wales, Merionethshire and Anglesey' had not supported Cymru Fydd.[59] To divide the opposed wings of Welsh Liberalism between 'reformist' and 'conservative' axes is therefore simplistic.

Finally, to characterize the opposition of D. A. Thomas and others to Cymru Fydd as purely materialist is unjustifiably deterministic, and a serious distortion of the complexities of the time. Mabon explained in November 1895 that although he and Thomas differed over a number of issues (including the Eight Hours campaign) they were united on the matter of Cymru Fydd.[60] Such opposition, shared by other miners' leaders, was due in part to a growing hostility towards the personal ambition being exhibited by Lloyd George, although it also seems likely that Thomas's dislike of what he saw as Cymru Fydd's cultural particularism and linguistic exclusivism may have been endorsed by Labour leaders catering for an increasingly cosmopolitan workforce.[61] Thomas accused Cymru Fydd of being nothing more than 'a small clique of wire-pullers' and asserted that '[t]hey, in the South, at all events, were determined that Liberal Wales should not have her policy dictated by a clique, but that it should be determined by the democracy'.[62] According to his daughter, 'When "Wales for the Welsh" was the great cry of the Cymru Fydd, he would laugh and say he preferred as the Welsh motto "The world is our oyster".'[63]

A clearer understanding of the issues at stake in the response to the Cymru Fydd movement can be obtained through a closer study of the personnel and tactics involved at local level. The Rhondda Valleys, as an acknowledged 'cockpit' for the battle over Cymru Fydd in the south, provides an appropriate case-study.

Clear divisions within the ranks of Rhondda Liberalism were revealed in May 1895 at two public meetings in Ferndale. Speaking at the first, Thomas and J. Bryn Roberts, both opponents of Cymru Fydd, argued for the retention of the South Wales Liberal Federation in its existing form, allowing the industrial south relative autonomy within the structures of the Welsh Liberal party. In this they were supported by the president of the

RLLA, the Revd O. Haelfryn Hughes of Tylorstown, who repeated the views of Mabon that labour questions should receive greater prominence in the Cymru Fydd programme.[64] Mabon himself explained to the *South Wales Daily News* that he did not wish to become embroiled in the controversy, but '[l]ooking at the things from a Labour standpoint, I believe more in the efficacy of the old Federation ... the vast majority in the Rhondda is in favour of the old organisation.' The following week Lloyd George, Alfred Thomas and Beriah Gwynfe Evans replied on behalf of Cymru Fydd, but were forced to deal with some hostile questioning from the Revd Hughes, who attacked what he considered to be the anti-democratic nature of the proposed Welsh National Federation, which in its composition would give equal weight to north and south Wales and thus drastically under-represent the much larger population of the latter.[65] Nevertheless, as at both meetings resolutions in favour of the opinions of the respective speakers were both carried overwhelmingly, honours might have been considered even at this stage.

The campaign took a different turn in November 1895 with Lloyd George undertaking a speaking tour of south Wales, to gather support for Cymru Fydd. Simultaneously, in the Rhondda Valleys, Mabon initiated a series of meetings with the avowed intention of enhancing the organization of the RLLA. Whether that was indeed the origin of the campaign it is difficult to determine: Mabon may have hoped that his campaign would forestall or dilute any local Cymru Fydd offensive. It is equally possible that he believed that only by bringing the RLLA organization up to scratch could he rely upon what would then be its renewed 'democratic' character to endorse his long-established restraint concerning the national question.[66]

Whatever Mabon's real intentions, his oft-stated desire during the campaign that the national question be set aside and only 'neutral' issues (such as disestablishment and the Labour question) be considered went unsatisfied. Inviting protagonists Lloyd George and D. A. Thomas to speak made some reference to the issue of the moment unavoidable. Lloyd George, lecturing at Ferndale on the subject of 'Llewelyn the Great' turned this into an analogy with Cymru Fydd.[67] Thomas responded in the midst of a speech on the coal trade, by calling for unity in the face of divisiveness, a sentiment that Mabon himself repeatedly endorsed.[68]

The presence on RLLA platforms of known opponents of Cymru Fydd such as MPs Roberts and Samuel T. Evans could only lend support to that cause, whether or not this was the Rhondda member's original intention.

Yet it was Lloyd George's two appearances, at Ferndale and Tonypandy on 11 and 20 November respectively, that seem to have had the greatest impact on the RLLA Executive.[69] When it met on 14 January 1896 it voted in favour of the Cymru Fydd plan for reorganization.[70] Two days later, however, came the Newport débâcle, and the collapse of the Cymru Fydd project. This episode itself stands in need of reassessment, as it has been subjected to severe and one-sided caricature, but with regard to the argument being considered here in respect of 'democracy' and the 'Lib-Labs', three points stand out.

First, the assertion by Cymru Fydd supporters, then and since, that had the meeting been properly representative the Cymru Fydd programme would have been carried is impossible to sustain. The Cardiff Liberal Association, for one, did not send any delegates to the Newport meeting: had it done so, contemporaries estimated that its sixty to eighty votes would have been cast against the Cymru Fydd proposals. Accusations of 'packing' by D. A. Thomas and others were countered vociferously by suggestions that it was Lloyd George and his supporters who had attempted to pack the meeting. According to the *South Wales Daily News*, Lloyd George's charges of malpractice were 'an unpardonable accusation'.[71]

The suggestion that Lloyd George was, unfairly and outrageously, 'howled down' is also difficult to uphold once one goes beyond partisan accounts of the meeting. Having been permitted to address the meeting once, his attempt to return to the platform in advance of other speakers was put to the vote, and lost. According to the *South Wales Argus*, the bad behaviour came more from the Cymru Fyddites, and for all Lloyd George's comments about the 'morbid footballism' of Monmouthshire:

> The howl that went up when Mr.Robert Bird said there was a large community in South Wales which would, not submit to domination and dictation was as bad as the pandemonium on a football ground when the referee decided against the home team. Some of the delegates were like raving lunatics for a time ... [72]

Finally, what the evidence from the Rhondda Valleys and elsewhere in the coalfield reveals is that far from representing a 'popular democratic' drive for Home Rule, Cymru Fydd may have appealed predominantly to middle-class rather than working-class elements within south Wales Liberalism, and precisely to those elements that worked against rather than towards working-class political representation. All three Rhondda leaders of the Cymru Fydd agitation – Tom John, the Revd Evan Richards, and William Gwrtydd Williams – had opposed Mabon during the 1885 election, whereas those siding with Mabon against Cymru Fydd included other Lib-Labs such as T. Daronwy Isaac, and those prepared to back Mabon on labour issues, such as the Revd O. Haelfryn Hughes.[73] This impression of a class divide in the Rhondda is corroborated by Demont's study of Tredegar, which reveals much less enthusiasm for Cymru Fydd than was apparent in the Rhondda, and argues that Home Rule for Wales was not 'a burning political issue' in the coalfield as a whole.[74] Overall, even if they entertained sympathies towards some form of devolution for Wales, Lib-Lab leaders were not prepared to submerge the interests of their 'democracy' in a political project that both bore the marks of cultural élitism and seemed very much to be beyond their control.

The understanding of the reception of Cymru Fydd at the hands of the Lib-Labs elaborated in this essay dovetails with the earlier stress upon the class identity and democratic principles of the Lib-Labs across the south Wales coalfield as a whole. Mabon and his fellow public representatives remained aware of their roots in that industrial democracy, and of the obligations placed upon them to serve its needs. Eventually, in some measure, their service was to outlast their contribution as new imperatives and practices first challenged and then destroyed the consensual and harmonious world to which they had contributed so much. The new generation of Labour leaders, socialist not Liberal in political ideology, combative not compromising in industrial matters, developed its own understanding of democracy to accord with the changed circumstances. In this redefined society, the working class was to be given due weight not simply because of its numerical superiority, but rather because of its qualitative importance as the only producer of wealth. Politicians were to be expected more to serve the movement as delegates than to personify their constituency as representatives.

Yet, in building upon the organizational foundations and discursive practices of the Lib-Labs, the new generation of MPs and councillors, of miners' agents and autodidacts, owed rather more to the 'shandygaff'[75] politicians than they cared to admit.

Notes

1 D. Howell, *British Workers and the Independent Labour Party* (Manchester, 1983), 18.
2 As a working definition, Lib-Labs were working men (thus 'Labour') candidates who nevertheless adhered to the national political programme of the Liberal party.
3 In 1909 the Mineworkers' Federation of Great Britain affiliated to the Labour party, and so the Welsh Lib-Lab MPs, all of whom were sponsored by the miners, nominally became Labour MPs, although their political beliefs and behaviour changed very little.
4 E. W. Evans, *Mabon: A Study in Trade Union Leadership* (Cardiff, 1959).
5 For Lib-Labs in local government, see C. Williams, *Democratic Rhondda: Politics and Society, 1885–1951* (Cardiff, 1996), ch.2.
6 D. Hopkin, 'The Rise of Labour in Wales 1890–1914', *Llafur* 6 (4) (1994), 120–41, is devoted entirely to tracing the slow growth of very small socialist societies and almost completely ignores the much more powerful and representative Lib-Lab tradition.
7 For T. J. McCarry, 'Labour and Society in Swansea, 1887–1918' (Ph.D. thesis, University of Wales, Swansea, 1986), 234, the Lib-Labs were 'a major obstacle to the expansion of socialist ideas'.
8 H. J. Davies, 'Mabon at Westminster: The Parliamentary Career of William Abraham M.P. 1885–1920', M.A. dissertation, University of Wales, Cardiff, 1990, 26.
9 R. Wallace, *Organise! Organise! Organise! A Study of Reform Agitations in Wales, 1840–1886* (Cardiff, 1991), 231.
10 Lib-Lab industrial strategy requires a much more extensive treatment than is possible here. Lib-Labs were prepared to engage in industrial conflict: Thomas Halliday led the Amalgamated Association of Mineworkers into three bitter strikes in the 1870s, and Mabon's contemporaries, William Brace, Isaac Evans and David Morgan, were much quicker than he to adopt aggressive postures. Recent contributions to the industrial relations history of the British labour movement have emphasized precisely the tradition of compromise and consensus that the Lib-Labs encapsulated. See the discussion in C. Williams, 'Britain', in *The Force of Labour: Western European Labour Movements in the Twentieth Century*, eds. S. Berger and D. Broughton (Oxford, 1995), 107–35.

11 E. F. Biagini, *Liberty, Retrenchment and Reform: Popular Liberalism in the Age of Gladstone, 1860–1880* (Cambridge, 1992); E. F. Biagini and A. J. Reid (eds.), *Currents of Radicalism: Popular Radicalism, Organised Labour and Party Politics in Britain 1850–1914* (Cambridge, 1991); Patrick Joyce, *Visions of the People: Industrial England and the Question of Class, 1848–1914* (Cambridge, 1991).
12 For a re-evaluation on a British scale, see J. Shepherd, 'Labour and Parliament: The Lib.-Labs. as the First Working-Class MPs, 1885–1906', in Biagini and Reid, *Currents*, 187–213.
13 Unofficial Reform Committee, *The Miners' Next Step* (Tonypandy, 1912).
14 Shepherd, 'Labour and Parliament', loc. cit., 197, argues that the Lib-Labs were caught between two different conceptions of their role as MPs: an older one in which they had a responsibility to 'the nation as a whole', and the newer view which saw them as representing simply the working class. Neither is accurate: the Lib-Labs saw themselves as representing all their constituents, but also being in a position to speak for their trades and occupations. Commenting on national policy was never considered their strength, or even purpose, and occasionally their perceived limitations in this respect were held to count against their suitability as MPs.
15 Occasionally, election candidates with no recognized link to the established Labour movement adopted the label of 'Lib-Lab' in an attempt to attract votes.
16 Cited in Shepherd, 'Labour and Parliament', 190.
17 The absence of such links in the cases of David Randell, MP for Gower 1888–1900, and Clement Edwards, MP for Denbigh Boroughs 1906–10, and for East Glamorgan 1910–18, is considered to invalidate any claim for them as Lib-Lab figures, as well as for Allen Upward, who stood as a 'Lib-Lab' candidate at Merthyr Boroughs in 1895.
18 As K. O. Morgan has argued, it was this 'Old Liberalism' rather than its newer varieties, that remained in place in Wales down to the Great War: 'The New Liberalism and the Challenge of Labour: The Welsh Experience, 1885–1929', *Welsh History Review* Vol.6 (1973), 288–312.
19 Cited in S. E. Demont, 'Tredegar and Aneurin Bevan: A Society and its Political Articulation, 1890–1929' (Ph.D. thesis, University of Wales, Cardiff, 1990), 76.
20 Williams, *Democratic Rhondda*, 29–48.
21 D. Cleaver, 'Labour and Liberals in the Gower Constituency, 1885–1910', *Welsh History Review* Vol.12 (1985), 388–410.
22 K. O. Morgan, *Wales in British Politics* (Cardiff, 1980 edn.), 209–10; Demont, 'Tredegar', 64–75.

23 Williams, *Democratic Rhondda*, 58–9; Wallace, *Organise!*, 233; Shepherd, 'Labour and Parliament', 194–6.
24 'H', in the *Glamorgan Free Press*, 30 August 1902.
25 Letter to *Cambria Daily Leader*, 31 September 1888, cited in McCarry, 'Swansea', 89.
26 Cited in Demont, 'Tredegar', 62–3. According to Demont, 'It is clear that Richards' politics centred around a belief in working class representation at all levels – in local and national government, and through a powerful trade union ... '.
27 *South Wales Daily News (SWDN)*, 8 April 1873.
28 *Workman's Advocate (WA)*, 6 September 1873. Halliday pointed out that he had himself been a coalminer for eighteen years, and that he knew 'what the life is'.
29 Ibid., 4 October 1873.
30 Ibid., 20 December 1873. In its inquest (7 February) upon Halliday's defeat, the *WA* regretted that 'the Nonconformist middle class have been so unmanly and cowardly, as to attack his candidature anonymously'. Later (21 February) another attack was made upon the 'disgraceful tactics' of the 'Liberal Nonconformists', 'the enemies of true freedom, and the upholders of the tyrannical conduct of the capitalists of this country'.
31 *SWDN*, 29 January 1874, 5 February 1874; *WA*, 7, 14 February 1874.
32 *SWDN*, 5 February 1874.
33 *SWDN*, 1 September 1873; *WA*, 6 September 1873. At a campaign meeting (*SWDN*, 29 January 1874) Mabon proclaimed '[t]hey must have men who could portray in living colours their hardships and sufferings and make their interest his own'.
34 *SWDN*, 12 May 1885; *Pontypridd Chronicle*, 15 May 1885.
35 Demont, 'Tredegar', 69–72, considers that in the election Richards's emphasis 'seems to have been evenly divided between the traditional Liberal issues ... and a strong appeal to the working classes to "elect one of their own" to defend their particular interests in an unsympathetic and hostile world'.
36 Davies, 'Mabon at Westminster', 46–96.
37 The main accounts are Morgan, *Wales in British Politics*; E. W. Williams, 'The Politics of Welsh Home Rule 1886–1929: A Sociological Analysis' (Ph.D. thesis, University of Wales, Aberystwyth, 1986); D. R. Hughes, 'Y Coch A'r Gwyrdd: Cymru Fydd A'r Mudiad Llafur Cymreig (1886–96)' ['The Red and the Green: Young Wales and the Welsh Labour Movement (1886–96)'], *Llafur* Vol.6 (4) (1995), 60–79. See also E. W. Williams, 'Liberalism in Wales and the Politics of Welsh Home Rule 1886–1910', *Bulletin of the Board of Celtic Studies* 37 (1990), 191–207. All references are taken from the thesis.

38 *SWDN*, 9 October 1888.
39 According to Hughes, 'Y Coch', 71–2, if Lloyd George had succeeded rather than failed at Newport in 1896 'y byddai hanes modern Cymru un wahanol o'r herwydd' ('the history of modern Wales would have been different').
40 Williams, 'Welsh Home Rule', 123–4. At the Newport meeting, the South Wales Liberal Federation (led by coalowners and businessmen including D. A. Thomas and Robert Bird) voted to resist Cymru Fydd's plans for the reorganization of the Liberal party across Wales as a whole. Such plans, if implemented, would have led to greater emphasis on 'nationalist' objectives, and, hypothetically, to a stronger movement for Home Rule for Wales.
41 Davies, 'Mabon at Westminster', 29–38, argues that 'Mabon' had a genuine concern for the importance of having Welsh-speaking mines' inspectors, and thus his use of Welsh was more than a rhetorical device.
42 The possibly apocryphal instance of 'Mabon' using the national anthem to subdue hecklers during the 1898 strike is related by R. Smillie, in *My Life for Labour*, (London, 1924), 62–3. I. Matthews, 'The World of the Anthracite Miner' (Ph.D. thesis, University of Wales, Cardiff, 1995), 198, substantiates the singing of hymns by Mabon at public meetings.
43 *SWDN*, 29 January 1874.
44 Ibid., 5 February 1874. 'Philo-Cambria' described Richard (ibid, 3 February 1874) as 'MP for all Welshmen and all Wales'.
45 Aled Jones, 'Trade Unions and the Press: Journalism and the Red Dragon Revolt of 1874', *Welsh History Review* Vol.12 (1984), 197–221.
46 A subtlety missed by Biagini, *Liberty*, 352, who portrays Mabon as 'completely identified with Welsh nationalism' and where this aspect of his public persona is equated with the rise of Cymru Fydd.
47 Morgan, *Wales in British Politics*, 104–6, 160.
48 *SWDN*, 9 October 1888.
49 Hughes, 'Y Coch', 66–7.
50 *SWDN*, 2 January, 7 May 1895, 23 January 1896.
51 Ibid., 23, 24 August, 11, 12, 20 September, 5 October 1894.
52 Ibid., 3, 5, 10 October 1888. Opposition was voiced by Beriah Gwynfe Evans, who 'held that allegiance should be given to the Welsh Parliamentary party above and before every other question'.
53 Ibid., 15 June 1894.
54 Williams, 'Welsh Home Rule', 111–15.
55 Hughes, 'Y Coch', 67–8.
56 Recognized by Morgan, *Wales in British Politics*, 106, and *Rebirth of a Nation: Wales 1880–1980* (Cardiff and Oxford, 1981), 118, who suggests that Cymru Fydd was 'an artificial construct of packed committees and pliant newspaper editors, not a genuinely popular movement for home rule'.

57 A. Jones, *Press, Politics and Society: A History of Journalism in Wales* (Cardiff, 1992), 41. The line taken by the *SWDN* with regards to Cymru Fydd, however, was variable, and the paper moved away from close identification with the movement from mid-1895, calling for 'peace' rather than for continued bitter in-fighting. See *SWDN*, 27 May 1895.

58 Morgan, *Wales in British Politics*, 164, sees Cymru Fydd as 'a network of paper organizations rather than a reflection of a genuine national call for home rule ... Lloyd George justifiably condemned the South Wales Liberal Federation as an unrepresentative and narrow caucus, but it is questionable whether his own Cymru Fydd had any broader popular basis ... '.

59 *SWDN*, 20 January 1896: letter by 'A Disgusted North Walian'.

60 Ibid., 16 November 1895.

61 See J. V. Morgan, *Life of Viscount Rhondda* (London, 1918), 203; Ll. Williams, 'Political Life', in *D. A. Thomas: Viscount Rhondda, by His Daughter* (Margaret, Lady Rhondda) and others (London, 1921), 77.

62 *SWDN*, 28 January 1896.

63 Margaret, Lady Rhondda, *D. A. Thomas*, 31. According to Morgan, *Life*, 107: 'He was not in bondage to the language, or to Welsh national ideals, though an ardent advocate of the claims of Wales to a larger recognition on the part of the state. ... He was a Briton first and a Welshman afterwards.'

64 *SWDN*, 13 May 1895. The Rev. Hughes (whose son, Philip, was to be a prominent figure in the Rhondda Labour party in the twentieth century) repeated his views in a letter to the *SWDN* on 12 November 1895:

> Truly, the warm-hearted miners of the Rhondda are 'Nationalists' in the highest sense. They want to see the 'working men' of the country – who are the nation – uplifted on all hands. They will see 'labour questions' put first and foremost on every programme.

65 Ibid., 20, 23 May 1895.

66 Indeed, it had been remarked in the *Glamorgan Free Press* on 27 July 1895 that the 're-organisation [of the RLLA] upon a new basis both popular and workable is absolutely necessary.' The same organ on 2 November 1895 opined that 'frequent complaints have been made that the Executive of the Association is non-representative', and the *SWDN* on 15 November 1895 related Mabon's preference for first reorganising and then deciding on the national question.'

67 *SWDN*, 12 November 1895; *Western Mail*, 12 November 1895.

68 *SWDN*, 15, 16 November 1895.

69 For the euphoric reaction of Lloyd George to these meetings see K. O. Morgan (ed.), *Lloyd George: Family Letters* (Cardiff and Oxford, 1973), 91–2. On Tonypandy:

> Last night's demonstration was simply immense – that is the word.

> Nothing like it in the Rhondda – not in the memory of the oldest inhabitant has anything to equal it been seen. Crowds from all parts of the Rhondda came down. Hundreds of D. A. Thomas's own colliers amongst them. Mabon looked blue. I talked Home Rule for Wales & all the nationalist stuff which the Mabon crew so detest – but the people cheered to the echo. The Rhondda has been captured.

70 Lloyd George believed this result represented a 'grand victory' which 'cripples Mabon's mischievousness' and would culminate in 'the turning of the scale at Newport' (Morgan, *Lloyd George Letters*, 93–4).
71 *SWDN*, 20, 23, 28 January, 8 February 1896.
72 Ibid., 17 January 1896.
73 For the continued involvement of the Revd E. Richards and Tom John, see *SWDN*, 7 February 1896. Emyr Wynn Williams's argument ('Welsh Home Rule', 111) that the fact that only one Lib-Lab MP had been elected to a south Wales constituency from 1885 onwards is evidence of unrepresentative south Walian Liberalism is thus substantiated, but in the opposite way to that intended. Similarly Mabon's opposition to Cymru Fydd undermines his argument (p.112) that the movement 'threatened to establish the dominance of working class political power at precisely the time when leading Liberal MPs were finding it necessary to resist political pressure from that quarter'.
74 Demont, 'Tredegar', 57–61; *Merthyr Express*, 23 November, 14 December 1895.
75 *Concise OED*: *shandygaff* 'n. a mixed drink of beer and ginger beer or lemonade. Nineteenth century. Origin unknown.'

~7~
History and the Triumph of Art: Manuel Azaña's Vision of Spanish Democracy

ROBERT STRADLING

You're not supposed to see an epic at short range, objectively. You should read it in history, with its fruits already known, or enjoy it when poetry has transfigured and elevated it ... artistic transmutation stands as a cornerstone of European culture. Who knows whether some day the Spanish mind will find inspiration, a national stimulus, in this upheaval ... Will we be capable of building a poetic and political monument of the present epic?

What spurred Azaña to seek to change the fate of his country was chiefly the longing for harmony and beauty, the preoccupation of the artist rather than the politician.[1]

Word into Subject

On 20 October 1935, Manuel Azaña achieved the fantasy of every intellectual. In the course of a lecture lasting over an hour he drove an audience of half a million wild with enthusiasm. The meeting, which took place at Campo de Comillas, near Madrid's huge working-class *barrio* of Carabanchel, in effect marked the opening of the Popular Front election campaign. Azaña was the leading architect of the electoral alliance destined to restore the Left to power in Spain; with a series of speeches 'en campo abierto' ('in the open air') he led the attack, as usual, from the front. Addressing his people in the familiar person, he told them that

> All Europe today is a battlefield between democracy and its enemies, and Spain is no exception. You have to choose between democracy, with all its fallibility, weakness, and mistakes, and tyranny, with all its horrors ... The people's silence expresses their misery and indignation, but the voice of the people can sound terrible, like trumpets on the Day

of Judgement. Let my words not slip casually over frivolous hearts, but penetrate yours like darts of fire. People, for Spain and for the Republic – Unite![2]

This seed was scattered exactly nine months before the generals' *pronunciamiento*, which – when it came – was announced encodedly as the birth of Helen's long-awaited and beautiful daughter.[3] Like her classical namesake, this fictitious female launched an epic struggle, a confrontation as central to our intellectual life as the Trojan War was to that of our forebears, and with cultural resonances almost as fabulous. In the Comillas speech, it was as if the speaker engendered a civil war to be conceived and delivered by his audience.

> A shudder in the loins engenders there
> The broken wall, the burning roof and tower
> And Agamemnon dead.
>   Being so caught up,
> So mastered by the brute blood of the air
> Did she put on his knowledge with his power
> Before the indifferent beak could let her drop?[4]

Yet few of his audience can have heard everything Azaña said; and, despite his eloquence, a majority failed to follow much of what they did hear.[5] Though deafening shouts greeted every phrase, it is unlikely that the crowd either understood or appreciated the most extensive section of the speech, in which Azaña explained why a victorious Popular Front government would need to balance the budget and could not commit itself to an untrammelled programme of social reform. Rather, they were enthused by the carefully-modulated emotion of his delivery, which seemed to voice their own feelings of righteous protest and justified vengeance, along with a kind of communitarian patriotism fired with enthusiasm for progress.[6]

It would hardly be surprising if Azaña believed at this moment that the uncompromising intellectual leadership he offered, reached – even represented – the masses. He may have felt (since he rarely desisted from awarding himself laurels for public performances) that he was indeed the spiritual father of his people. He was by no means the first Spanish politician to see himself as patriarch and prophet, and his gift for oratory was not unusual in the context of contemporary politics. However, his mission was not, at least in the conventional usage of the word, political; rather it was humanistic, ethical and utopian. Azaña's objective was far more ambitious and long-term than that sought by any other Spanish politician, or arguably by any other modern democratic leader. Of course, he wished to educate the people in politics, and to create a politically mature society in Spain. In more recondite terms, he sought to model a harmonious arcadia which, like a masterpiece of Art, would be beautiful and indestructible. Only in a general and somewhat commonplace sense can his ideals be said to have adumbrated the stable but mundane democracy which came into existence in the 1980s, half-a-century after he flourished as the recognized leader of the Second Republic. For this reason, one might hesitate before counting him – along with Francisco Franco, King Juan Carlos, Adolfo Suárez and Felipe González – as one of the founders of contemporary Spain. His career was in many ways bizarre and remains elusive. He practised politics through extreme principles of aesthetics, and wished for a society projected on the premises of a radical interpretation of Spanish history, which he self-consciously subjectified.

Subject into History

Manuel Azaña Díaz died in exile in France in the midst of modern mankind's darkest days – October 1940. Everything he had hoped and worked for was in bloody ruin and apparently terminal overthrow. It is said that his death anticipated by only a few hours the arrival of the Gestapo, on a visit inspired by Hitler's associate and potential ally, General Franco. Fifty years later, a spate of books and other writings issued in the new Spain of democracy and socialism hailed him as one of the greatest figures of modern Spain and a warrior for universal freedom. Yet controversy over Azaña's political legacy was so potentially disruptive that only a decade earlier, in a more delicate phase of Spain's 'transition' to democracy, the centenary of his birth (in 1880) had been allowed to pass almost without comment. A thoroughgoing act of atonement for this deliberate oversight was made with the celebrations of 1990. Even the Catholic-monarchist newspaper *ABC* – which the arch-republican atheist prime minister had closed down for a spell in 1932 – embraced his memory and admitted him to the pantheon of greatness. The restoration of Azaña seemed to be a sign that his vision had been realized: a plural, tolerant society, which at last felt itself to be secure. In fact, the strongly contrasting reactions of the nation to the opportunities offered in 1980 and 1990 serves to expose the central contradiction of Azaña's life and career.[7]

Not long after his death, Azaña was the subject of a eulogy by the celebrated British hispanist, Gerald Brenan, in *The Spanish Labyrinth* – a book familiar to generations of students of modern Spanish history, and which can still have a revelatory impact on those approaching the subject for the first time. Brenan's treatment established some characteristic priorities. He pointed out that Azaña was a writer,

> but in the first place he was a man of action ... He showed, more than any other Republican politician, the qualities of statesman and parliamentarian without ever compromising his honesty. It was mainly due to his drive and persistence that the huge mass of new legislation was piloted through an increasingly recalcitrant *Cortes*. But the cause of Azaña's greatness lies deeper than this. Just as Abraham Lincoln lived for American democracy and came to stand as a symbol for it, so Azaña lived for and embodied the idea of the Spanish Republic.[8]

Manuel Azaña was thus nominated as a crucial subject for the attention of scholars of the liberal-humanist tradition: that is to say, virtually any historian recognized as such by professional colleagues. Yet fifty years after Brenan's encomium, Azaña remains an obscure figure outside Spain. In the first edition of *The Penguin Dictionary of Modern European History*, which I procured as a 1960s undergraduate, he had no entry. (The new edition of 1979 repaired the omission, but gave a wrong date for his birth, in addition to several other errors of fact.) In the *Larousse Encyclopaedia of Modern History*, he is mentioned only once – incorrectly – as the leader of the Spanish socialists who dominated the government in the period 1931 to 1933.[9] Of his voluminous and diverse writings, only one substantial item has been translated into English.[10] In the 1960s – of all decades in the history of liberal-academic hegemony – the British Library neglected to obtain for its stocks a copy of the standard edition of the *Obras Completas*, published in Mexico. Though he arguably deserved inclusion more than any contemporary, Azaña was absent from the constellation of *Intellectuals in Politics* memorably studied by James Joll in 1964. Even today, only one biography of this putatively great hero of Europeanism and democracy exists in English, and no study of his literary work is available in an English version.[11]

So profound was the silence about Azaña which prevailed for decades under the Franco regime that he was referred to as 'the unknown one'.[12] In contrast, he had earlier been the cynosure of politics – the object of fanatical hatred and adulation. He was admired and feared as reformist ideologue, political tactician and parliamentary performer in the opening 'reform period' of the Republic (1931–3), for most of which he was prime minister. He became the target of virulent denigration from the Right, as a result of his radical reorientation of the state's relations with the military and clerical interests. His reputation was damaged by the 'massacre' of anarchist terrorists at Casas Viejas in 1933, a scandal over which he failed to exculpate himself. Thereafter, he presided over a paralysed coalition government which eventually collapsed in mutual recrimination. His enemies on the Centre-Right, let into power by these events, rescued Azaña from the doldrums by arresting him for complicity in the 'revolution' of 1934 – when, in fact, he was virtually the only major figure on the Left to be innocent of any involvement. He served three months' confinement on board a warship anchored in Barcelona harbour, coming on deck at intervals to wave benevolently to well-wishers and photographers on the quayside. In the true style of the charismatic political hero, he wrote a defence of his conduct which became a best-seller.[13] At his release he was a superstar, a martyr for democracy and defender of the people, insatiably in demand as writer and speaker. Azaña's 'open-air' speeches in 1935 were the culmination of an astonishing wave of popularity.[14] Crisis, decline and collapse followed, with the coming of the civil war. Although now president of the beleaguered republic, Azaña lost the capacity to influence events. Long before the victory of Franco, which re-established (*a fortiori*) all the principles he most excoriated, he had virtually relinquished an interest in practical politics.

The stark division of opinion over his general reputation was reflected in the earliest studies of Azaña to be published, in the wake of the Republic's defeat in 1939. Here, even before his death, commentators set out to vilify his personality and career in the most uninhibited terms. Some of these were Francoist hacks whose main job was character-assassination of 'the monster' – a term which had become ubiquitous within the Nationalist 'Movement'. To them, Azaña was

> the repulsive caterpillar of red Spain, inspirer of the killings and the secret police, organiser of the most refined and satanic cruelties ... He had a devilish pride in dominating others ... In his appearance he resembled a deformed reptile.[15]

But the triumphalist propaganda of Francoism was not just extended insult. It was deeply concerned to emphasize the insidious evils of intellectualism, and above all to establish its alien origins and subversive purpose.

> He knew well the weaknesses of the perverted and amoral intellect, and that it had no place in the essential core of Spain ... Yet he falsified everything, playing and speculating with falsehoods and foreign cretinisms for the pure pleasure of it ... He came to be the instrument of the Satanic terror of the Russians in Spain.[16]

Moreover, these views were not exclusive to the Right. Other voices of radically different allegiance joined in the chorus of condemnation. Indeed, at least one socialist utterance echoes with remarkable fidelity those we have already sampled: 'He was a negative force who lied and calumniated merely for the sadistic pleasure it brought him ... His reptilian pen was employed seductively to defame all those who fought with courage in Spain.'[17]

Thus his erstwhile Popular Front allies now accused Azaña of betraying the masses. His nationalist enemies had also indicted him as a traitor in a more traditional sense: 'according to one, he represented 'the most notorious type of anti-patriot'.[18] But there was worse still; with crudely transparent euphemisms they repeated allegations – freely disseminated on both sides during the war itself – of Azaña's homosexuality. In this way, the complex cross-hatch of fault-lines which was the Spanish Civil War reduced itself to the elemental collision of cultural terrors represented in the genderized discourse of 'the body politics'. Azaña was demonized not only through his ugly physical appearance, but also by being vested with sexual 'otherness'.[19]

History into Politics

In more than one sense the victim had courted his fate – to be caught and crushed between the upper millstone of Rightist disgust and the nether of Leftist resentment. Azaña's ideas are so full of anomalies, inconsistencies and downright contradictions that they defy coherent interpretation. Yet the problems arise more from prevailing modes of evaluative analysis than the subject's own discourse. Not only was Azaña himself never confused about political issues or his own role in them, having a more intense conviction of rectitude than is the norm even among politicians; he also believed that the power of his personality – above all, as artist and seer – absolved him from rules. To use the platitude which art-critics often apply to 'genius', the only relevant sanction was that he should be true to himself. His thought-processes were instinct with the rhetoric of nineteenth-century Philosophy of Art, a version of Nietzschean–Darwinian determinism, or, more contingently of Whitman's: 'Do I contradict myself? Very well then, I contradict myself'. That is to say, even when he was wrong, he was right.[20]

What (however) did Azaña stand for which the sordid world of pragmatic politics might recognize? His private criticism of his closest associate in the creation of the Popular Front, the moderate socialist Indalecio Prieto – 'he believes in nothing, not even in himself' – has been turned on Azaña too, often by Catholic opponents who in the process implied the aptness of scriptural injunctions against judging others.[21] Arguably, a sense of history provided his political credo. It was this which gave him at once an empathy with the Spanish past and the ability to supervene it. It can best be described as a sense of patriotic republicanism.

The elemental principles to which Azaña subscribed were inherited from the Jacobinism of the French Revolution. His own forbears had been supporters of the first liberal Constitution of 1812 which was overturned by the restored monarchy. To that extent, Azaña belonged to a mainstream of *progresista* patriotism which ceaselessly ran against, over, and around – without ever dislodging – the stones of autocratic conservatism.[22] But as the tempo of 'modernist' revolution increased, to culminate in the crescendo of 1936, such ideals could easily be made to seem intransigent, anachronistic, or even reactionary. Azaña's national-political feelings were encapsulated in the main visual representation of the Republic. The Goddess of Reason wears a cap of Liberty, holds the scales of justice, and carries a tricolour flag. To the left, a shield bears the words 'Libertad, Igualdad, Fraternidad'. This nineteenth-century patroness is surrounded by symbols of twentieth-century 'modernity'. Yet it may be noted that the palette and brushes of the artist are nearest to her feet, together with the architect's tools and the piled-up books of the scholar.[23]

The Jacobin ideal of 'La Patrie' appealed to Azaña, and he mixed a commitment to democracy and progress with the proverbial national pride. 'No-one has in his veins a sense of Spanishness which is more profound, pure and passionate than mine' he announced in 1931.[24] No chauvinist, he wanted Spain to be part of the international community and the League of Nations. Yet he was no pacifist, and his reforms of the army were inspired by the need to bring it up to date in technical as well as political terms.[25] A modern, efficient Spain, then; organized democratically; with wealth redistributed from rich to poor. But for Azaña, Cultural, not economic, deprivation was at the root of Spain's malaise. His commanding heights were not the institutions of industry and commerce, but rather the *institutos* of learning – secondary schools, and education generally. Here also he conformed to a pre-mediated image of the Spanish character, essentially spiritual, only demeaned by overt attention to questions of material improvement. Under his government, the provision for free state education advanced tremendously, despite haemorrhages of personnel and other resources brought about by the war against the Church, and acute financial restraints. Yet, despite the latter, little change was made in Spain's fiscal system, which continued as ever to favour the wealthy.[26]

The rigorous self-examination which Azaña often applied to his dialectical processes was by no means infallible in producing a radical outcome. Behind the colourfully extreme language, many of his attitudes remained instinctually conservative. For Stanley Payne, Azaña was almost as much a product of the nineteenth century as his older colleague, Niceto Alcalá-Zamora (the republic's first president, an Andalusian landowner), and also one of the last great Castilian élitists.[27] Certainly Azaña often referred to the special meaning of Castile in Spanish history, and was reluctant to relinquish a view of the peninsula as seen from Madrid.[28]

He admired the Catalans, to whose self-image as close to the civilized temperament of the French he was susceptible. But he supported autonomy statutes in Catalonia and the Basque Country more from pragmatic necessity than inner conviction, and was worried by the prospect that the regions might go further in the direction of independence. He rarely left Madrid, except to address audiences or lobby political allies in the reassuring urban environments of Bilbao, Barcelona or Valencia. Just as he lacked any grasp of the peculiarly intense localism of his country, so he had little awareness of poverty or class grievance. During the prolonged Casas Viejas affair, which exposed the fundamental flaws of Republican politics, he never visited the seat of the crisis, Andalusia. He was far too much the patrician even to affect the compassion which is an indispensable attribute of the modern politician: but – unlike that of Don Niceto – Azaña's was not the patriarchism of the conventional ruling class.

Perhaps the issue which most threatens Azaña's claim to liberal statesmanship is that of the notorious Law for the Defence of the Republic, introduced as the first act of his government in October, 1931. However worthy its intentions to protect democracy, the view that Azaña utilized it too freely and partially is difficult to resist. There were two discrete but equally damaging tendencies. The first concerned workers' organizations. The law was often employed against the anarchist union (CNT) – not infrequently in order to break strikes – but was rarely invoked against its socialist equivalent (UGT). Azaña's coalition government depended upon support of the PSOE, the political wing of the latter, and bitter rivals of the anarchists. (As we have seen, Azaña was a good *Madrileño*, and the bulk of the UGT's membership was in Madrid, whilst the CNT was overwhelmingly provincial and/or rural.) The second tendency concerned the weapon of media censorship which the Defence Law placed in the government's hands. Azaña is often judged to have been over-enthusiastic in its use; his ministerial lieutenant, Santiago Casares Quiroga, sequestrated newspapers and jailed journalists with a will.[29] Both tendencies reflected the intolerance the prime minister expressed so provocatively in public and private. Both evoked a counter-productive backlash, fusing together to undermine his government over the incident at Casas Viejas (early 1933), when the responsibility for the 'execution' of 'anarchist saboteurs' was unfairly pinned on Azaña by a sustained press campaign.[30]

The fact that the Republic was personified by the Goddess of Reason may represent an anomaly, for Azaña had little sympathy for the political aspirations of women. Only three women entered the *Cortes* (parliament) during the *bienio reformador* (1931–3), and its main inspirer did not lament this state of affairs. In his diary, he dismissed Victoria Kent's prescient warning against conceding the franchise to a womanhood still under the domination of the clergy, and noted that 'it would be an atrocity to deny women the vote through suspicion that they might not vote in favour of the Republic'.[31] Yet he observed the *Cortes* debates over the female franchise with condescending disdain. His own party (*Acción Republicana*), whose policies he controlled absolutely, remained committed against female suffrage, and presumably Azaña voted accordingly in the divisions.[32] He expressed no concern when the Catholic parties joined with the Socialists (PSOE) to force through the reform. He seems not to have noticed when Kent became the first Spanish woman to occupy a senior administrative post (director-general of prisons); but did not hesitate to sack her as soon as she became a liability to his government. After the civil war began, he accused Spanish women in general of helping 'to create a climate favourable to violence when votes alone could not bring down the government'.[33]

If on some issues he was unable to escape from the gravitational pull of history and culture, Azaña was acutely sceptical of the assumptions moulded by a past mediated through a nationalist context. It is this facility which makes him so fascinating to any historian with a post-structuralist interest. He centred his historical-cultural understanding – with all its ambivalence – on what might be called 'The Escorial Effect'. Philip II's austere headquarters, set in its lofty mountainside landscape just north of Madrid, was his imaginative obsession. Both palace and monastery, the building was originally designed as a power-centre of imperial administration and religious orthodoxy, and situated near the geographical nucleus of the Iberian peninsula. Here the royal dynasty of Spain had been sepulchred since the seventeenth century in a series of subterranean vaults sacred to the idea of monarchy. Here the Augustinian friars ran an exclusive *instituto*, which the future leader of the Republic attended between the ages of 14 and 18.

During the years of adolescence, doubt, and rebellion, he was thus in the care of teachers who were specialists in inculcating conventional religious obedience and social discipline. His novel *El Jardín de los Frailes*, which reflects this environment, was an attempt to exorcize its influence on his psyche by transmutation into art.[34] In later life, the republican agnostic revisited the place constantly, revealing, in spite of himself, his love of its ambience, almost as if performing an act of penance for his political sins. Yet it was this Spain, the Spain of Absolutism, Empire, and Inquisition, the Spain which the historian Menéndez Pelayo had exhorted his countrymen not to abnegate, but on the contrary to celebrate as the essence of *Hispanidad*, which was the focus of Azaña's political mistrust. This was the Spain embraced by Francisco Franco, who was to construct his own grandiose sepulchre on a site not far from the Escorial.[35]

Azaña often referred to this tradition with a calculated loathing which made him seem almost a mouthpiece of the foreigners, against whose contempt for things Hispanic Menéndez Pelayo and others had consciously reacted. It was for this reason that the Francoists found him easy to characterize as the very reverse of a patriot. But in a speech to young republicans in April 1934, at a time when he was in the political cold, Azaña stated a credo which has the ring of honesty:

> I certify before you the principles I have always sustained: Republic! Democracy! Authority! – Ah, yes, authority – but republican authority. A republic for all? Yes, conceived patriotically – the Spanish Republican Fatherland (*Patria Republicana Española*).[36]

Politics into Art

In June 1931, Manuel Azaña and his fellow-intellectual, José Ortega y Gasset, were elected as deputies to the Constitutional *Cortes* of the fledgling Republic. Azaña had already been appointed war minister in the provisional government. The new regime was quickly dubbed by an anonymous hand as 'The Republic of Professors'; though it referred to itself in its Constitution as 'a Republic of Workers of all kinds'. In fact, the parliament contained fifty professors and only twenty-seven workers. In addition to the academics, forty-one doctors of medicine, thirty journalists and no less than 123 lawyers were present among the massive Left–Republican majority.³⁷ It would seem that Spain was on course for Utopia even before Azaña began the work of reform. However, the fact that, as minister, he was provided with such a sound base of operations was partly due to the precursor activities of Azaña himself, along with other intellectuals. In the 1920s – though (unlike Ortega) never an academic – he had been journalist, 'creative' writer and political scientist. He had spent some years in France studying the relationship between the state and the army, and his doctoral thesis was an examination of 'The Political Responsibility of the Masses'. During the 1920s he published (*inter alia*) two novels of an autobiographical character, and Spanish translations of George Borrow's *Travels in Spain* and Bertrand Russell's *Marriage and Morals*. His books often contained trenchant attacks upon the Catholic-clerical traditions of Spanish society and culture. None attracted much attention. In 1924, however, he was selected as secretary of the Madrid intellectuals' club, the *Ateneo,* where came many a Socrates in order to deride the military dictatorship of Primo de Rivera from a position of relative safety. Sparta silenced Athens; Primo closed the club, thus achieving Azaña's objective of making the intellectuals into martyrs of resistance and potential generators of a new order. He founded a political party, and was in the front rank of delegates to the San Sebastian Congress (summer 1930) which designed the basic programme of a republican dispensation even before the Monarchy had fallen.³⁸

In nearly all his subsequent political interventions, several of which proved to be crucial for the future of Spain, Azaña rationalized his position and action by reference to intellectual considerations – typically aesthetic or historical. His military reforms, pushed through with a series of speeches and decrees in 1931, were based on the conviction that the army should be terminally depoliticized. Such a rationale was common to his type and generation. In Azaña's case, the 'historical' fear of Napoleonism was accentuated by his artistic sense that the pen must not only be mightier than the sword, but also must be seen to be mightier. The result was a combative desire to defeat (in his own words, 'to pulverize') the army. A press photograph showed the war minister lecturing the assembled staff officers of the Military Academy of Zaragoza, which – in an act which could be seen as almost a ritual revenge for Primo's closure of the *Ateneo* – he was about to close down.[39] Athens defeated Sparta, but Sparta had an even more powerful ally – Rome. Thus, the most ominous intervention of Azaña's career came on 13 October 1931, when, after months of controversy, the recommendations of the commission on the religious aspects of the constitution came before the *Cortes*. That morning, examining his own feelings with an almost confessional rigour, Azaña concluded that his objections to the radical proposals arose not from independent reason but from his Catholic conditioning, which induced a false cultural consciousness.[40] On this basis, he delivered the celebrated speech in which he sought to impose the true consciousness, asserting that 'Spain has ceased to be Catholic', changing the course of the debate in favour of the extreme anti-clerical option, and (some argue) sealing the ultimate fate of the Republic.[41] Moreover, Azaña's role in the resolution of the religious issue not only gave the Constitution its fatally compromising tone of cultural intolerance, but also propelled him to the premiership. In succession, general-dictator, king, and cardinal-primate had all been driven into exile. Once the most important of these – the last – had gone, the artist-intellectual could properly take over.[42]

Earlier that year, Ortega y Gasset had organized a political party exclusively for intellectuals which he called the *Agrupación al Servicio de la República* and which included (amongst others) the pathologist-historian Gregorio Marañón, the philosopher-journalist Ramón Sender, and the poets Antonio Machado and Federico García Lorca.[43] Ortega himself had claimed that as society got ever more complex, only trained intellectuals would be equipped to cope with its political management.[44] For his part, however, Azaña saw Ortega's group not as an ally but as a threat. Some of its members, like Pedro de Ayala, had in fact deserted to Ortega from *Acción Republicana*, but Azaña's attitude was coloured by artistic as well as political jealousy. Several luminaries of Ortega's group were 'recognized' artists, who wore the halo of spiritual greatness which Azaña deeply coveted. The fact that Ayala and Marañón had signed Ortega's letter protesting at the government's inaction over a spate of church-burnings which broke out in May, undoubtedly influenced Azaña's speech to the *Cortes*, which may therefore be read – in one dimension – as a denunciation of intellectual adversaries and artistic rivals.[45]

Azaña once described himself as 'a writer without readers', eliciting the biting response from Miguel de Unamuno, Spain's most distinguished thinker and academic, that he had become prime minister in order to correct this state of affairs.[46] There was more than a grain of truth in this remark. Many writers claimed that his promiscuous resort to the censorious provisions of the Republic Defence Law seriously inhibited publishing both in authorial and industrial terms. Azaña himself, meanwhile, continued a prolific rate of writing and publishing. Moreover, in 1932, he was the first incumbent chief minister since Cardinal Richelieu (and the last before Vaclav Havel) to have a play performed by a professional ensemble in the capital city.[47] When the veteran politician, Alejandro Lerroux, the best-known opportunist in public life, accused him of being an opportunist, Azaña replied 'If I had been ambitious, do you think I would have spent so many years in a library writing books which are not important to anybody, not even to myself?'[48] In the face of such complacent arrogance it is not surprising that the eminent writer Azorín – more sympathetic to the Right than Unamuno or Lerroux – felt the need to go even further in his attempt to vindicate his profession and to puncture Azaña's artistic ego.

> The Republic has made the intellectuals possible, not the other way around. Those of you who occupy power may have been the midwives of the Republic, but allow us to tell you that it is we who have engendered it, not you. We the people, some humble and others elevated, have made it, little by little, over thirty years of work.[49]

When – as a result of the feelings of Azorín and the activities of Sender, among others – he was relegated to the opposition benches in 1934, Azaña revealed to the *Cortes* that his underlying motivation as prime minister had been 'the ineffable pleasure of creating things', specifically likening it to the work of an artist.[50] His words were appropriately self-reflexive, for he approached the act of oratory itself as primarily an aesthetic experience. Privately, he complained that 'my tragedy is that I have been able to find no interlocutor', admitting that this was the result of a puristic intellectual disdain he had cultivated for so long that 'there was no longer any remedy'.[51] One of Azaña's modern biographers castigates his subject for his excessively, obsessively academic approach to politics. For example, 'what he insisted on explaining to the *Cortes* could have been better left to the professorial chair, the lecture-theatre or the *Ateneo*, or to some international congress of scholarly specialists'.[52]

But similar criticisms were made at the time; indeed, Azaña sought openly to answer them. On one occasion, speaking to an audience in Bilbao, he described his love of politics as not an academic but an emotional affair, actually resorting to the analogy of sexual attraction. 'Of a man who does not feel a thrill face to face with a beautiful woman we can say without calumny that he does not have the erotic faculty ... I am Spanish – virile – emotional – individual – Don Juan – Primo'.[53] Here he was consciously going 'down market' – and possibly attempting to counter rumours about his private life. He knew that many would react favourably to this identification of his character with a sort of composite 'stage' Spaniard, the platitudinous 'macho' individualism which covers a multitude of ethnic sins. But it was this peculiar egoism – as a Spanish friend of the present writer put it 'un gran hipertrófia de su "Yo"' ('a hugely inflated ego') – which lay behind his irresistible flair for hurting his opponents. He used words as weapons in the press, in parliament and on public podium with the same nimble skills as the *banderillero* wields his darts in the bullring. When a cabinet colleague who had parted from him on the religious issue challenged Azaña about this tendency, the prime minister proclaimed that 'I do it because it amuses me'.[54] In his best-known literary work he makes one of his speakers assert that 'We do not fight, except with words, and words do not kill'.[55] The author's meaning and intention here was exactly the same as Auden's contemporary disclaimer, over the same conflict: that 'poetry makes nothing happen'. This was a palpable plea of innocence of 'the necessary murder', an exculpation based on the privileged autonomy of High Art, a genius which endowed its possessors with built-in absolution.[56]

Art into Power

My final task is to locate the contradictions of Azaña's ideas and career, not in the context of normative categories of 'modernization' and 'transition' central to current political history, but rather in a certain cultural (and Cultural) ambience which we can now see as central to his time.[57] Of course, in abstract terms, he recognized the importance of material progress both as function and symbol of the twentieth-century state; but he was not directly concerned with the nuts and bolts of technological change or the infrastructures of economic 'modernization'. Azaña's politics did not derive from the social anxiety of the liberal reformer, and related far less to the excited revolutionary, fired by unbearable compassion for the downtrodden masses. He did not feel – or at any rate did not feel deeply – the almost genetic guilt which often gives subliminal drive to the political attitudes of the hereditary middle-class. He had little or no emotional response to suffering, nor any gut reaction to exploitation or oppression on a human level. His diaries and other writings make no references to the miserable condition of large numbers of his compatriots, nor even (more surprisingly) to the broad historical causes of their misery. Though he hardly approved of them more than any other extrinsic interest, he never expressed special distaste for the landowning class whose entrenched socio-economic position was the fundamental obstacle to democratic progress, and he regarded the whole agrarian issue as beneath his exalted vision.[58] What, then, fuelled the vital radicalism, the passionate utterances, the revolutionary profile which moved the masses and horrified the classes? It was Azaña's hatred of the ordinary and the routine, derived from his philosophical-artistic psyche, which led him to seek extremes, to flirt with a mephistophelian chiasmus. In this sense he was as much, 'sin entrañas' (the Castilian expression for 'cold-blooded') as one to whom the term is far more frequently applied – his exact antipathetic opposite, Francisco Franco. Yet who can doubt, at the same time, that his was a politics of conviction?

Manuel Azaña was intellectual, artist, and teacher: Spain was his subject, his artefact, his pupil. Yet at the same time he was a warrior, a crusader, a Cid. He belonged to a generation of Europeans which I have elsewhere termed 'the artistocracy'.[59] A new (but hardly homogeneous) caste of metropolitan society, its members were *ilustrados* who believed themselves to have inherited the mainsprings of power once possessed by assorted princes, peers, priests, and entrepreneurs. The task of this élite was to abolish politics in favour of a Utopia of Truth and Beauty under the benign dictatorship of the Olympian artistocrats.[60] Ortega y Gasset expressed the apprehension of the old ruling élites when he wrote about the 'Rebellion of the Masses'.[61] Azaña's career itself, fuelled by his talents as a campaigning journalist, demonstrated how the classes were losing control of the media of communication, as they had already lost control of physical space to the invasive and ubiquitous presence of the crowd. The ethical perception he had of these media, and the uses to which he put them, brought about a bloody conflict in which the aspirations of Art to abolish its master, Politics, were definitively overthrown.[62]

Of course, Azaña himself was by origin and physical disposition a bourgeois: a story is told of him losing his temper when acclaimed by a crowd with the cry of 'death to the bourgeoisie'.[63] Yet his politics supervened Marxism – class considerations and economic determinants being unimportant to the point of irrelevance. Some may (therefore) conclude that he was not truly of his time – that, in the context of the 1930s, he can only have been a throwback. However, this interesting issue is not central to my purpose. Azaña was nobody's 'compadre', but neither was he 'Don Manuel'. He represented an approach to society quite distinct from that implied in either label, a type whose moment, prophesied by Nietzsche, seemed to have arrived precisely during the period of *entre deux guerres*, when most parts of western Europe were achieving universal education and literacy, with populations which were also acquiring a degree of public leisure (if, for many, a condition enforced by default).

The transcendental reputation of 'the artist', that ultimate product of the rise of the affective subject, a process which had been the irresistible work of history since the Renaissance, was never higher than in the 1930s. The present writer recalls, when at school, marvelling at a science teacher's revelation that in our generation there were more scientists at work than had ever lived in all past generations put together. In the 1930s, at least, something equally stupefying (and incapable of proof) could have been said about artists. This was the period when T. S. Eliot asserted that poetry was the truly democratic art, and when writers, painters and composers flourished in every section of society and every region of Europe. Artefacts of Beauty, Experiment and Aspiration were competing for attention everywhere. It was a time when everybody, and especially characters in novels, seemed to be writing a novel. Schools and societies of artists pullulated: the twenties and thirties actually proclaimed themselves as the age of 'Isms'. Yet despite the apparent democratization of Art, the autonomous world of the intellect began to provide a new medium of justification of the élite. Since the lower classes, at least via their self-proclaimed representatives, were grasping control of politics, High Art became an escape from politics, or rather a higher medium or division of politics. Intelligent middle-class people who had come to reject social distinctions based on mere birth or prosperity, were seeking – perhaps subliminally – ethically superior explanations for their obvious superiority. They found it in 'the creative spirit', the expression and/or worship of Artistic Greatness. But the project of Great Art faced in both political directions. During the first third of this century, in all its now-exalted spheres, it achieved such a pinnacle of social esteem that it sought freedom from its master, politics. Indeed, Prometheus was not satisfied with release from his chains: he demanded lordship and supremacy. Thus many artistic protagonists made common cause with revolutionary movements, whose ideologies were more blatantly orientated towards power, but apparently rooted in philosophy, and which promised a future above and beyond sordid political realities.[64]

The forces Azaña unleashed were to make Spain the laboratory of the artist and the battleground of ideas. Even before the civil war, curious minds, from Laurie Lee, disingenuous farmboy fiddler, to Gwyn Thomas, miner's son and Oxford student, to the Bloomsbury set and Robert Graves – not to mention Hemingway – 'discovered' Spain. After July 1936, artists and writers flocked to the peninsula, many to fight in the International Brigades, others to attend propaganda congresses where they were lionized by the loyalists.[65] Indeed, one of the outstanding successes of Azaña's doomed Republic was the mobilization of virtually the whole world of art and letters in its cause. For this reason, although the republic lost the war of guns and bombs, it won the war of words and images, the war of transmutation and representation to which Azaña desperately – and, as it proved, prophetically – pinned his hopes in 1937. The belated triumph of Spanish democracy in the 1980s, to the extent that it may be seen as the posthumous vindication of the Second Republic, was in many ways a function of this strange victory. It was a victory based on the projection into the deep consciousness of the liberal west that the republic stood for Art and Beauty as well as for Freedom and

Democracy. It represented mind against mindlessness, the civilization of the imagination, not that of modernization. The most overworked word in Azaña's vocabulary was 'intelligent': he evaluated everything by the extent to which it excited his intelligent interest.[66] Little wonder the enemies of the Republic focused their hatred upon the intelligentsia, and that the extreme Right more and more conformed to its given profile of philistinism. One of the slogans of the Nationalist movement was 'Death to the Intelligentsia'. It was no accident that an almost custom-designed anti-Azaña model leader emerged in the figure of Franco – Catholic, monarchist, military careerist, unpretentious in character, lacking any imaginative intelligence, and profoundly suspicious of intellectuals and foreigners alike.[67] During the most 'representative' war in history, Tragedy and Hubris replaced Utopia, traditional Spanish values reasserted themselves via the military, and Art was defeated. In one respect, writers like Orwell who prophesied that the overthrow of Utopia in Spain would mean defeat in the rest of Europe too proved to be right. In the war of 1939–45, one cost of defeating Nazism was the complete surrender by its guardians of Art's vaunted autonomy. Orwell himself did his duty on the BBC, and 'transmuted' this and his Spanish traumas into *Nineteen Eighty-Four*.

The idiosyncratic excesses of Manuel Azaña contributed centrally to the failure of the Second Republic and to the onset of a ferocious civil war which cost hundreds of thousands of lives and left millions of others permanently blighted. Democratic politicians often make honest mistakes which have terrible and/or unforeseen consequences. What inspires a unique horror in this case is that Azaña knew the risks he was running; indeed, he appreciated, frigidly appraised, even consciously dramatized them in his memoirs. In a book dedicated mainly to illustrating how miserable a fate the war was for ordinary Spaniards, one recent writer seeks (once again) to make Azaña the heroic centre of attention. For Azaña, we are told, 'the war was an authentic tragedy, a personal drama'.[68] But as the metaphorical discourse implies, his was the public face of tragedy – a tragedy in the specifically theatrical sense. His fate had (and has) an audience, which is the destiny he most craved. What kind of tragedy is that for a dramatist? Most of those who died or had their lives ruined by the Civil War had no witnesses. They craved justice, not an audience.

In a recent distillation of his views on our subject as an 'Intellectual in Politics', the doyen of *azañistas*, Juan Marichal, does not examine his subject's role in creating the context for Civil War. However, concerning the period after 1936, Marichal writes: 'I dare to suggest that he underwent a species of political-intellectual conversion which was determined by an intense feeling of guilt.'[69] In his apologia, *Vigil in Benicarlo*, Azaña repeatedly betrayed, through the mouths of his characters, an awareness of personal responsibility. I give a selection of examples:

> If you don't limit the artist to merely exercising his profession, his special talents can clarify the true hierarchy of values by which we should judge a people's life and aspirations ... We achieve this concept of hierarchy by thought, not by political and journalistic canting.
>
> Did the League of Nations ever exist? [It was] a Professor's dream brought to life [and] never more than an illusion.
>
> We have many such academic republicans ... They speak softly, sip cups of tea ... the English way ... like a very polite game of cards ... They've helped to re-establish politics as a game.
>
> Our moral evaluation of the actors' conduct in this drama will soon become blurred ... our present crisis represents nothing but a pulsation of History.[70]

The pervasive sympathy for his cause – and his predicament – which is in the atmosphere breathed by scholars and writers should not lead us uncritically to consider that Azaña's sacramental act of transmutation is enough to absolve his memory from guilt. Of course, neither should Azaña's accurate perception of his own errors serve to condemn all intellectuals in politics. It was a Spanish writer who first suggested that the science of Politics should be taught in the universities, and the record suggests that Spain has been ruled by academics for rather more of its history than has seen the domination of the army. The ever-present danger is that intellectuals tend to regard the vocation of politics as though it were merely an academic discipline. Experiment, risk and constant flux are essences of scholarship; but none of these properly belongs in the domain of applied politics, where the stakes involve rather more than intellectual excitement, academic *amour propre* and individual reputations.[71]

Notes

1. The opening quotation is from M. Azaña, *La velada en Benicarló* (trans. J. and P. Stewart as *The Vigil in Benicarlo*, East Brunswick, NJ, 1982), 97–8. This dramatic dialogue was completed in April 1937, during the civil war, when its author was president of the republic. The second quotation (originally from A. Ramos Oliveira's *Politics and Economics in Modern Spain*) is quoted in F. Sedwick, *The Tragedy of Manuel Azaña and the Fate of the Spanish Republic* (Ohio, 1963), 20.
2. M. Azaña, *Discursos en Campo Abierto* (Madrid, 1936), 239–42. The original texts (prepared by the author for publication) appear frequently punctuated by spontaneous expressions of approval and applause from the audience. That of the Comillas speech occupies over fifty pages (189–242).
3. H. Thomas, *The Spanish Civil War* (3rd edn., Harmondsworth, 1977), 209.
4. W. B. Yeats, 'Leda and the Swan', from the collection *The Tower* (1928).
5. P. Preston, 'The Creation of the Popular Front in Spain', in idem and H. Graham (eds.), *The Popular Front in Europe* (London, 1987), 99–100.
6. Sedwick, *Azaña*, 146–52.
7. 'Cincuenta Años de Manuel Azaña', supplement in *ABC* (Madrid), 3 November 1990. Most other national dailies published similar tributes. At a conservative group conference on Azaña held in the Escorial Palace, a distinguished contributor, Ricardo de la Cierva, resisted a moderate consensus which was supported even by clerical colleagues; see R. Morodo, 'Revisión y Actualización', ibid. La Cierva's attitude seemed perverse since years earlier he had ventured a more positive assessment. In a notably irenic gesture, he endorsed Gabriel Jackson's view that Azaña was more sinned against than sinning – in other words, that the unrestrained anti-Azaña campaign did more to precipitate civil war than any foible of the man himself; see 'Los factores desencadenantes de la guerra civil española', in idem, V. Palacio Atard and R. Salas Larrazábal, *Aproximación a la guerra española (1936–39)* (Madrid, 1970), 61–3.
8. G. Brenan, *The Spanish Labyrinth: An Account of the Social and Political Background of the Civil War* (Cambridge 1943, repr. of 2nd edn., 1990), 239. For its perennial influence, see 'Speaking Volumes: Paul Heywood on Gerald Brenan's *The Spanish Labyrinth*', *Times Higher Education Supplement*, 14 October 1994. It is fair to add that Brenan's overall inscription of Azaña fell short of the hagiographic. For example, though he chose to picture him as the symbol or epitome of the Republic, he also pointed out that Azaña himself had encouraged the development of this notion.

9   A. Palmer, *The Penguin Dictionary of Twentieth Century History, 1900–1982* (2nd edn., Harmondsworth, 1983), 36; M. Dunan (ed.), *Larousse Encyclopedia of Modern History from 1500 to the Present Day* (New York, 1981), 371.
10 Cited above, n.1.
11 The relevant biography is cited above, n.1. In fact, scholarship is exclusively American in terms of national origin. Whilst this essay was being written, two faculty colleagues, both modernists and 'active researchers', were unable to place its subject. A copy of Azaña's speeches (published 1936, see above n.2), borrowed from the British Library lending stores, had its pages still uncut. Given the sustained level of interest in the Second Republic and the civil war as subjects for teaching and textualization, such ignorance of its outstanding figure is puzzling.
12 This was the title of a study by Azaña's brother-in-law, the theatre director C. de Rivas Cherif; *Retrato de un desconocido: Vida de Manuel Azaña* (Mexico City, 1980) but was used elsewhere, see G. Villapalos, 'Tragedia de un desconocido' *ABC*, 3 Nov. 1990. The former has recently been reissued in English: P. Stewart (ed.), *Portrait of an Unknown Man: Manuel Azana and Modern Spain* (Madison and London, 1995).
13 M. Azaña, *Mi Rebelión en Barcelona* (Madrid, 1935). The book, however, did not sell on the same scale as *Mein Kampf*.
14 M. Espín, *Azaña en el poder. El partido de Acción Republicana* (Madrid, 1980), 274–5.
15 J. Arrarás, *Memorias íntimas de Azaña* (Madrid, 1939), 5–6. This is a version of Azaña's diaries, skilfully edited from authentic material sold to Franco by an ex-Republican diplomat; see J. Marichal, 'El Secuestro de Manuel Azaña' in *Diario 16* (Madrid) 'Culturas' Supplement, 27 Oct. 1990.
16 F. Casares, *Azaña y ellos. Cincuenta semblanzas rojas* (Granada, 1939), 20–5, 36.
17 A. Toryho, *Después de la Tragedia: La traición del señor Azaña* (New York, 1939), 6–7, 13–16 – the bitterly resentful voice of millions on the Left whose expectations Azaña's government had raised only to disappoint. A more effective attack from the broad 'revolutionary' perspective is made by the POUMista journalist 'Victor Alba' (pseudonym of P. Pagés Elías) in *Los Sepultereros de la República* (Barcelona, 1977).
18 Casares, *Azaña*, 26.
19 Toryho, *Después de la Tragedia*, 13–14; cf. Arrarás, *Memorias*, 293–6. There was little subtlety about Roy Campbell's approach, in 'Hard Lines Azaña' (1937):

>   The Sodomites are on your side,
>   The Cowards and the cranks;

> You've got the cowards on your front
> But you've got these behind
> For fat though your belly, your Popular 'Front'
> Is surely your Fat 'Behind'.

Quoted in V. Cunningham (ed.), *Spanish Front: Writers on the Spanish Civil War* (Oxford, 1986), 71-2. In 1960, researching his book on *The Spanish Republic and the Civil War* (Princeton, 1967), Gabriel Jackson interviewed a prominent Francoist who referred to Azaña as an 'invertido'. When asked to corroborate this, he cited 'his fat, womanish hands, his lack of courage during the civil war, his face like a toad's. And he married late, much later than a real man'; idem, *An Historian's Quest* (New York, 1969), 52-5.

20 'The important thing is to be right': Azaña's dictum is the keyquote to Sedwick's *Azaña*. For background to the present hypothesis, see J. Tussell and G. G. Queipo de Llano, *Los Intelectuales y La República* (Madrid, 1990) and S. Balfour, 'The Solitary Peak and the Dense Valley: Intellectuals and Masses in *Fin de Siecle* Spain', *Tesserae* 1 No. 1 (1994), 1–19.

21 M. Azaña, *Memorias políticas y de guerra* (2 vols., Madrid, 1978), I, 320. (Hereafter cited as *Memorias* followed by vol. and p. nos.)

22 See J. Marichal, 'La tradición liberal española', *ABC*, 3 Nov. 1990.

23 The best-known version provides cover illustration for several works on the Second Republic, including the 50th anniversary number of the magazine *Historia 16* and J. Gil Pecharromán's study from the same publishers (see below, n.25). It was displayed in many homes and shops; two examples decorate a CNT vehicle in Barcelona (1936) in a photograph reproduced in D. Mitchell, *The Spanish Civil War* (London 1982), 39. The artist here was J. Barraine; but other varieties existed of the basic 'Marianne' model; see e.g. R. Carr et al., *Images of the Spanish Civil War* (London, 1986), 26.

24 Quoted in J. Marichal, *El intelectual y la política en España (1898-1936)* (Madrid, 1990), 79.

25 J. Gil Pecharromán, *La Segundă República* (Madrid, 1989), 95.

26 Alba, *Sepultereros*, 76–8.

27 S. Payne, *Spain's First Democracy: The Second Republic, 1931-1936* (Madison, 1993), 383–4.

28 Sedwick, *Azaña*, 120; see also I. Herreros, 'Un Madrileño', *ABC*, 3 Nov. 1990.

29 Pecharromán, *Segunda República*, 129; Brenan calls Azaña's approach 'heavy-handed' (op.cit., 240). For Alba, his use of this and other repressive laws puts him in the same league as Franco's police chief, Martínez Añido, notorious assassin of the workers; see *Sepultereros*, 72–5.

30 R. Abella, 'Casas Viejas: Cincuenta aniversario de la tragedia que

minó a la II República', *Historia* 16 No. 82 (1983), 11–18.
31 *Memorias*, I, 199–200. Cf. however, Sedwick, who rationalizes Azaña's opposition to female suffrage on the basis of his support for Kent's argument; see *Azaña*, 89.
32 S. Ben Ami, *The Origins of the Second Republic in Spain* (Oxford, 1978), 305.
33 *Memorias*, I, 469–70; idem, *Vigil in Benicarlo*, 59–61.
34 E. Aguado, *Don Manuel Azaña Díaz* (Barcelona, 1972, repr. Madrid, 1986), 61–2. See also S. Juliá, 'Su sentimiento religioso' in *ABC*, 3 Nov. 1990. In the novel by C. Rojas, starring Azaña as the eponymous hero (*Azaña*, Madrid, 1973), he returns to the Escorial not only physically but also in his dreams (see, for example, 39–40).
35 The 'official' portrait of José Antonio Primo de Rivera, founder of the Falange, poses him on the Guadarrama mountainside with the Escorial glowing like a shrine in the distance; see Carr, *Images*, 30. For the importance of Menéndez y Pelayo in this connection, see (variously) J. Saínz Rodríguez, *Evolución de las ideas sobre la decadencia española* (Madrid 1962); J. Vicens Vives, *Approaches to the History of Spain* (Berkeley and Los Angeles, 1970); and R. A. Fletcher, *The Quest for El Cid* (Oxford, 1989).
36 Quoted in J. Ferrer Solá, *La pasión intelectual de Manuel Azaña* (Barcelona, 1991), 171. Another expert refers to 'a non-conservative patriotism, an idea of a republican community united in defending radical laicism from the forces of the Right'; Espin, *Azaña*, 232–3.
37 Sedwick, *Azaña*, 83–4. The Republic's extravagant intellectual profile is a recurrent theme of scholarship. The first extended study, by an International Brigade veteran, Aldo Garosci, appeared in Italy in 1959; tr. G. Guijarro as *Los intelectuales y la guerra de España* (Madrid, 1981), with a chapter on Azaña. A conference held at Segovia in 1986 devoted more time to this issue than to that of agrarian reform! The published proceedings are adorned with Azaña's features; M. Tuñón de Lara (ed.), *La II República Española: el primer bienio* (Madrid, 1987).
38 Details mainly from Sedwick, *Azaña*, 3–81 passim.
39 On the issue generally, see M. Alpert, *La reforma militar de Azaña (1931–1933)* (Madrid, 1982). The photograph referred to in the text was reproduced in the 'Azaña Supplement' of the Madrid Sunday *El Independiente* on 4 Nov. 1990.
40 *Memorias*, I, 218.
41 For example, M. Muela, *Azaña, Estadista* (Madrid, 1983), 109–11.
42 General Primo de Rivera resigned in January 1930 and died in exile later that year; King Alfonso XIII left Spain definitively (though without abdicating) in April 1931, during the events which gave birth to the Republic; and Cardinal Segura, primate of Spain, was deported in June after a pastoral letter which pungently criticized the Republic.

43 A. Ortega Klein, 'La decepción política de Ortega', *Historia 16* No. 48 (1980), 67–78; F. J. Laporta, 'Los intelectuales y la república', ibid, No. 60 (1981), 86–93.
44 Marichal, 'La tradición liberal', loc. cit.
45 See Ben Ami, *Origins*, 54–5. For examples of Azaña's senior common-room backbiting about Ortega, see *Memorias*, I, 135–7, 319–23, 487.
46 Alba, *Sepultereros*, 39.
47 Sedwick, *Azaña*, 46–8. Azaña's play *La Corona* (The Crown), was directed by Rivas Cherif. It concerns the outcome of a civil war, and the sordid compromising of political principles. For acute and suggestive treatment of the relationship between art and politics in Azaña's personality, see J. M. Marco, *Azaña* (Madrid, 1990), esp. 136–42.
48 Sedwick, *Azaña*, 97.
49 Quoted in P. Aubert, 'Los intelectuales en el poder (1931–33)' in Tuñón de Lara, *II República*, 174. Azorín's caveat (in the magazine *Crisol*) was repeated in one of the occasional 'Spanish Chronicles', which Antonio Marichalar – a disciple of Ortega – contributed to T. S. Eliot's review *The Criterion*: 11, No. 3 (Jan. 1932), 296–303 (at 302). By implication, this also argued that only because Azaña was a second-rate artist could he be an authentic politician (at 296–7).
50 Quoted in Sedwick, *Azaña*, 123–4.
51 Quoted in Alba, *Sepultereros*, 53–4.
52 Aguado, *Azaña*, 213–14.
53 Quoted in Sedwick, *Azaña*, 132.
54 M. Maura, quoted in Payne, *Spain's First Democracy*, 67–8. See also F. Lázaro Carreter, 'Azaña el Joven y el Orador', *ABC*, 3 Nov. 1990; and *Memorias*, I, 346.
55 Azaña, *Vigil in Benicarlo*, 74.
56 Auden used the quoted phrase in his poem 'Spain' – but later, stung by criticisms from Orwell and others, he amended the text. See E. Maslen, '"The Menacing Shapes of Our Fever". Looking Back at Auden's Spain' in S. Hart (ed.), *No Pasarán!: Art, Literature and the Spanish Civil War* (London, 1988), 65–82, and R. Stradling, 'Orwell and the Spanish Civil War: A Historical Critique', in C. Norris (ed.), *Inside the Myth: Orwell – Views from the Left* (London, 1984), 103–25. The other Auden quotation in this paragraph is from his 'Ode on the Death of Yeats' (1939).
57 The 'insights' of the cultural historian, like those on offer in any other department of the historians' store, are made possible by 'hindsight'. We can now examine the ideological struggles of the 1930s from a point of perspective situated beyond the events of the late 1980s. For the moment, dust has settled and things are clearer. As recently as 1991, atmospherical disturbance prevented Ferrer

Solá from obtaining a good view of the relationship between Azaña's intellectual and political lives (see *La pasión intelectual,* esp. 225–7). Nowhere more than in the study of the civil war and its origins is the Spanish proverb 'aquellos polvos traeron estos lodos' ('dust raised in the old days has left us stuck in this mud today') more meaningful.

58 See, for example, *Memorias,* I, 342.
59 R. A. Stradling and M. Hughes, *The English Musical Renaissance, 1860–1940: Construction and Deconstruction* (London, 1993).
60 The rightist newspaper *ABC* characterized Ortega's group in the *Cortes* as 'the Olympian delegates'; Ortega Klein, 'Ortega', 73.
61 J. Ortega y Gasset's essay 'La rebelión de las masas' was first published in 1928 (Madrid).
62 Azaña had been a practising journalist for many years before 1931. At the age of seventeen, he founded his own magazine and later helped edit a satirical weekly, titled *La Avispa* – 'The Wasp'. In the 1920s, his stinging attacks on politicians appeared in the journal *España*. Once in power, however, he became contemptuous of the profession – particularly what he called 'el reporterismo' – a feeling he did not trouble to hide; see, for a number of instances, *Memorias,* I, 320, 326, 335–41, 490–2, 549.
63 Muela, *Azaña,* 124.
64 In 1932, Marichalar anticipated a Nietzschean utopia of artist-leaders able to unite the 'Apolline' and 'Dionysiac' aspects of their genius; 'Chronicle', loc. cit., 296. For dispersed and sporadic hints towards the hypothesis advanced here, see W. Gerhardie, *God's Fifth Column: A Biography of the Age 1890–1940* (London, 1990) and R. Graves and A. Hodge, *The Long Weekend: A Social History of Britain, 1918–39* (London, 1939, repr. 1963); J. King, *The Last Modern: A Life of Herbert Read* (London, 1990); and, above all J. Carey, *The Intellectuals and the Masses: Pride and Prejudice among the Literary Intelligentsia, 1880–1939* (London, 1992).
65 For details, see V. Cunningham, *British Writers of the Thirties* (Oxford, 1988), 419–61.
66 Sedwick, *Azaña,* 54.
67 As early as August 1931, assessing the reactions of various military personnel to his army reform decrees, Azaña identifed Franco as his most dangerous adversary among the general staff; see *Memorias,* I, 100.
68 A. Reig Tapía, *Violencia y terror: Estudios sobre la guerra civil española* (Madrid, 1990), 180.
69 Marichal, *El intelectual y la política,* 80.
70 Azaña, *Vigil in Benicarlo,* 65, 99, 101, 114, 130–1. In a series of essays composed during the war, Azaña consistently and meticulously avoided allocating any blame for its causes – even to the Nationalists. It was all due to a 'pathological phenomenon in

Spanish society'; this, in its turn, was caused by abstract considerations, resembling the Gods of some Greek tragedy; see *Causas de la Guerra de España* (ed. G. Jackson, Madrid, 1986), esp. 9–11. For another perspective on Azaña's role in the civil war, and the polarity between his identities as writer and politician and those of General Franco, see R. Stradling, 'The propaganda of the deed: history, Hemingway and Spain', *Textual Practice* 3 No. 1 (1989), 15–35.

71 In 1939, Azaña prophesied that: 'in a hundred years, many people will not know who Franco and I were; but all the world will still know who Velázquez and Goya were'; quoted in Reig Tapía, *Violencia*, 171. This was unusually modest, but it seems not to have been modest enough. It is true that, twenty years after his death, many Spanish schoolchildren do not know who Franco was: but Azaña disappeared far more rapidly and completely from popular memory. Both these phenomena were assisted by censorship of a kind. Spaniards who were of mature age when Franco died, today are happy for their children not to ask awkward questions about why they did not oppose him. The premature demise of Azaña's reputation was largely due to the suffocating censorship of the Franco regime. One example is worthy of remark. In October 1936, as General Varela pushed north towards Madrid after the relief of the Alcázar of Toledo, his army found in its path a tiny pueblo 'Azaña'; see *El Adelanto de Salamanca*, 23 Oct 1936. It was much rumoured at the time – but never proven – that the distant forefather of Manuel Azaña hailed from this poverty-stricken community. (It was not unusual in certain parts of Castile, even in the 1930s, for illegitimate children to be given the name of their place of origin.) What happened to the village in 1936 is also unknown; but sometime later, after Franco's victory, the place was renamed as 'Numancia de la Sagra'. The Sagra is a dirty stream which (at best) trickles through the settlement. Numancia is the epic site, near faraway Soria, and on the mighty River Duero, where the 'original race' of Spaniards were supposed to have resisted the Roman invaders to the death. These heroes figured in Francoist propaganda as models for those of the Alcázar, and the event was fixed upon by hack historians as the key to Spain's subsequent destiny. The fate of Azaña – *pueblo* – represents an ironic comment on the attempt of Azaña – *hombre* – to change the history of Spain by changing Spain's view of history. For the former, see P. Madoz, *Diccionario Geográfico-Estadístico-Histórico de España y sus posesiones de Ultramar* (Vol. 3, Madrid, 1846, repr. 1989), 207. For the modern *pueblo*, just off autovia 401 near Illescas, see *Military Maps* 604 and 605.

~8~
The Myths of José Antonio Primo de Rivera

PAUL PRESTON

Sixty years after his death, José Antonio Primo de Rivera is virtually unknown among his compatriots. Yet, he was the founder of Spain's Fascist party, the Falange Española, which was to be the political instrument with which Franco ruled Spain for nearly four decades. After his execution by a Republican firing squad on 20 November 1936, he was converted into a symbolic martyr, the fulfilment of whose alleged plans for Spain provided a spurious justification for almost every act of the *Caudillo*. The case for assessment of the career of José Antonio Primo de Rivera in life and in death is overwhelming and is not in any way diminished by the fact that the cult of his memory so cynically and deafeningly built up by the regime was already an obsolete irrelevance before the demise of the dictator. Indeed, the importance of José Antonio Primo de Rivera as both man and myth is underlined by the existence of several contradictory myths enthusiastically used by the adulators of Franco, by Falangist opponents of Franco and even by anti-Francoist democrats.

Although none of these myths correspond precisely to historical reality, all feed on different aspects of José Antonio's multifaceted personality, the fascination of which cannot be gainsaid. The most elaborate montage was constituted by the official Francoist myths of José Antonio as the saintly predecessor of the *Caudillo*, a Christ-like martyr in *la Cruzada*. Many streets and squares, schools, university halls of residence and other official buildings were named after him. Virtually every church in Spain, with the exception of the Cathedral of Seville, had painted or carved on its walls the words 'José Antonio Primo de Rivera, ¡Presente!' - a reference to the practice in the early days of ending meetings by shouting out the names of the absent (*ausente*) Falangist dead. Alongside the vaguely religious symbolism, there was a more direct political objective to this myth. The legends of a romantic and poetic leader of a Falange which was both revolutionary and *franquista* were carefully cultivated by the Franco régime to provide a populist mask for its own commitment to traditional oligarchic interests. The régime thus cried crocodile tears at José Antonio's absence while deriving immense benefit from the fact that he could not be an awkward presence.

Altogether more subtle and still pervasive are the myths of José Antonio, agent of reconciliation, above parties, certainly not a fascist, concerned only with the welfare of all Spaniards. This José Antonio would have opposed Franco and carried out 'la revolución pendiente', the Falange's great unfinished revolution.[1] In support of this view, there exists José Antonio's own dismissal of his suitability as a populist leader. In his first political manifesto, as a candidate in the June 1931 elections, he said 'God knows that my vocation is among my books, and to leave them to throw myself into the sharp vertigo of politics causes me real pain.'[2] He wrote to a friend

> I could be anything but a fascist caudillo. The attitude of doubt and the sense of irony which never leaves those of us who have had some intellectual curiosity renders us incapable of making the robust and categoric statements needed by the leaders of the masses.[3]

His political partner, Ramiro Ledesma Ramos, shared this view, regarding José Antonio's suave, rational scepticism, 'with his polite temperament and his legal education', as inclining him to parliamentary politics rather than fascism.[4] Falangist opponents of Franco propagated the idea that the young Primo de Rivera represented Spain's great lost opportunity, that somehow he could have led a Spain free of both the divisiveness of the Republic and the brutality of Francoism. This view can also be found in the writings of the exiled Socialist leader, Indalecio Prieto. Musing on the transfer of the mortal remains of José Antonio from the monastery of El Escorial to the Valle de los Caídos in 1959, he wrote

> He was a good hearted man, unlike the man who will be his bed-fellow in the tomb at Cuelgamuros. José Antonio has been condemned to

dishonorable company, which he certainly does not deserve, in the Valle de los Caídos. He is dishonoured by being associated with the atrocities and corruptions of others.[5]

Both sets of myths, his official posthumous role as the holy predecessor of Franco and the unofficial as the revolutionary reconciler, have grains of truth, but they should not obscure certain inconvenient facts about José Antonio Primo de Rivera's political activities and his personal relationship with Franco. A detailed examination of his role during the Second Republic suggests that he was neither so poetic nor so progressive as the myths imply. It is reasonable to assume that the extremely shrewd Prieto wrote in the way he did in the hope of intensifying further the existing tensions between Franco and part of the Falange. Even if Prieto's outrage on behalf of Franco's bed-fellow is deemed to have been sincere, to sustain his conclusion would require several counter-factual speculations. José Antonio Primo de Rivera would have to be exonerated from any connection with the role played in the Spanish Civil War by the Falange as the blood-stained auxiliary repressive force which freed the military from the task of politically purging conquered territory.[6]

José Antonio was undoubtedly an attractive figure, cultured, personally courageous, loyal to his friends and a wickedly amusing journalist.[7] The American Ambassador, Claude Bowers, found him 'courtly, modest and deferential' and the English journalist Henry Buckley wrote that 'soft-voiced, courteous José Antonio was one of the nicest people in Madrid'.[8] The son of the dictator General Miguel Primo de Rivera, his loyalty to the memory of his father and his bravery in defending it, was what pulled him into politics.[9] An elegant lawyer-about-town, his saturnine good looks made him the heart-throb of many young women in the high society of 1930s Spain.[10] Smart, witty and charming, he shared little of the buffoonery of Mussolini or of the loud vulgarity of Hitler, and the attractions of his personality have seduced more than one Anglo-Saxon scholar.[11] Equally, the dignity of his death at the age of thirty-four facilitated the subsequent Francoist invention of a cult of his memory.

The founder of the Falange contributed significantly to the atmosphere of political violence which preceded the military uprising of 1936. Behind José Antonio's smooth and polished exterior there was an apparently barely controllable violence which occasionally turned him into a cheap brawler and even found its way into his theoretical statements. As a student in the 1920s, he was often involved in violent altercations. On several occasions in the 1930s, he was involved in fist fights and duels because he took criticisms of the dictatorship as personal insults of his father.[12] Jealous of his own dignity, he refused to permit anyone to call him by the usual diminutives associated with his name to the extent of once declaring 'If anyone called me Pepe or Don Pepe, I believe that I would be capable of shooting them.'[13] On one occasion, he leapt the benches of the *Cortes* to get to Indalecio Prieto whom he perceived to have insulted the memory of his father. In the ensuing brawl, 'he functioned like a punching machine'. On another, he knocked down the Radical deputy for Cuenca, José María Alvarez Mendizábal. As his victim reeled backwards towards the government benches, José Antonio sneered 'Thank me because for once in your life, albeit rolling on the floor, I've helped you get to the front bench.'[14] It is likely, however, that the use of violence was coldly fabricated in search of an appropriately 'fascist' image. According to a perceptive monarchist observer,

> he made a show of a strong and violent attitude but, really, if he acted on it, it was because he believed it to be for the good of his organization. He was violent not because he was impulsive, incapable of reason and given to risking, because of his aggression, something for which he carried the responsibility. He was cold, moderate and of sound judgement.[15]

This view was shared by his friend José Finat y Escrivá de Romaní, the Conde de Mayalde, who said that he 'conceived and carried out violence with his surprisingly cold head'.[16] With this in mind, after his car was damaged in a bomb attack on 10 April 1934, he refused to have it repaired.[17]

He seems to have derived some pleasure from what were called 'laxative sanctions', the forcing of castor oil on the Falange's enemies and referred to the 'joyful irresponsibility necessary for assaults on newspaper kiosks'.[18] His cult of violence facilitated the destabilization of the politics of the Second Republic. His blue-shirted militias, with their Roman salutes and their ritual chants of *¡ARRIBA ESPAÑA!* and *¡ESPAÑA! ¡UNA! ¡ESPAÑA!*

¡LIBRE! ¡ESPAÑA! ¡GRANDE!, aped Nazi and Fascist models. From 1933 to 1936, Falange Española functioned as the cannon fodder of the haute bourgeoisie, provoking street brawls and helping to generate the lawlessness which, exaggerated by the right-wing press, was used to justify the military rising. The intrinsic violence, personal and political, of José Antonio undermines his posthumous image as an agent of reconciliation in November 1936.

Similarly, the notion of a progressive, left-wing José Antonio propounded by opposition Falangists is impossible to sustain.[19] To begin with, it is difficult to explain away the close links between José Antonio and the southern landowning oligarchy. He was born on 24 April 1903 into a distinguished and comfortably wealthy Andalusian military family. His great-uncle, Fernando Primo de Rivera y Sobremonte, was made Marqués de Estella for his part in the siege of that Navarrese town during the second Carlist war. On General Fernando Primo de Rivera's death, successive holders of the title, including José Antonio himself, held the title of 'grandes de España'. There were aristocratic connections too through his mother, Doña Casilda Sáenz de Heredia.[20] An instinctive snobbery *de señorito* rendered José Antonio an unlikely leader of Spain's hungry masses. He frequented the best restaurants and bars, cultivated an exquisite elegance of dress, and would wear only English suits. His great passions were horses, riding and hunting. He collected English equine prints. In early 1934, two Falangists were assassinated. The first, Vicente Pérez Rodríguez, was killed on 27 January. The news reached José Antonio when he was at a ball at the fashionable Madrid country club at Puerta de Hierro. The second, Matías Montero, had been killed on 9 February. José Antonio was late for the funeral because he had been out hunting.[21]

He regarded the ability to ride well as crucial. Accordingly, he discounted the monarchist leader José Calvo Sotelo as a potential caudillo because 'he couldn't ride' (*porque no sabía montar a caballo*). He commented that he never understood how 'it could be possible to be chief of anything of importance without being able to cut a dashing figure in the saddle astride a nervous and potent brute which must be dominated by one's thighs and knees, with one's ankles and with one's intelligence'.[22] This haughty disdain sat ill with the young Primo de Rivera's populist pretensions. In fact, José Antonio's first experience in politics was as vice-secretary general to the Unión Monárquica Nacional, a monarchist organization of ex-ministers and collaborators of his father. He also stood unsuccessfully as a monarchist candidate for Madrid in a by-election in October 1931.[23]

Indeed, the monarchist aristocrat José Antonio Primo de Rivera had little to do with the first pioneering efforts to create a Spanish fascism made by the deranged surrealist Ernesto Giménez Caballero, the eccentric Dr José María Albiñana, the would-be Nazi and translator of *Mein Kampf,* Onésimo Redondo Ortega, or the post-office functionary and energetic student of German philosophy, Ramiro Ledesma Ramos. Giménez Caballero was author of surrealist classics like *Yo, inspector de alcantarillas* and innumerable political works drenched in overt sexual metaphors which constitute a kind of erotico-fascism. During the Spanish Civil War, he became a slavish sycophant for Franco, producing panegyrics to the *Caudillo* along the lines of: 'Who has penetrated the innermost parts of Spain like Franco to the point where it is not clear if Spain is Franco or Franco is Spain? Oh Franco, our Caudillo, father of Spain!'[24] His contribution to the introduction of fascism into Spain derived from his love affair with Rome. In 1927, he founded the literary magazine *La Gaceta Literaria* through which he imported into Spain many of the ideas of Italian fascism. He was in many respects the principal ideological precursor of Spanish fascism, although Ledesma Ramos would eventually split with him precisely because of his excessive Italophilia.[25]

Albiñana, a Valencian neurologist and admirer of General Primo de Rivera, was the author of more than twenty novels and books on neurasthenia, religion, the history and philosophy of medicine and Spanish politics, and a number of mildly imperialist works about Mexico. In April 1930, he launched his Partido Nacionalista Español, 'Hispanic brotherhood of energetic action' with the aim of 'annihilating the internal enemies of the fatherland'. Its objectives were the defence of religious principles, of the political unity of Spain, of the monarchy and of the army. A fascist appearance was provided by a blue-shirted, roman-saluting Legionarios de España, a 'citizen volunteer force to act directly, explosively and expeditiously against any initiative which attacks or diminishes the prestige of the fatherland'. Although he declared himself 'a new man' and announced the need for the seizure of power, Albiñana, for all his authoritarianism, nationalism and antisemitism, was essentially a conservative. Eventually, Albiñana linked up with the monarchists of Renovación Española.[26]

In February 1931, ten men met in a squalid room in an office block in Madrid. The light had not been connected and the only furniture was a table. They signed a manifesto composed by Ledesma Ramos called *La Conquista del Estado*. José Antonio was not one of their number. An eleventh, Giménez Caballero, telephoned his support from Barcelona. A newspaper of the same name was launched on 14 March and published over the next year despite public indifference and police harassment.[27] Three months later, Onésimo Redondo, a functionary of the sugarbeet growers' association, founded a fascist group in Valladolid under the name La Junta Castellana de Actuación Hispánica. In October 1931, these two diminutive organizations fused into Las Juntas de Ofensiva Nacional-Sindicalista (JONS), a tiny, penurious outfit whose greatest asset was their symbol, the yoke and the arrows. They could not pay the 100 pesetas per month rent on their modest Madrid HQ and could barely afford to produce propaganda leaflets.[28] According to the Italian Ambassador Raffaele Guariglia, although they could fight university students, they were too weak to take on Socialist or Communist labour organizations in the streets.[29]

While these early attempts were being made to launch fascism in Spain, José Antonio Primo de Rivera was busy working for the Unión Monárquica. It was during this period that José Antonio first met General Franco. After the Falangist leader's death, the idea of Franco as the representative on earth of the absent José Antonio was built up assiduously by the regime. This was done despite the fact that there was considerable personal acrimony between them and despite the fact that, in power, Franco systematically ignored the legacy, such as it was, of Primo de Rivera's thought. Their first meeting took place in Zaragoza in the early 1930s. At the time, Franco was the Director of the General Military Academy in Zaragoza where he had become friendly with a brilliant lawyer, Ramón Serrano Suñer. When, in February 1931, Serrano Suñer married Zita Polo, the beautiful sister of Franco's wife, Carmen, in Oviedo, the bride's witness was her brother-in-law, Francisco Franco; the groom's was José Antonio Primo de Rivera.[30] Despite the encouragement of Serrano Suñer, the dour, hard-working general and the rising young lawyer did not become friends. Although both opposed the Second Republic, their style and attitudes could not have been more different. Even when involved in the creation of Falange Española, José Antonio remained a popular socialite and a witty journalist. He was the antithesis of the dour, and ten years older general whose eminence owed nothing to the advantages of birth or of verbal brilliance and everything to hard work and bravery. Concerned exclusively with safeguarding his military career in a hostile environment, and never a man to look backwards, Franco was not inclined to sympathize with José Antonio's efforts to defend his father.

By 1933, inspired by the success of Hitler, José Antonio had developed an interest in fascism. Along with his father's one-time collaborator, Manuel Delgado Barreto, editor of the conservative daily *La Nación*, he had been involved in an attempt to launch a paper called *El Fascio*. They were joined in February 1933 by Giménez Caballero, Ledesma Ramos, Rafael Sánchez Mazas and Juan Aparicio, their 'adolescent eyes opened by the triumph of Hitler' and the Nazi victory marches portrayed on cinema screens. Only one issue of *El Fascio* was ever printed. It carried an article on the New State by José Antonio Primo de Rivera entitled 'Orientaciones' and signed 'E'. As Juan Aparicio wrote later, 'The Marqués de Estella remained reluctant to give up the historic links of his family past.' Not that it mattered, since most copies were seized by the police. Nevertheless, the group continued to meet and was soon joined by the famous aviator Julio Ruiz de Alda and the young university professor and disciple of the philosopher José Ortega y Gasset, Alfonso García Valdecasas.[31] They formed a group called the Movimiento Español Sindicalista whose propaganda carried the subtitle Fascismo Español.[32]

José Antonio Primo de Rivera seems by this time to have decided that if there was ever to be a significant fascist option in Spain, he would have to supply it. He therefore embarked in the course of 1933 on a three-pronged plan which involved seeking support from the traditional Right, gaining the backing of fascist Italy and finding ways of unifying the existing fascist embryos. The link with fascist Italy was not simply a question of immediate finance but rather lay at the heart of José Antonio's imperialist project. The Falangist alternative to the class struggle was empire.

However, an awareness that Spain alone would be unable to challenge the international hegemony of Britain and France led José Antonio and his followers to think in terms of an alliance with other powers anxious to overturn that hegemony. In José Antonio's sympathy for Italy and Germany can be seen the hope, shared by Franco, that, in conjunction with Fascists and Nazis, Falangist Spain could overthrow the possessing powers and seize an empire.[33] As Herbert Southworth has shown, the ambition of Franco was directed against Britain and France far more than against Soviet Russia.[34] Like Franco, José Antonio loathed the League of Nations. On one occasion, as a friend, Juan Antonio Giménez Arnau, was leaving for Switzerland, he asked him 'Is there anything I can do for you in Geneva?' José Antonio replied 'If you have time, burn it down.'[35]

In search of links with like-minded groups, José Antonio Primo de Rivera entered into contact with the JONS and, through García Valdecasas, with Frente Español, a group consisting of young followers of Ortega y Gasset, including the historian Juan Antonio Maravall. Having formed the Agrupación al Servicio de la República, Ortega had become disillusioned by the reality of democracy. Frente Español had emerged in March 1932 and never acquired more than the couple of dozen members who took turns waiting in vain at their offices for new recruits to turn up. Most of them would finally pull back from the prospect of creating a full-blown fascist organization but García Valdecasas was convinced that the name Frente Español and particularly its initials (FE spells faith in Spanish) had a political value. He was open to the idea of fusing this moribund shell with the dynamic, but unstructured Movimiento Español Sindicalista – Fascismo Español. His erstwhile comrades from the organization opposed the use of its title for a new fascist group. The name Falange Española was chosen in an attempt to retain part of the original cachet and the statutes of the Falange were those of Frente Español.[36] José Antonio Primo de Rivera derived from Ortega y Gasset several of his central ideas – the nation as a community of destiny, the need to 'give Spain a backbone' (vertebrar España), the relation of the élite to the masses. However, he was never to forgive Ortega for failing fully to embrace Spanish fascism.[37]

The leadership of the new party Falange Española consisted of José Antonio and García Valdecasas, along with the aviator, Julio

Ruiz de Alda. At a meeting in San Sebastián in late August 1933, organized by the Basque extreme rightist, José María de Areilza, they tried unsuccessfully to secure the participation of Ledesma Ramos. The JONS leader, endlessly suspicious of the upper class connections of Primo de Rivera, simply insisted that the newcomers join his party. Ledesma did, however, despite his suspicions of the haute bourgeoisie, accept from the monarchists of Acción Española the gift of a motorbike which he rode on his propaganda trips around Spain.[38] More successful was the agreement made in August 1933 by José Antonio Primo de Rivera with representatives of the Traditionalist Communion and the monarchists of Renovación Española represented by Pedro Sainz Rodríguez and José Antonio de Sangróniz – the so-called Pacto de El Escorial. The monarchists undertook to finance the Falange to the tune of 10,000 pesetas per month in return for the Falange not opposing the restoration of the monarchy and for an undertaking that the Falange would consult with them on major policy initiatives. Even before Falange Española was officially launched it was already tied to the most conservative sectors of the old patrician Right. A cordial arrangement seems to have existed for some time thereafter with Sainz Rodríguez nominated as the monarchist liaison with the Falange. Sainz Rodríguez even helped José Antonio in the drafting of the Falange's programme.[39]

Primo de Rivera was fortunate that the Italian Ambassador in Madrid, Raffaele Guariglia, was a firm advocate of Rome providing material help for the establishment of a Spanish fascist party. Armed with a letter of introduction from Guariglia, José Antonio Primo de Rivera went to Italy in mid-October 1933 'to obtain information about Italian fascism and the achievements of its régime. And also to get, as far as possible, advice on the organization of a similar movement in Spain.' He was received by Mussolini on the evening of 19 October. A few minutes before the meeting, he told an Italian journalist 'I am like a pupil about to see the teacher. How much good he could do, if he wanted and I am sure that he will want to, for me, for my movement and for my country. He was a friend of my father, he will surely help me.' The meeting itself was evoked by José Antonio in his introduction to the Spanish translation of Mussolini's *La Dottrina del fascismo*, a reverential piece in which he describes the Duce in a corner of his immense, cold marble-clad office, working while Rome relaxed, 'watching over

Italy, listening to her breathing as if to that of small daughter ... the hero made father, beside the eternal lamplight, keeping vigil over the anxieties and the slumber of his people.' While in Rome, he visited the offices of the Partito Nazionale Fascista and was given all the information that he sought.[40] The Duce presented him with a dedicated photograph that he hung thereafter in his office next to a portrait of his father.[41]

The creation of Falange Española was announced by José Antonio during the campaign for the elections of November 1933. Recruiting had started in early October. New militants were required to fill in a form which asked if they had a bicycle – a euphemism for pistol – and were then issued with a truncheon (porra). The formal launch took place on Sunday 29 October at the Teatro de la Comedia in Madrid. Defence squads around the building were organized by the chief of the Falange militias, Lieutenant Colonel Ricardo de Rada.[42] In his otherwise poetically flowery inaugural speech, José Antonio made much of his commitment to violence:

> if our aims have to be achieved by violence, let us not hold back before violence. Because who has ever said – when speaking in terms of 'anything other than violence' – that the highest of values is to be found in amiability? Who has ever said that, when our feelings are insulted, rather than react like men, we are obliged to be amiable? The dialectic is all very well as a first instrument of communication. But the only dialectic admissible when justice or the Fatherland is offended is the dialectic of fists and pistols.[43]

Although violence was to become a commonplace of the politics of Spain in the 1930s, no politician incorporated the rhetoric of violence so lyrically into his oratorical repertoire. This was frequently evident at the funeral rituals which, in emulation of the practice of the Italian Fascist Squadristi, followed the participation of Falangists in street violence.[44] Paradoxically, after the meeting, José Antonio told Felipe Ximénez de Sándoval, 'The masses embarrass me. The idea of hundreds of eyes fixed on me causes me real distress ... How I suffered on seeing the arms raised to salute me!'.[45]

Within four weeks of the party's foundation, García Valdecasas had disappeared on an interminable honeymoon with a wealthy aristocratic bride.[46] José Antonio also took advantage of all his conservative connections in running on a monarchist slate for a seat in the Cortes for Cádiz, where his family enjoyed enormous influence. Thanks to the electoral power of the local ultraconservative landowners, he was elected with 49,028 votes, 18.5 per cent of the total cast, a figure far in excess of anything that he could have managed running as a Falangist. His decision reflected the financial weakness of the Falange although there is no reason to suppose that either he or the Cádiz monarchists were uncomfortable with the arrangement.[47] Indeed, he told the Italian *chargé d'affaires*, Geisser Celesia, of his disappointment that neither the leader of the Catholic authoritarian CEDA party, José María Gil Robles, nor 'the grandes de España' would finance the Falange. This was an unusually frank admission to Mussolini's representative and one which revealed the limitations of his desire to break free of conservative influences. For Celesia, José Antonio was a señorito who could never appeal to the masses precisely because he looked to the oligarchy for his finance.[48]

The appearance of a new fascist party to rival the JONS caused financial problems for both and stimulated thoughts of union. At first, Ledesma Ramos was reluctant to see the JONS join with the Falange, but some of his lieutenants, notably Francisco Bravo Martínez and Ernesto Giménez Caballero, persuaded him that the logic of eventual fusion was unavoidable.[49] The rich had not been prepared to fund Ledesma Ramos. When he managed to secure an interview with Francesc Cambó in the Ritz, he was quickly seen off.[50] In contrast, monarchists had been prepared to finance the Falange as an instrument of political destabilization. José Antonio's credentials as a southern land-owner, a grande de España, an eligible socialite, and above all as the eldest son of the late lamented military dictator, seemed to offer a guarantee to the upper classes that Spanish Fascism would not get out of their control in the way of its German and Italian equivalents. However, monarchist enthusiasm for José Antonio diminished somewhat when, on 15 February 1934, he fused Falange Española with the Juntas de Ofensiva Nacional-Sindicalista. The new FE de las JONS was to be ruled over by a three-man executive consisting of Primo de Rivera, Ruiz de Alda and Ledesma Ramos. It was not long before José Antonio was able to please his new allies with a gesture which seemed to manifest some of the radicalism associated with the JONS. In May 1934, he rejected an attempt to join the Falange by José Calvo Sotelo, who had recently returned from exile after being amnestied. Ledesma Ramos fondly believed that Calvo Sotelo was excluded because José Antonio regarded him as too closely linked to the grand bourgeoisie. In fact, José Antonio felt a simmering hostility to the monarchist leader whom he believed had fled like a coward rather than defend the record of the Dictatorship. Thus patrician disdain and personal resentment, rather than any inclination to prevent the radicalism of the new party being tainted by Calvo Sotelo's conservatism, lay behind the rejection.[51]

The link with the JONS intensified the contradictions between José Antonio's aristocratic instincts and his populist ambitions. This was to have economic consequences. Partly in reaction to these financial difficulties, José Antonio began in early 1934 to fish for an invitation to Nazi Germany. There was also an element of sympathetic curiosity behind his visit – he had been an avid reader of *Mein Kampf* and Alfred Rosenberg's *Der Mythus der zwanzigsten Jahrhunderts* (*The Myth of the Twentieth Century*). He met Hitler in Berlin in May 1934 but the Germans had little interest in giving him financial assistance.[52] In some frustration, the Italian Embassy reported regularly throughout 1934 that the new party had financial problems and that its violent acts of retaliation against the Left were clumsily handled. Celesia attributed the party's lack of popular impact to the fact that José Antonio Primo de Rivera was a señorito and that his speeches had little appeal to the masses, since they were either theoretical disquisitions or defences of his father. Guariglia lamented that 'in questo immenso manicomio politico che si chiama la Spagna', the new Fascists could do nothing beyond issuing verbal statements and leave the hopes of the right in the Catholic CEDA.[53]

Accordingly, the FE de las JONS remained dependent on monarchist charity. In April 1934, for a nominal rent, one of the party's few rich backers, Francisco Moreno y Herrera, the Marqués de La Eliseda, had permitted use of one of his houses, at Marqués de Riscal 12, as Falange headquarters.[54] Eliseda complained to Celesia in September 1934 that cash was tight, but recruitment booming, because the Falange was going towards the Left. Eliseda abandoned the party two months later and endeavoured to evict the Falange from his property. José Antonio used every possible legal subterfuge to permit his men to go on using the premises. Eliseda retaliated by cutting off the gas and the electricity which were surreptitiously and illegally reconnected. Always happier to direct violence against the Left than the Right, José Antonio then intervened to stop enraged comrades giving Eliseda a dose of castor oil.[55]

The marriage of the two parties, financial difficulties aside, was never an easy one. Conflict derived from the different ambitions of José Antonio and Ramiro Ledesma Ramos, the one élitist, the other populist. Tensions were provoked in the summer of 1934 by the monarchist adventurer Juan Antonio Ansaldo. A well-known aviator and playboy, Ansaldo had joined the Falange in late April at the invitation of José Antonio. He was given the title of Jefe de Objetivos, a euphemism which covered his organization of terrorist squads. Although uneasy about his reactionary monarchism, Ledesma approved of the efficacy with which Ansaldo toughened up what was called the Falange de la Sangre ('the Falange of Blood'):

> His presence in the party was of undeniable utility because he found a place for that active, violent sector which the reactionary spirit produces everywhere as one of the most fertile ingredients for the national armed struggle. Remember what analogous groups meant for German Hitlerism especially in its early stages.

During the summer, a plan to blow up the Casa del Pueblo of Madrid reached an advanced stage. The followers of Ansaldo were disappointed that José Antonio did not throw greater weight into the terrorist destabilization of the Republic. There was even talk of a group of militia officials led by Ansaldo threatening him with expulsion from the leadership if he did not drop what was perceived as his policy of appeasement. Matters grew worse after the discovery by the police, on 10 July 1934, of large quantities of guns, ammunition, dynamite and bombs at the Marqués de Riscal headquarters. Eighty militants, mainly Jonsistas and members of Ansaldo's squads, were imprisoned for three weeks. During the days spent in prison, criticisms of Primo de Rivera's leadership surfaced. Moreover, Ansaldo and the militia leaders, together with the Jonsistas, were particularly incensed by José Antonio's evident enjoyment participating in *Cortes* debates. They were even more outraged by the fact that, on 3 June 1934, José

Antonio had crossed the chamber in order to shake Prieto's hand, after the Socialist leader had opposed the lifting of his parliamentary immunity and that of the Socialist Juan Lozano, parliamentary deputy for Jaén, which would have permitted their being tried for illicit possession of arms (*tenencia ilícita de armas*). The Ansaldo-inspired mutterings widened into a broader conflict between *Falangistas* and *Jonsistas*.[56]

When he found out what was happening, José Antonio immediately expelled Ansaldo before the end of July commenting that the conspirators involved in this 'dirty intrigue' matched 'their felony with their imbecility'. Thereafter, the hit-squads continued to carry out reprisals against the Left with equal frequency and efficiency, albeit with greater loyalty to José Antonio Primo de Rivera. With apparent reluctance, he then moved in September 1934 to abandon the triumvirate and assume sole leadership of the Falange.[57] He cannot have been unaware of the involvement of Ramiro Ledesma in the conspiracy. The Falange's student leader, Alejandro Salazar wrote in his diary in the summer 'For some time now Ramiro Ledesma is no longer one of ours'.[58] In fact, Ledesma Ramos was always resentful of Primo de Rivera's aristocratic background and his wealth. The resentment was intensified by the fact that he was prevented from ever matching José Antonio as a fascist orator by a speech defect – a defect cruelly mocked by José Antonio later.[59]

In the late summer of 1934, when Left-Right tension was reaching a peak, José Antonio took an initiative which substantiated the suspicions of Ledesma Ramos that he could never break free of his family background and aristocratic instincts. He wrote an hysterical letter to Franco. In an attempt to incline Franco to make a coup against the Left, he claimed that Socialist victory was imminent and equivalent to 'a foreign invasion' since France would seize the opportunity to annex Catalonia. Franco did not deign to reply. Now well-established as a major general and a favoured confidant of the Minister of Defence, Diego Hidalgo, Franco was not remotely interested in assuming the risks involved in association with small-time fascist organizations. Believing that only the Army had the right and the might to determine the political destiny of Spain, franco can have felt little but disdain for the nascent Falange.[60]

The outbreak of the left-wing uprising on 6 October 1934

coincided with the first meeting of the Consejo Nacional of the Falange convened to ratify José Antonio's assumption of the role of Jefe Nacional. On 7 October, José Antonio led a demonstration from Falange headquarters to the Puerta del Sol. Climbing onto the scaffolding which surrounded the site of the metro, he made a speech in support of the government which Ledesma Ramos regarded as feeble and inappropriate. There seems to have been little more by way of anti-revolutionary initiatives in Madrid although, in the provinces, Falangists appear to have acted as auxiliary forces of order.[61] Dining out on the evening of one of the sessions, José Antonio, his friend Raimundo Fernández Cuesta and Julio Ruiz de Alda had threatened to beat up the Catalan student leader Antonio María Sbert if he did not leave the fashionable restaurant where they had just taken a table. Sbert had been the leader of the student opposition to the dictatorship of Miguel Primo de Rivera.[62] Celesia commented sarcastically that Falangists could be heard boasting in Madrid of having collected the odd dustbin or given a lift to an army officer in their cars.[63] Even after the crushing of the Left after the rising, the Italians complained of the failure of the Falange to impose itself on the situation. The Falange played some small role in the repression after Asturias.[64]

José Antonio's conservative inclinations and his awareness of his ultimate dependence on the oligarchy was most starkly seen in the elaboration of the programme of the new party which followed the Consejo Nacional. A first, and radical, draft was drawn up by Francisco Bravo on behalf of the Junta Política (the permanent executive committee of the Consejo Nacional) which was chaired by Ramiro Ledesma. The final version was the work of José Antonio who had not only improved the prose but also rendered the programme more abstract and altogether less radical.[65] Friction over the programme fed into a struggle for power. In late November, Geisser Celesia informed Rome that Ledesma Ramos was about to leave the Falange. In this he was being encouraged by one of the most radical of the Jonsistas, the ex-anarchist Nicasio Alvarez de Sotomayor.[66] In consequence, on 14 January 1935, Ledesma, Alvarez de Sotomayor and Onésimo Redondo announced that they would be reorganizing the JONS outside the Falange. Rather than accept this split, José Antonio announced to the Junta Política two days later that Ledesma had been expelled because of persistent factionalism. The bulk of the JONS, including Onésimo Redondo, remained within FE de las JONS.[67] In his own accounts, Ledesma denied that he had been pushed out and claimed that he had left of his own initiative because of 'irresolvable differences' with José Antonio over the deradicalization of the 27-point programme.[68] In his own version, José Antonio spoke contemptuously of the factionalism of a few lumpenproletariat mercenaries: 'a few people brought up in the lowest depths, revolutionaries for hire, are those who have had to leave the Falange de las JONS not to establish any unity of thought, but for reasons of hygiene.' So intense were the divisions that allegedly only the intervention of José Antonio prevented a Falangist assassination attempt on Ledesma Ramos.[69] None the less, José Antonio led a Falangist hit-squad to seize the offices occupied by the JONS in the Calle del Príncipe.[70] He also published a savage attack on Ledesma, ridiculing his speech defect.[71] Only a small number of Jonsistas accompanied Ledesma. He threatened legal action against José Antonio Primo de Rivera to recuperate the name of his party,[72] but his effort to start a new party eventually came to naught and he returned to his job in the Post Office only to be shot as a fascist at the beginning of the Civil War.

The removal of radical elements did not endear the Falange to the middle and upper classes. Satisfaction with conservative governments in 1935 ensured that financial support remained exiguous. Efforts to create a daily newspaper foundered.[73] José Antonio used his own money and received inadequate gifts from friends. The Falange in Gijón rented a flat which belonged to Franco's wife Carmen. When the general found out the use to which it was being put, he instructed his brother-in-law Ramón Serrano Suñer to tell José Antonio to evict his followers.[74] By the end of 1934, the Falange could not pay its lighting and heating bills. Shivering members of the leadership held meetings by candlelight.[75]

Primo de Rivera was finally obliged to turn to Mussolini. At the end of April 1935, he visited Italy again and was received in Genoa by Eugenio Coselschi, one-time secretary to D'Annunzio, the head of the Comitati d'Azione per la Universalità di Roma. Mussolini's equivalent of the Nazi *Auslandorganization*, the CAUR, was placed within the Italian Ministry of Press and Propaganda under the direction of its under-secretary, Galeazzo

Ciano, the Duce's son-in-law. Mussolini himself authorized funds for José Antonio. Between June 1935 and January 1936, he received It.£50,000 per month (i.e. about ptas 30,000 of the day) – a significant sum – in money deriving from police slush funds. José Antonio collected the money himself in bi-monthly instalments during visits to Paris in June, August, November 1935 and January 1936 receiving it from Amadeo Landini, the energetic press attaché at the Italian Embassy in Paris. From February 1936, with Italy suffering a crisis of its foreign currency reserves, the amount was to be reduced by half. He was unable to collect his payments for February and March, due in March, because by then he was in jail.[76]

Perhaps it was Italian criticisms of Falangist weakness and indecision which impelled José Antonio to make the ill-advised move to armed struggle to overthrow the Second Republic. Alarmed at the moderate scale of the repression after the October insurrection, José Antonio was anxious to take action before the Left could return to power.[77] The decision was taken at a meeting of the Junta Política at the Parador de Gredos in mid-July 1935. He reported on his contacts with sympathetic army officers. He then put forward a plan for an uprising against the government to take place near the Portuguese frontier at Fuentes de Oñoro in the province of Salamanca. An unnamed general, possibly Sanjurjo, was to have secured 10,000 rifles in Portugal which would then be handed over to Falangist militants. The initial coup would then be followed by a 'march on Madrid'.[78] It was fraught with risk. With the Left recently defeated and suffering ongoing repression, with an authoritarian right-wing government in power, with the most right-wing elements of the military in positions of power, the timing could not have been more inappropriate. Accordingly, José Antonio seems to have presented the idea in a half-hearted manner, hoping perhaps that it would never get beyond the planning stage. Senior military encouragement was not forthcoming and, probably to José Antonio's relief, the idea was quickly dropped. The head of the Falangist student organization, Alejandro Salazar, wrote bitterly in his diary 'We returned from Gredos with wild enthusiasm only to see it converted into disillusionment on finding out that all we had done there was pass the time.'[79] The main consequence of this decision was ultimately the establishment by José Antonio of contacts with the ultra-rightist

Unión Militar Española in an unsuccessful quest for weapons.[80]

Presumably it was in the knowledge that funds were now forthcoming from Italy, that José Antonio Primo de Rivera made a speech at the Cine Madrid on 19 May 1935. He declared that the monarchy was dead and dissociated the Falange from 'monarchist reaction'. He complained that the counter-revolutionary forces in Spain 'had hoped at first that we would be the vanguard of their endangered interests, and so they offered to protect and help us at that time, and even to give us some money. And now they are crazed with despair when they see that what they thought would just be the vanguard has turned into a whole independent army.' Confident of Italian funding, he could declare his belief in the miracle of eventual success despite the fact that the Falange was 'attacked on all sides, without money, without newspapers'.[81] However, his tone changed in the course of the year. In his closing address to the second Consejo Nacional of the Falange in the Cine Madrid on 17 November 1935, he spoke in horrified terms of the Soviet assault on family life and religious values. He described the Russian revolution as the 'invasion of the barbarians'.[82] As Southworth has pointed out, José Antonio, recognizing that his party could go nowhere without the financial support of the oligarchy, was trying to create an ambience of fear which might induce its members to finance the Falange as a means of self-defence.[83] However, it was too late. The damage had been done and boats had been burned.

On 2 October 1935, José Antonio spoke up firmly in the *Cortes* in favour of the Italian attack on Ethiopia. It is possible that he was to some extent expressing gratitude for the financial assistance that he was receiving from Mussolini. He used the occasion for a fervent reminder of the indignity of British occupation of Gibraltar.[84] Elsewhere, he wrote, in terms reminiscent of Mussolini's rhetoric about Italian servitude in the Mediterranean, 'in foreign policy, weakness, servility, forgetting Gibraltar and Tangier. In a nutshell: spiritual and material ruin. Shame!'[85]

Perhaps because more serious elements of the army had shown no interest in Falangist overtures, José Antonio Primo de Rivera took a singularly hare-brained step at the end of 1935. In mid-December 1935, in complex circumstances, the government of Joaquín Chapaprieta fell, and with it José María Gil Robles, the CEDA leader who had been Minister of War since May. Several right-wing politicians tried to persuade senior generals to intervene in order to prevent new elections being called. The view held by General Franco, that the relative success of the working class during the events of October 1934 did not bode well for a military coup, prevailed. However, on 27 December, taking up a suggestion by the Jefe Provincial of Toledo, José Sainz Nothnagel, the Jefe Nacional proposed that several hundred Falangist militants join the cadets in the Alcázar of Toledo to make a *pronunciamiento*. It was a ridiculous idea in itself and one of the Junta de Mando, José María Alfaro, tried to dissuade him by pointing out that the enterprise could be defeated in Toledo's narrow streets by people dropping flowerpots on the insurrectionaries. Nevertheless, José Antonio was filled with enthusiasm for the idea, declaring 'we will place machine-guns in the Puerta Visagra. I will handle one of them.' He sent his lieutenants Raimundo Fernández Cuesta, Alfaro and Sainz Nothnagel to Toledo with this ill-considered proposal to Colonel José Moscardó, military governor and director of the Escuela Central de Gimnasia (Central School of Physical Education) there. Their departure was delayed until after a dinner held by a gourmet dining club to which José Antonio and Alfaro belonged along with a number of prominent monarchists. As soon as Alfaro changed out of his dinner jacket, they set off at 2.00 a.m., spending the remains of the night in an hotel in Toledo. Moscardó, whom they saw early the next morning, was a third-rank figure at best which perhaps explains why he did not dismiss the idea out of hand. Instead, he drove to Madrid to discuss it with Franco. It was José Antonio's good fortune that Franco, having just turned down rather better supported proposals, rejected the scheme as impracticable and badly timed.[86] Franco resented what he regarded as premature initiatives from civilians.[87]

Franco and José Antonio met again in February 1936 at the home of Ramón Serrano Suñer's father and brothers, just before the Popular Front elections in mid-February. José Antonio argued passionately in favour of a military coup in order to establish a counter-revolutionary national government. His charm was lost on Franco, who was cautiously evasive and rambled interminably. Regarding him as a dangerous dilettante, Franco had no intention of getting involved in conspiracy with him but typically failed to say so clearly. José Antonio was bitterly disillusioned and irritated, saying 'my father for all his defects, for all his political disorientation, was something else altogether. He had humanity, decisiveness and nobility. But these people ...'[88]

Despite the efforts of José Antonio, who visited Gil Robles on three occasions, the Falange was unable to reach an agreement with the conservative Right in the preparations for the elections of mid February 1936. He wanted more safe seats than the Falange's exiguous electoral support seemed to Gil Robles to justify. José Antonio refused to accept a few token seats which would, he claimed, have taken the Falange's votes while depriving the party of any role other than that of the guerrilla forces of the conservatives.[89] Since the safest seats were the Galician rotten boroughs and the Andalusian fiefs controlled by the ultra-conservatives of Renovación Española, José Antonio believed that his exclusion was influenced by a Calvo Sotelo seeking revenge for the rejection of his own attempt to join the Falange.[90] Had the Falange formed part of the broad right-wing front, it is likely that José Antonio would have been elected. Alone, and lacking substantial popular appeal, he had little chance.

José Antonio campaigned tirelessly but, for all the rhetoric about being neither of the Left nor the Right, his sympathies were clear. The Falangist dissident and poet, Dionisio Ridruejo, demolished the idea of a left-wing Falange when he described the fury of José Antonio on witnessing a working-class demonstration in Madrid shortly after the Popular Front electoral victory of February 1936. José Antonio commented 'With a pair of good marksmen, a demonstration like that can be dissolved in ten minutes'. Ridruejo wrote 'Such reactions were a useful way to persuade those who deny the necessarily and viscerally rightist or reactionary character of the Falangist movement that, "cold", kept its distance from the wider counter-revolutionary movement and even felt repulsion for it, but that, "in the heat of the moment" found itself dragged along behind it'. His distaste for Calvo Sotelo aside, José Antonio was prepared to let the Falange act as the instrument of the upper classes. As he said to Ridruejo, 'We are ready to take the risks (*dispuestos a poner las narices*), no? Well let them, at least, provide the money'.[91]

That the allegedly left-wing José Antonio sought money from bankers and industrialists is no more surprising than that the indisputably nationalist José Antonio accepted money from Mussolini. Both facts remind us of the reality so conveniently forgotten by Francoist apologists, that the exiguous scale of support enjoyed by the Falange in 1936 hardly boded well for its leader's chances of becoming a serious political option by legal means. It is worth remembering that, whereas the cerebral Azaña attracted hundreds of thousands of Spaniards to his meetings 'en campo abierto' during 1935, José Antonio never hypnotized a mass audience. Geisser Celesia complained of the 'scholastic and philosophical mentality' revealed in speeches by José Antonio that he regarded as 'more technical than political'.[92] His attractions were most intense in the salon and the *tertulia* rather than in the mass arena. This was reflected in his electoral fortunes. In the elections of 19 November 1933, when as a candidate for Cádiz as part of a broad right-wing platform, he had been elected with 18.5 per cent of the vote. In February 1936, he ran as an independent Falangist candidate and gained only 7,499 votes, 4.6 per cent of the total, while the conservative Ramón de Carranza of Renovación Española, gained 64,326 votes. The only other occasion when he gained sufficient votes for a parliamentary seat was also as part of a broad right-wing candidacy in the partial elections of Cuenca in May 1936, a seat he was prevented from occupying because of irregularities.

However, despite his failure in the February elections, the changed circumstances after the victory of the Popular Front saw things begin to go dramatically better for the Falange. Perhaps as many as 15,000 members of the CEDA youth movement, the Juventud de Acción Popular, swung over to FE y de las JONS.[93] Unfortunately, José Antonio Primo de Rivera was unable to capitalize on this change of conjuncture. Nevertheless, he took various other opportunities provided by his friend Ramón Serrano Suñer to make clear to senior military figures his interest in, and sympathy for, their conspiracy. He had an interview with General Mola, apparently to offer the services of the Falange. Earlier on the same day, 8 March, Mola had been designated 'El Director' of the projected military uprising by the principal conspirators, including General Franco. He also met Lieutenant Colonel Juan Yagüe, Mola's liaison with the linchpin of the rebellion, Spain's Moroccan Army.[94] The role of the Falange would be that of acts of terrorism to provoke left-wing reprisals, the two things combining to justify right-wing jeremiads about disorder. On 12 March, a three-man Falangist hit-squad, almost certainly acting with the knowledge of José Antonio, attempted to assassinate Luis Jiménez Asúa, a distinguished jurist and PSOE parliamentary deputy. Jiménez Asúa survived but his bodyguard was killed.[95] On 14 March, having been denied parliamentary immunity, José Antonio Primo de Rivera, together with other members of the senior leadership of FE de las JONS, was arrested on a technicality. In prison, he played centre-forward in the Falangist prisoners' football team,[96] but principally devoted his time to directing the Falangist strategy of tension. From prison, he was in touch with Carlists and with Renovación Española. As he told Antonio Goicoechea, prison did not stand in the way of his organization of the Falange's role in the preparations for civil war.[97] He remained in contact with Mola, offering him 4,000 men as a shock force.[98]

There were exceptions – in April, for instance, he prevented an assassination attempt against Largo Caballero in the hospital where he used to visit his dying wife.[99] In general, however, he was using the Falange in the role of street-fighting cannon-fodder so crucial to the political scenario of the military uprising. At the end of May 1936, he gave José Luis de Arrese responsibility for organizing the Falange in Granada. The three squads so organized played a crucial role in the repression in Granada.[100] Other subordinates of José Antonio were sent as emissaries to the provinces to organize co-ordination between the Falange and the military. José Sainz Nothnagel was active in New Castile, Zaragoza, Murcia, Albacete and Alicante. Manuel Hedilla was tireless in Santander and Galicia.[101] Rafael Garcerán was sent by José Antonio to Pamplona with a letter for General Mola containing details of the proposed participation of the Falange in the imminent rising.[102] In the meanwhile, however, Calvo Sotelo had emerged as the strong man of the Spanish Right which was, in any case, placing its hopes on a military coup.

Ironically, despite the efforts of Francoist propagandists to write a different story, his relationship with Franco, far from the cooperation of two heroes, was one of mutual contempt. What really put the seal on their antipathy was their involvement in the re-run elections in Cuenca in April 1936. After the Popular Front elections of 16 February 1936, the results had been declared null and void in certain provinces including Cuenca, where there had been falsification of votes. In the re-run elections scheduled for the beginning of May 1936, the united right-wing slate included both José Antonio Primo de Rivera and General Franco. The Falange leader was included in the hope of securing for him the parliamentary immunity which would ensure his release from jail where he had been since 17 March.[103] However, José Antonio Primo de Rivera made it known that he regarded the inclusion of Franco in the list as a 'crass error'. Believing that Franco would be a failure as a parliamentary orator, José Antonio said to Serrano Suñer: 'This is not what he's good at and, given that what is brewing is something more conclusive than a parliamentary offensive, let him stay in his territory and leave me where I have already proved myself'. In the event, the Cuenca election was declared at the last minute to be technically a re-run and, although José Antonio Primo de Rivera gained sufficient votes to win a seat, he was disqualified because he had not been a candidate in the original election.[104] However, Franco would never forgive the Falangist leader's part in what he regarded as a humiliation.[105]

If José Antonio Primo de Rivera had been freed from prison as a result of the Cuenca elections, we do not know how he would have behaved. His 'Carta á los Militares de España' of 4 May 1936 did little to suggest that he was a figure of either peace, reconciliation or progressive ideals: 'when that which is permanent is itself in danger, you no longer have any right to be neutral. The time has then come in which your arms have to come into play to save fundamental values'. This document was a logical sequel to José Antonio's advocacy of a military coup before the February elections itself the instinctive resort to family traditions. He always believed in the necessity of military assistance; his concern was only that the Falange not be submerged by reactionary army officers.[106] He was also worried about their determination, saying 'It is useless to rely on generals on active service. They are just mother-hens and Franco is the biggest mother-hen of the lot'.[107] On the other hand, his two circulars to the Jefes provinciales on 24 and 29 June 1936 indicated his worries that the Falange would be destroyed even by a successful military uprising.

The Falangist leader was transferred from Madrid to Alicante during the night of 5 June despite strenuous protests which he himself, in a letter to a female 'comrade', described as a 'biblical rage'.[108] There he was treated extremely well, receiving the press, vast quantities of correspondence and hundreds of visitors without any official interference until three weeks into the war. The CEDA deputy, his friend José Finat Escrivá de Romaní, the Conde de Mayalde, smuggled two pistols into his cell. Throughout June and the first half of July, he was able to play an active role in the preparation of the uprising sending Finat to Pamplona with an imperious letter telling Mola to make haste with the uprising. He sent instructions for Falangists in Madrid to take to the streets with the military rebels. Informed of the precise date of the uprising, he wrote a manifesto, dated 17 July 1936, in which he expressed the Falange's unreserved participation in the rebellion. He spent the days immediately before the outbreak of war tidying his voluminous papers clearly under the impression that the coup would be successful in Alicante and that he would soon be leaving the prison. Later on, at his trial, he was to deny that he had played any part in the preparation of the uprising.[109]

What he would have done about the behaviour of the Falange during the civil war can only be a matter for speculation. The scene narrated by Ridruejo sows doubts as to whether he would have objected to a greatly expanded Falange, flooded with newcomers, becoming one of the instruments of state terror which annihilated the Left in the nationalist zone. It does, however, seem reasonable to suppose that he would have regarded with disgust its subsequent incorporation into the Movimiento Nacional, Franco's bureaucratic claque. Moreover, it is difficult to believe that he would have approved of the way in which Falange Española, once converted into Falange Española Tradicionalista y de las JONS, deteriorated into a parasitical organization whose main function was to provide jobs in the Organización Sindical and elsewhere for its members. On the other hand, there is little evidence to support the belief that he could have done something to put a stop to the orgy of killing in which the Falange quickly became involved.

The idea that José Antonio was the great lost opportunity was based firstly on the fact that, in the prison in Alicante, he expressed an interest in reconciliation, secondly on a reasonable supposition that he could not have coexisted politically with Franco and finally on a much-exaggerated mutual sympathy between him and Prieto. On 9 August 1936, José Antonio Primo de Rivera wrote to the President of the Cortes, Diego Martínez Barrio, requesting an audience. Martínez Barrio sent an intermediary to whom José Antonio unsuccessfully pleaded to be sent to the Nationalist zone in order to work to bring an end to the war. He gave his word of honour that, if released for this mission, that he would return to prison, which was an implicit, if not cynical, recognition of the legitimacy of the Republic. Given the circumstances, the Republican authorities could not accept his offer. In any case, Martínez Barrio was convinced that a peace mission, even one consisting of the Jefe Nacional of the Falange, could have had little impact on the military rebels.[110]

It was presumably in the hope of sowing discord in the Francoist camp that Prieto sent copies of José Antonio's prison writings to his two executors (*albaceas*), Ramón Serrano Suñer and Raimundo Fernández Cuesta.[111] The alleged sympathy between Prieto and Primo de Rivera rested on only three flimsy premises. There had been their celebrated handshake in June 1934. The second connection was the fact that, in prison in Madrid, Primo de Rivera wrote an article in response to Prieto's famous speech on 2 May 1936, during the Cuenca election campaign. Then, in early August 1936, Prieto intervened to prevent José Antonio, his brother Miguel and his sister-in-law Margot being shot without trial by the revolutionary Comité de Orden Público in Alicante.

The article, entitled 'Prieto se acerca a la Falange' ('Prieto draws near to the Falange'), was published in the obscure Falangist journal *Aquí Estamos* in Palma de Mallorca on 23 May. Prieto did not see it until after José Antonio's death and, when finally he wrote a response in late December 1938, he protested that, far from 'drawing near to the Falange', he had said nothing that he had not been saying for the previous twenty-five years. However, Prieto was sufficiently moved by José Antonio's article to write 'Perhaps in Spain, we have not calmly compared ideologies to find out where they coincide, perhaps in the fundamentals, and measure the divergencies, probably secondary, with a view to finding out if these differences have to be resolved on the battlefield'.[112]

That Prieto himself might have considered that José Antonio could have been a serious inconvenience for Franco indicates why so little was done in Salamanca to facilitate attempts to save him from execution. Once he was dead, of course, Franco would not scruple to allow his death to be mythologized into martyrdom as a means of attracting supporters. The man who once declared that 'We want a happy and short-skirted Spain' ('Nosotros queremos una España alegre y faldicorta') was hardly likely to be to Franco's taste.[113] His execution was a gross political error on the part of the Republic.[114] Since he had been in jail since mid-March, four months before the military uprising, he was to an extent being tried for what it was assumed that he might have done had he been at liberty.

An escape bid or a prisoner exchange, although clearly hazardous, had not been entirely out of the question. Although ultimately rejected, the notion of an exchange of José Antonio for the son of the Republican Prime Minister Francisco Largo Caballero was mooted.[115] Several prominent Nationalists crossed the lines. José Antonio's close friend Raimundo Fernández Cuesta was officially exchanged for a minor Republican figure, Justino de Azcárate. His brother Miguel was exchanged for the son of the Republican General Miaja. Among the more significant escapees was José Antonio's other close friend, Ramón Serrano Suñer. Obviously, given the pre-eminence of José Antonio Primo de Rivera, his release or escape would be far from easy. Yet there were attempts to liberate him. The first had been the work of isolated groups of Falangists in Alicante. Then in early September, when the Germans had come to see the Falange as the Spanish component of a future world political order, more serious efforts were made, largely under the auspices of their Consul in Alicante, Hans Joachim von Knobloch. A band of Falangists led by José Antonio's cousin, the twenty-four-year-old Agustín Aznar arrived on a German torpedo boat on 17 September. However, their plans for a *coup de main* were changed into an attempt to get Primo de Rivera out by bribery which failed when Aznar was caught and only narrowly escaped himself. In October, von Knobloch and Aznar continued their efforts but came up against a less than enthusiastic backing from the newly elevated Head of State.[116]

This was hardly surprising. Franco needed the Falange both as a device for the political mobilization of the civilian population and as a way of creating a spurious identification with the ideals of his German and Italian allies. If the charismatic José Antonio Primo de Rivera were to have turned up at Salamanca, it would have made it significantly more difficult for Franco to have dominated and manipulated the Falange as he wished. It was certainly the case that José Antonio Primo de Rivera's disappointing encounters with Franco before the war, and his personal acquaintance with many generals, had left him cautious about too great a co-operation with the Army lest the Falange simply be used as cannon fodder and political trimming for the defence of the old order. He gave his last ever interview to the American journalist Jay Allen, on 3 October 1936 and it was published six days later in *The Chicago Daily Tribune*. The Falangist leader had spoken in terms of outrage because the defence of oligarchical interests had swamped his party's rhetorical ambitions for sweeping social change. He also told an incredulous Jay Allen that his responsibility for political violence in Madrid could not be proven.[117] The Nationalists 'will throw Spain into the abyss'. Even taking into account the possibility that José Antonio was exaggerating his revolutionary aims to curry favour with his jailers, the implied clash with the political plans of Franco was clear. Jay Allen found José Antonio's attitude anything but conciliatory and he terminated the interview 'because of the astounding indiscretions of Primo'.[118]

José Antonio Primo de Rivera was shot in Alicante prison on 20 November 1936. Eye-witness accounts testified that he died with courage and dignity.[119] The news of the execution reached Franco's headquarters, the *cuartel general*, shortly afterwards.[120] Franco would make full use of the propaganda opportunities thereby provided by the eternal absence of the hero who could not now be an awkward presence.[121] For two years, he chose, at least publicly, to refuse to believe that José Antonio was dead. The Falangist leader was more use 'alive' while the *Generalísimo* made his political arrangements. As long as the provisional leadership of the Falange entertained the hope that he might still be alive, they did nothing to create an alternative leadership. In Herbert Southworth's expressive theatrical metaphor, the stage properties, costumes, décor, scripts and *mise en scène* of FE y de las JONS were stolen to mask the doctrinal poverty of Francoism. Certain of Primo de Rivera's writings were suppressed and his designated successor, Manuel Hedilla, was imprisoned under sentence of death. Once the death was officially accepted, Franco used the cult of *el ausente* to take over the Falange.

The execution of José Antonio Primo de Rivera was a significant contribution to Franco's political security. Had he somehow reached Salamanca, it is possible that he would have worked to bring an early end to the carnage. The months in prison, conversations with his jailers, the bloodshed of the war and the looming shadow of his own execution had mellowed the violent figure of only eight months previously. He was open to the idea of national reconciliation in a way that Franco would never be. His testament included the phrase 'would that mine might be the last Spanish blood to be shed in civil strife' (*ojalá fuera mía la última sangre española que se vertiera en discordias civiles*).[122] In his last days in prison, José Antonio was sketching out the possible membership and policies of a government of 'national concord' whose first act was to have been a general amnesty. His attitude to Franco was revealed clearly in his comments on the implications of a military victory which he feared would merely consolidate the past. He saw such a victory as the triumph of 'a group of generals of depressing political mediocrity, committed to a series of political clichés, supported by old-style intransigent Carlism, the lazy and short-sighted conservative classes with their vested interests and agrarian and finance capitalism'.[123] On the other hand, at his trial, he refused to condemn the military for anything done since the uprising.[124]

Had José Antonio been saved, Franco's exploitation of the Falange as a ready-made political base would have been made significantly more difficult. What the role of his friend Serrano Suñer – Franco's principal political adviser – would have been if José Antonio had lived remains an interesting question. However, it takes far too much for granted simply to assume that Franco would not have disposed of Primo de Rivera in the same way as he was to dispose of so many rivals. As José Antonio himself said to Jay Allen 'I do know that if this movement does win and it turns out to be nothing but reaction, I'll withdraw my Phalanx and I'll ... I'll probably be back here in this or another prison in a very few months'.[125] None the less, the execution of José Antonio Primo de Rivera was a major political error for the Republic. The trial itself was not illegal. It was a court martial which had followed due process and, José Antonio Primo de Rivera, having been found guilty of military rebellion, was sentenced to death. The sentence went to the Supreme Court and was confirmed. However, he was executed before the cabinet had given final approval. The Republican prime minister, Francisco Largo Caballero, along with every member of his government, was outraged.[126]

José Antonio cannot be judged for what was done with his memory after his death. Even less can he be judged on the basis of what many of his followers did in the service of Franco. To paraphrase Herbert Southworth once more, 'they sold their shares in the ideals of Falange Española in return for lifetime pensions from Franquismo S.A.' The politics of Spain between 1937 and 1942 provide ample evidence that to think of José Antonio as the great lost opportunity is to underestimate the cunning and ruthlessness of Franco. In this sense, while the remarks of Prieto quoted earlier may be valid as an assessment of the humanity of José Antonio, they have to be seen in the light both of the political context in which they were written and of the enormous difficulties that José Antonio would have had if he had opposed Franco. The Falange which was spawned in the first months of the war owed little to José Antonio. In the eight months since his arrest, the caravan had moved on. It is impossible to know what authority he would have enjoyed among his erstwhile followers and, even if he did, whether Franco would have permitted him to exercise it.

Notes

1. M. García Venero, *Falange en la guerra de España: la Unificación y Hedilla* (Paris, 1967), 38; R. Serrano Suñer, *Entre Hendaya y Gibraltar* (Madrid, 1947), 365; idem, *Política de España 1936–1975* (Madrid, 1995), 81.
2. F. Bravo, *José Antonio: el hombre, el jefe, el camarada* (Madrid, 1939), 7.
3. Primo de Rivera to Julián Pemartín, 2 April 1933, in S. Dávila and J. Pemartín, *Hacia la historia de la Falange: primera contribución de Sevilla* (Jérez, 1938), 24–7.
4. R. Ledesma Ramos, *¿Fascismo en España?* (2nd edn., Barcelona, 1968), 178–9.
5. I. Prieto, *Convulsiones de España*, 3 vols (México DF, 1967–9) I, 127–33.
6. On the Falangist role in the repression, see García Venero, *Falange/Hedilla*, 227–37; H. R. Southworth, *Antifalange; estudio crítico de 'Falange en la guerra de España' de Maximiano García Venero* (Paris, 1967), 3–4; D. Ridruejo, *Escrito en España* (2nd edn., Buenos Aires, 1964), 83; A. Bahamonde y Sánchez de Castro, *Un año con Queipo* (Barcelona, n.d. [1938]), 89–136.
7. The most vivid short portrait of José Antonio Primo de Rivera is to be found in D. Ridruejo, *Casi unas memorias* (Barcelona, 1976), 53–62.

8   C. Bowers, *My Mission to Spain* (London, 1954), 28; H. Buckley, *Life and Death of the Spanish Republic* (London, 1940), 127.
9   A. del Río Cisneros (ed.), *Textos de doctrina política: Obras de José Antonio Primo de Rivera* (Madrid, 1966), 3–13. See also H. Thomas, 'The Hero in the Empty Room: José Antonio and Spanish Fascism' in *Journal of Contemporary History* Vol.1, No.1 (1966), 174–82.
10 Bravo, *José Antonio*, 76.
11 G. Jackson, *The Spanish Republic and the Civil War* (Princeton, 1965), 178–80; S. G. Payne, *Falange: A History of Spanish Fascism* (Stanford, 1961), 24–30; Thomas, 'Hero in the Empty Room', loc. cit. See also idem, introduction to *José Antonio Primo de Rivera: Selected Writings* (London, 1972), 11–16; and 'Spain' in S. J. Woolf (ed.), *European Fascism* (London, 1968), 289–96.
12 F. Ximénez de Sandoval, *'José Antonio' biografía* (2nd edn., Madrid, 1949), 41-2, 90; I. Gibson, *En busca de José Antonio* (Barcelona, 1980), 189–207; R. Fernández Cuesta, *Testimonio, recuerdos y reflexiones* (Madrid, 1985), 31; Southworth, *Antifalange*, 4; R. Garriga, *La España de Franco: Las relaciones con Hitler* (2nd edn., Puebla, México, 1970), 15–18; G. Cabanellas, *La guerra de los mil días* (2 vols., Buenos Aires, 1973), 166–7.
13 Ximénez de Sandoval, *'José Antonio'*, 15.
14 Interview with R. Serrano Suñer in *Dolor y memoria de España en el segundo aniversario de la muerte de José Antonio* (Barcelona, 1939), 224; Fernández Cuesta, *Testimonio*, 32; Gibson, *En busca de José Antonio*, 196–7.
15 Sainz Rodríguez, *Testimonio*, 222.
16 Gibson, *En busca de José Antonio*, 206.
17 Ximénez de Sandoval, *'José Antonio'*, 252–4.
18 Gibson, *En busca de José Antonio*, 201–2.
19 Most eloquently by M. Cantarero del Castillo, *Falange y socialismo* (Barcelona, 1973) which uses the writings of José Antonio Primo de Rivera to establish 'the socialist vocation of the Falange' (9), of 'the Falangist negation of the Right' (177–200), of 'Falangist revolutionism' (211–22), of 'the predominant leftism of the Falange' (237–51) and of the influence of Marx and Engels on José Antonio Primo de Rivera (254–6). See also M. Ramos González, *La violencia en Falange Española* (Oviedo, 1993), 19–58; C. Rojas, *Prieto y José Antonio: socialismo y Falange ante la tragedia civil* (Barcelona, 1977).
20 Ximénez de Sandoval, *'José Antonio'*, 12–13.
21 *F.E.*, 18 January, 22 February 1934; E. Vegas Latapie, *Memorias políticas: el suicido de la monarquía y la segunda República* (Barcelona, 1983), 194–6; Ximénez de Sandoval, *'José Antonio'*, 24.
22 Ibid., 23, 573; Southworth, *Antifalange*, 267–8; Ridruejo, *Memorias*, 54–5.
23 Ximénez de Sandoval, *'José Antonio'*, 92–108; P. Sainz Rodríguez,

Testimonio y recuerdos (Barcelona, 1978), 196; Bravo, José Antonio, 18–22; S. Ellwood, Prietas las filas. Historia de Falange Española, 1933–1983 (Barcelona, 1984), 22–5.

24 E. Giménez Caballero, España y Franco (Cegama, Guipúzcoa, 1938), 31.

25 I. Saz Campos, Mussolini contra la II República: hostilidad, conspiraciones, intervención (1931–1936) (Valencia, 1986), 97–101; M. Pastor, Los orígenes del fascismo en España (Madrid, 1975), 24–37; E. Selva Roca de Togores, 'Giménez Caballero en los orígenes ideológicos del fascismo español', Estudis d'Història Contemporània del País Valencià, No.9 (1991), 183–213.

26 For a list of his publications, see Dr Albiñana, Confinado en las Hurdes (una víctima de la Inquisición republicana (Madrid, 1933), 7–10. The manifesto of the PNE is printed in J. María Albiñana, Después de la dictadura: Los cuervos sobre la tumba (2nd edn., Madrid, 1930), 252–9. See also Saz, Mussolini contra la II República, 95–7; Pastor, Los orígenes, 38–61; Southworth, Antifalange, 29–30.

27 Ledesma Ramos, ¿Fascismo?, 77–81; T. Borrás, Ramiro Ledesma Ramos (Madrid, 1971), 216, 248–50; H. R. Southworth, 'The Falange: An Analysis of Spain's Fascist Heritage' in P. Preston (ed.), Spain in Crisis: The Evolution and Decline of the Franco Regime (Hassock, 1976), 6.

28 Onésimo Redondo Caudillo de Castilla (Valladolid, 1937), 18–37; Ledesma Ramos, ¿Fascismo?, 99; Payne, Falange, 15–18.

29 R. Guariglia, Ambasciata in Spagna e primi passi in diplomazia 1932–1934 (Naples, 1972), 288–9.

30 J. María Pemán, Mis encuentros con Franco (Barcelona, 1976), 14–16; R. Garriga, La Señora de El Pardo (Barcelona, 1979), 57–9; R. Serrano Suñer, Entre el silencio y la propaganda, la Historia como fue. Memorias (Barcelona, 1977), 54–6.

31 F.E., 22 February 1934; Ledesma Ramos, ¿Fascismo, 104–8; Guariglia to MAE, 24 febbraio 1933, in Guariglia, Ambasciata, 263–4; J. Aparicio, 'Mi recuerdo de José Antonio' in Dolor y memoria, 255–6; Ximénez de Sandoval, 'José Antonio', 124–6; A. Corniero Suárez, Diario de un rebelde (Madrid, 1991), 42; Saz, Mussolini contra la II República, 105–8; Gibson, En busca de José Antonio, 43–56.

32 F.E., 22 February 1934; Ximénez de Sandoval, 'Jose Antonio', 130–4; G. Montes Agudo, Pepe Sainz. Una vida en la Falange (n.p. [Barcelona?], n.d. [1939?]), 24–8; Gibson, En busca de José Antonio, 56–64.

33 Southworth, Antifalange, 15–19, 39–53; E. Giménez Caballero, Genio de España (Madrid, 1939), note to 276.

34 Southworth, Antifalange, 50; J. María de Areilza and F. María Castiella, Reivindicaciones de España (Madrid, 1941), 48–52.

35 Ximénez de Sandoval, 'José Antonio', 412.
36 On the antidemocratic and nationalistic tendencies of Ortega y Gasset, see A. Elorza, *La razón y la sombra: una lectura política de Ortega y Gasset* (Barcelona, 1984), 191–213; A. Dobson, *An Introduction to the Politics and Philosophy of José Ortega y Gasset* (Cambridge, 1989), 95–105. On *Frente Español*, see Elorza, *La razón*, 213–24.
37 J. Antonio Primo de Rivera, 'Homenaje y reproche a Don José Ortega y Gasset' in *Textos de doctrina política*, 745–9; 'El Gran Inquisidor', 'Autos de F.E.: Antifascistas en España Don José Ortega y Gasset' in *F.E.*, 7 December 1933, 12.
38 J. María de Areilza, *Así los he visto* (Barcelona, 1974), 92–4; Saz, *Mussolini contra la II República*, 109–12; Ledesma Ramos, *¿Fascismo?*, 122–3; Sainz Rodríguez, *Testimonio*, 220.
39 The only reliable contemporary report of this agreement is Guariglia to MAE, 1 settembre 1933, in Guariglia, *Ambasciata*, 304–5. There is confusion about the date of the agreement – see Saz, *Mussolini contra la segunda República*, 111–12, Sainz Rodríguez, *Testimonio*, 220–2; J. M. Gil Robles, *No fue posible la paz* (Barcelona, 1968), 442–3. There is also doubt as to whether the money was actually handed over, see J. A. Ansaldo, *¿Para qué...? (de Alfonso XIII a Juan III)* (Buenos Aires, 1951), 89.
40 Guariglia to MAE, 24 novembre 1933, Guariglia, *Ambasciata*, 323–4; Primo de Rivera, *Textos*, 53–5; R. Guariglia, *Ricordi 1922–1946* (Naples, 1949), 203–5; Saz, *Mussolini contra la II República*, 113–18.
41 Bravo, *José Antonio*, 68; Ximénez de Sandoval, *'José Antonio'*, 138.
42 Corniero, *Diario*, 47–9, 66–8.
43 J. A. Primo de Rivera, 'Discurso de la fundación de Falange Española' in *Textos*, 61–9.
44 Southworth, *Antifalange*, 27–9; Ximénez de Sandoval, *'José Antonio'*, 204–5, 210–12, 316–17, 358, 437–40.
45 Quoted by Gil Robles, *No fue posible la paz*, 436.
46 Undated letter of García Valdecasas to Sainz Rodríguez, in Sainz Rodríguez, *Testimonio*, 221; Ledesma Ramos, *¿Fascismo en España?*, 136–7.
47 Bravo, *José Antonio*, 31–2.
48 Saz, *Mussolini contra la segunda República*, 120–1.
49 Bravo, *José Antonio*, 64–6; Ximénez de Sandoval, *'José Antonio'*, 218–30; Payne, *Falange*, 46–7.
50 Southworth, 'The Falange', loc. cit., 6.
51 Ledesma Ramos, *¿Fascismo?*, 159–60, 164–5; Ximénez de Sandoval, *'José Antonio'*, 564–74.
52 A. Viñas, *La Alemania nazi y el 18 de julio* (Madrid, 1974), 155–60, 496–9; Ximénez de Sandoval, *'José Antonio'*, 288–91.

53 Saz, *Mussolini contra la II República*, 121–2; Guariglia to MAE, 20 marzo, 26 aprile 1934, Guariglia, *Ambasciata*, 349, 372.
54 Corniero, *Diario*, 72, 74. According to Ledesma Ramos, *¿Fascismo?*, 167–8, between May 1933 and the merger in February 1934, the JONS had 12,000 pesetas to cover all of its activities including propaganda and publications. The Falange had been significantly more prosperous having 150,000 pesetas at its disposal in the three months between its foundation and the fusion. After the merger, the monthly needs of the new party were 40,000 pesetas.
55 Corniero, *Diario*, 96; Ximénez de Sandoval, '*José Antonio*', 364, 369–70; Southworth, *Antifalange*, 81–2; Saz, *Mussolini contra la II República*, 122–3.
56 Ledesma Ramos, *¿Fascismo?*, 161–2, 169–71, 173–80; Ansaldo, *¿Para qué?*, 84–6; Bravo, *José Antonio*, 57; Ximénez de Sandoval, '*José Antonio*', 577–82; Ramos González, *La violencia*, 75–80.
57 *F.E.*, 12, 19 July 1934; Ledesma Ramos, *¿Fascismo?*, 186–7; Ansaldo, *¿Para qué?*, 86–7; Bravo, *José Antonio*, 58–9, 75; Payne, *Falange*, 59–61.
58 Alejandro Salazar, *Diario*, in Ibáñez Hernández, *Estudio y acción*, 34.
59 Gibson, *En busca de José Antonio*, 63, 208–9.
60 Primo de Rivera, *Textos*, 297–300; F. Franco Bahamonde, '*Apuntes' personales sobre la República y la guerra civil* (Madrid, 1987), 9.
61 G. Montes Agudo, *Vieja guardia* (Madrid, 1939), 217–36; Corniero, *Diario*, 87–8; Ledesma Ramos, *¿Fascismo?*, 188; Bravo, *José Antonio*, 78–81; R. Ibanez Hernández, *Estudio y acción: La Falange fundacional a la luz del Diario de Alejandro Suárez (1934–1936)* (Madrid, 1993), 65–8; M. Suárez Cortina, *El fascismo en Asturias (1931–1937)* (Gijón, 1981), 164–6.
62 Fernández Cuesta, *Testimonio*, 37; Corniero, *Diario*, 41, 93–4.
63 Saz, *Mussolini contra la II República*, 122.
64 García Venero, *Falange/Hedilla*, 52–6; Francisco Bravo, *Historia de la Falange* (2nd edn., Madrid, 1943), 77–80.
65 Ledesma Ramos, *¿Fascismo?*, 197–8; Bravo, *José Antonio*, 182–3; Southworth, *Antifalange*, 80–1.
66 Saz, *Mussolini contra la II República*, 123–4; Ibáñez Hernández, *Estudio y acción*, 74–5.
67 Bravo, *José Antonio*, 82–4; Ibáñez Hernández, *Estudio y acción*, 75–6.
68 'Las J.O.N.S. rompen con F.E. Manifiesto de las J.O.N.S.', *La Patria Libre*, No.1, 16 February 1935; undated letter of Ledesma Ramos to Francisco Bravo, in Bravo, *José Antonio*, 83; R. Ledesma Ramos, *Discurso a las juventudes de España* (2nd edn., Bilbao, 1938), 6; idem, *¿Fascismo en España?*, 200–2.
69 Ximénez de Sandoval, '*José Antonio*', 373–7; J. M. Sánchez Diana, *Ramiro Ledesma Ramos: biografía política* (Madrid, 1975),

210–13; Bravo, *José Antonio*, 82–4; Corniero, *Diario*, 102.
70 Fernández Cuesta, *Testimonio*, 44.
71 *Arriba*, 21 March 1935.
72 *La Patria Libre*, 2 March 1935.
73 *Arriba*, 11 April 1935; Corniero, *Diario*, 109; García Venero, *Falange/Hedilla*, 265–8.
74 Interview of the author with Serrano Suñer, Madrid, 1993. See also Serrano Suñer, *Política*, 34; Cortina, *El fascismo en Asturias*, 156–7.
75 Ledesma Ramos, *¿Fascismo?*, 199–200; Fernández Cuesta, *Testimonio*, 44.
76 Correspondence between Celso Luciano, Capo Gabinetto di S.E. il Ministro per la Stampa e la Propaganda, and Amadeo Landini, press attaché at the Italian Embassy in Paris, Archivio Centrale dello Stato, Ministero Cultura Popolare, Busta 170 bis, fasc.36. The pioneering account of this episode is by Viñas, *La Alemania nazi*, 152–5. The definitive version is by Saz, *Mussolini contra la II República*, 138–45. See also John F. Coverdale, *Italian Intervention in the Spanish Civil War* (Princeton, 1975), 57–8; Max Gallo, *Spain Under Franco: A History* (London, 1973), 48–9.
77 Bravo, *José Antonio*, 100–2.
78 Ibid., 159–65; Corniero, *Diario*, 120; Fernández Cuesta, *Testimonio*, 51–2; Montes Agudo, *Pepe Sainz*, 56–7; García Venero, *Falange/Hedilla*, 66; Ibáñez Hernández, *Estudio y acción*, 98–101. There has been speculation that generals such as Franco, Mola and Goded had been contacted – J. Arrarás, *Historia de la Cruzada española* (8 vols., 36 tomos, Madrid, 1939–43) II, 358–9. However, it is likely that the idea derived from a *post-factum* desire to stress the links between the Falange and the Army. The uprising was allegedly to have been started by Captain José Luna, Jefe Provincial of Cáceres, who was later to be involved in the violence at Begoña in 1942. See Gibson, *En busca de José Antonio*, 130–4.
79 Salazar, *Diario*, in Ibáñez Hernández, *Estudio y acción*, 36.
80 Antonio Cacho Zabalza, *La Unión Militar Española* (Alicante, 1940), 24–5.
81 Primo de Rivera, *Textos*, 567–70.
82 *Arriba*, 21 November 1935; Primo de Rivera, *Textos*, 705–22.
83 Southworth, *Antifalange*, 95.
84 Primo de Rivera, *Textos*, 651–9.
85 Primo de Rivera, 'A los maestros españoles', *Textos*, 815–16.
86 The versions of all the protagonists coincide in broad lines but differ in detail. For Moscardó's accounts, see García Venero, *Falange/Hedilla*, 66 and B. Gómez Oliveros, *General Moscardó* (Barcelona, 1956), 104. Fernández Cuesta's version appears in a letter to Felipe Ximénez de Sandoval, 9 February 1942, in Ximénez de Sandoval, *'José Antonio'*, 209–10, and Fernández Cuesta,

Testimonio, 52–3. See also Montes Agudo, *Pepe Sainz*, 57–62. There are excellent accounts in Southworth, *Antifalange*, 91–4, and Gibson, *En busca de José Antonio*, 136–141, which included testimonies from both Alfaro and Fernández Cuesta.
87 Franco, *Apuntes personales*, 21–2.
88 Serrano Suñer, *Memorias*, 56. As part of the political operation undertaken in 1937 to link the names of Franco and José Antonio, Arrarás gives a version of this interview, placing it in early March and portraying the two protagonists as decisive collaborators in the preparations for the rising, Joaquín Arrarás, *Franco* (7th edn., Valladolid, 1939), 228.
89 *Arriba*, 19 December 1935.
90 Gil Robles, *No fue posible la paz*, 444–6; Ximénez de Sandoval, '*José Antonio*', 624–6.
91 Ridruejo, *Memorias*, 60.
92 Saz, *Mussolini contra la segunda República*, 121.
93 Gil Robles, *No fue posible la paz*, 573–5, 688; Southworth, *Antifalange*, 113–17; Paul Preston, *The Coming of the Spanish Civil War: Reform, Reaction and Revolution in the Second Republic 1931–1936* (2nd edn., London, 1994), 256–7; Payne, *Falange*, 104–5; R. Valls, *La Derecha Regional: Valenciana 1930–1936* (Valencia, 1992), 227–31; Serrano Suñer, *Entre Hendaya y Gibraltar*, 25.
94 Interview with Ramón Serrano Suñer in *Dolor y memoria*, 204; B. Félix Maíz, *Mola, aquel hombre* (Barcelona, 1976), 206–7, 238. On the generals' meeting of 8 March, see Gil Robles, *No fue posible la paz*, 719–20; Arrarás, *Cruzada*, II, 467; B. Félix Maíz, *Alzamiento en España: de un diario de la conspiración* (2nd edn., Pamplona, 1952), 50–1; F. Bertrán Güell, *Preparación y desarrollo del alzamiento nacional* (Valladolid, 1939), 116.
95 Ximénez de Sandoval, '*José Antonio*', 706–8; Corniero, *Diario*, 150; Southworth, *Antifalange*, 95; J. Simeón Vidarte, *Todos fuimos culpables* (México DF, 1973), 66–7.
96 Fernández Cuesta, *Testimonio*, 59–62; Ximénez de Sandoval, '*José Antonio*', 709–10, 728.
97 Ibid., 733–4; Southworth, *Antifalange*, 101–2; Sainz Rodríguez, *Testimonio*, 222.
98 Arrarás, *Cruzada*, II, 511; Maíz, *Mola*, 158; García Venero, *Falange/Hedilla*, 197–8.
99 Bravo, *José Antonio*, 96–9; Corniero, *Diario*, 155.
100 Arrarás, *Cruzada*, III, 275; Southworth, *Antifalange*, 106.
101 Ibid., 108, 131–3; García Venero, *Falange/Hedilla*, 141; Montes Agudo, *Pepe Sainz*, 62–76.
102 Félix Maíz, *Alzamiento*, 129.
103 Gil Robles, *No fue posible la paz*, 561–2; M. García Venero, *El general Fanjul: Madrid en el alzamiento nacional* (Madrid, 1967),

208–12.
104 Gil Robles, *No fue posible la paz*, 563–72; García Venero, *Fanjul*, 226–8; Serrano Suñer, *Memorias*, 56–8.
105 See P. Preston, *Franco: A Biography* (London, 1993), 127–8; Franco, *Apuntes personales*, 34–5.
106 García Venero, *Falange/Hedilla*, 49; Southworth, *Antifalange*, 76.
107 Ansaldo, *¿Para qué?*, 121.
108 Reproduced in Bravo, *José Antonio*, 130.
109 Gibson, *En busca de José Antonio*, 149–59; Primo de Rivera, *Textos*, 951–2.
110 *Homenaje a Diego Martínez Barrio* (Paris, 1978), 185–9; Gibson, *En busca de José Antonio*, 250–3.
111 José Antonio Primo de Rivera's prison writings are reproduced by Prieto, *Convulsiones*, I, 137–44. A heavily censored version, which omits his projected government of conciliation, is reproduced in Primo de Rivera, *Textos*, 951–7.
112 Ibid., 933–8; Prieto, *Convulsiones*, I, 136–7.
113 Bravo, *José Antonio*, 104.
114 J. Zugazagoitia, *Guerra y vicisitudes de los españoles* (2 vols., Paris, 1968) I, 256–9.
115 Ibid., 176–7.
116 Ximénez de Sandoval, '*José Antonio*', 784–5; A. Viñas, *Guerra, dinero, dictadura: ayuda fascista y autarquía en la España de Franco* (Barcelona, 1984), 69–97; taped testimony of Hans Joachim von Knobloch to S. Ellwood; García Venero, *Falange/Hedilla*, 200–7.
117 *The News Chronicle*, 24 October 1936; Gibson, *En busca*, 161–70; Southworth, *Antifalange*, 144–8.
118 Claude G. Bowers to Acting Secretary of State, 20 November 1936, *Foreign Relations of the United States 1936*, II (Washington, 1954) 568.
119 See affidavit by a member of the firing squad reproduced in Southworth, *Antifalange*, 162–3.
120 García Venero, *Falange/Hedilla*, 255.
121 Southworth, *Antifalange*, 164–5.
122 Primo de Rivera, *Textos*, 955.
123 Facsimile of letter from José Antonio Primo de Rivera to Serrano Suñer and Fernández Cuesta, 19 November 1936, A. Alcázar de Velasco, *Serrano Suñer en la Falange* (Madrid/Barcelona, 1941), 166–7; Zugazagoitia, *Guerra*, I, 256–64; Prieto, *Convulsiones*, I, 130–53; Southworth, *Antifalange*, 203; Serrano Suñer, *Memorias*, 483–4.
124 Southworth, *Antifalange*, 148.
125 *News Chronicle*, 24 October 1936.
126 F. Largo Caballero, *Mis recuerdos* (Mexico D.F., 1954), 208–9.

~9~
'Primitive Rebels' in Spain: Historians and the Anarchist Phenomenon

EDDIE MAY

The aim of this chapter is to present an overview of the recent historical research on Spanish anarchism. In the process, I will outline the major themes arising from this body of research, which cumulatively call for a rethinking of traditional historical perspectives on Spanish anarchism and the anarchists.

In the immediate post-Second World War period historians generally, but more especially those on the Left, wrote from far more secure intellectual foundations than we do today. For British social democrats, the social and political situation was more promising than at any time since the heady days of 1919. The 'Forward March of Labour' in Britain, for example, had reached majority office and the post-war Labour government was busily – or so it seemed – placing the cornerstones of a new social order. For liberal historians, the ability of capitalism to compromise with the demands of social justice similarly rewarded their faith in their political beliefs. Likewise, Communist intellectuals in Europe found sustenance in the fact of 'actually existing communism' in the USSR and its east European satellites. As the Cold War acted to influence thinking and shape allegiances, it seemed that society was clearly on the march towards a future where liberalism and socialism would be able to keep in step with historical development, although not necessarily peacefully co-exist.[1]

It appeared that history had also made its judgement on those social and political movements that rejected both political liberalism and socialism. And there was a sense in which the Spanish anarchist movement was approached as a historical novelty or artefact of another, premodern world. Its rejection of the state and of centralized political authority and of the political party as the means of mobilizing social and political interests and capturing the state, appeared anachronistic in the age of the superpowers and the Cold War. Anarchism, because of its rejection of the key institutions and concepts of the modern era, was therefore considered by most commentators as clearly being a premodern movement, one that was ideologically and politically ill-equipped for survival in the contemporary world. Its vitality in 1930s Spain was thus viewed as the outcome of its implantation in a backward country, where economic, social and political developments had not kept pace with those of its northern European counterparts. In the light of such attitudes, it is not too surprising that the picture presented of Spanish anarchism as being the product of a premodern society, and hence antipathetic to the modernizing world of interwar Europe, gained general academic acceptance.[2]

By the 1960s and 1970s, however, the post-war foundations of the intellectual and political Left in Europe began to crumble. Within the Left there was a fundamental loss of confidence in the post-war trajectory taken by the majoritorian currents of social democracy and communism. Social democracy appeared to have reached the limits of reform and the reality of 'already existing communism' in eastern Europe and elsewhere had been exposed. A 'New Left' appeared, ready to rediscover the radical mainsprings of the European Left, which resulted in the recovery of marginalized alternative traditions within the pre-war Left. This coincided with, and fed into, new intellectual departures within the arts and social sciences. Social and oral history, labour history, women's history – 'history from below' – brought a new concern to study the 'losers' and the 'undifferentiated' masses beyond the formal leaders and institutional structures that were the concern of traditional history. In particular, feminist research challenged received wisdom and opened new avenues of research. In sum, the old certainties vanished and history became a more open and negotiable process. These new concerns and approaches renewed interest in dissident movements such as anarchism and syndicalism, and led to new departures in the study and assessment of such movements. In the process, previous views on Spanish anarchism began to be rethought. The remainder of this essay will deal with the fruits of this new research.

The 'Primitive Rebel' Paradigm

The two most influential works on Spanish anarchism by non-Spanish writers are those by Gerald Brenan and Eric Hobsbawm. Drawing heavily on the pioneering work of early Spanish observers such as Juan Díaz del Moral, these authors presented Spanish anarchism as essentially an irrational and millenarian form of primitive rebellion.[3] For Brenan, the *desamortización* (sale of Church lands) and the introduction of capitalist socio-economic relations had served to destabilize the traditional peasant lifestyle in southern Spain. As a result, the peasantry became alienated from both the Church and the landowner, and anarchism filled the resulting moral and political vacuum. Brenan wrote that anarchism was ideally suited to the Spanish national temperament, marked by its fierce independence, its individualism and its loyalty to the *patria chica*, and anarchism's popularity was largely 'moral-religious' in its appeal. With its promise of an imminent new world and the *reparto* (when land would be redistributed) and its unceasing preaching of hostility towards the priest and the landlord, anarchism articulated the peasants' sense of rejection and alienation from the modern world, giving them the hope of a better life that sustained them during the miserable present.[4]

Eric Hobsbawm was in agreement on the importance of the role of the introduction of capitalist socio-economic relations consequent upon the *desamortización* in explaining the growth of Andalusian anarchism. Hobsbawm, however, placed Spanish anarchism into a broader Marxist structuralist theory of social change and social protest.[5] He argued that forms of social protest are determined by the socio-economic structures of the society within which they operate. As capitalism developed, Hobsbawm argued that the changing modes of production produced more advanced forms of social organization and social protest. In other words, as capitalist society modernized so did the forms of protest that it engendered. Those workers engaged with the most progressive modes of production would accordingly adopt the most advanced modes of organization and ideology. Therefore in the early – craft and small workshop – stage of capitalist development, workers' movements exhibited 'primitive' characteristics of organization and ideology. They were spontaneous and pre-political protests, messianistic, with quasi-religious undercurrents, often led by charismatic figures, and were entirely appropriate to the general level of the development of the modes of production. Advanced capitalist societies, with more advanced modes of production, such as mass automated factory production, would produce more advanced forms of protest, such as the mass centralized and bureaucratic trade unions and socialist/social democratic political parties. These are organizations capable of formulating rational programmes and strategies based upon a full understanding of the complex reality of power and exploitation in advanced industrial nations. There were, therefore, ideologically and organizationally equipped to wage the class war in advanced capitalist societies.

In his comparative study of what he termed primitive rebellion, Hobsbawm focused on social and political protest movements in premodern and modernizing societies. Andalusian anarchism, Hobsbawm argued, was a good example of a premodern and primitive form of rebellion. The movement was characterized as being more a moral than a political revolt and Hobsbawm concluded that 'it is misleading to express the anarchists' aspirations in terms of a precise set of economic and political demands. They were for a new moral order.' It was this alleged vagueness – the absence from Andalusian anarchism of a political programme or organization, that marked the movement as millenarian. The Andalusian anarchist was a 'revolutionary in the most total sense conceivable to Andalusian peasants, condemning everything about the past. He was, in fact, a millenarian.' Accordingly, Andalusian anarchism generally, and specifically the anarchist insurrections of Jérez (1892) and Casas Viejas (1933), exhibited many of the features of primitive rebellion, he argued. Against the background of the most rudimentary and exploitative modes of production, workers' protest movements, illustrated by such events as Casas Viejas, were characterized by spontaneous outbursts of anger at deteriorating conditions, accompanied by millenarian expectations of immediate social transformation, and were led by charismatic anarchist leaders. The appeal of anarchism (a primitive form of protest because of its rejection of the need for centralized and bureaucratic union and political organization) to the Spanish peasantry was linked to the backward socio-economic situation in a premodern Spain. For Hobsbawm, therefore, millenarianism was the connecting link between the anarchism of the Andalusian peasants' movement and the 'social banditry' of men such as Francisco Sabaté Llopart in Francoist Spain. Indeed, the tragedy of the Spanish situation was that anarchism encouraged rather than resisted such primitive forms of protest and rebellion.[6]

The description of Andalusian anarchism as a premodern, millenarian movement of primitive rebellion formed the interpretative paradigm through which subsequent historians viewed the anarchist movement more generally. If historians differed on the exact causes of the strength of anarchism in Andalusia – some stressed the ignorance and poverty of the *braceros* (landless labourers) of the *latifundia* (the vast estates of the south, often owned by absentee landlords),[7] whilst others pointed to the premature implantation of liberal ideology within a society that lacked the level of economic and cultural development necessary to sustain it and meet the expectations it generated[8] – there was a consensus on the linkage between the socio-economic retardation of Spain and the rise of the anarchist movement. There was also general agreement on the nature of the praxis of the anarchist movement in southern Spain. Various authors stressed the 'quasi-religious' and 'naïvely millenary' character of a movement that eschewed anything more than a rudimentary organization and placed everything on the spontaneous realization of its aim of total social transformation, for which little more than propaganda was considered to be necessary. Complementing the 'social psychology' of the peasantry, the movement was characterized as one of short bursts of frantic enthusiasm followed by long sojourns of passive inactivity. The one sustaining thread being the missionary work of the *concientes obreros* (conscious workers).[9]

Descriptions of the movement and its tactics were similarly framed by the primitive rebel paradigm. Characterized as a morally austere movement, it was generally held that the anarchists eschewed all action not aimed at the final overthrow of the existing order, for which little more preparation than the spreading of the idea of revolution was deemed necessary. Motivated by the 'Idea', the anarchist movement apparently launched periodic attempts to inaugurate the millennium.[10]

The primitive rebel paradigm was also influential in analyses of the growth of the anarchist movement in Catalonia. The small scale of Catalan industry, it was argued, was particularly appropriate for a movement which stressed individualism and local organization above the collectivism and centralization typical of Spanish socialist organization to be found in the larger-scale, more developed and complex heavy industry of the Basque Country and Asturias. It was also considered significant that anarchism found its first recruits in the Catalan capital amongst migrants from Andalusia. The strength of anarchism in Catalonia was, therefore, linked to the backward nature of the Catalan economy and the presence of immigrants from Andalusia who translated their political traditions from a rural to an urban environment.[11]

It is in this vein that most historians interpreted anarchist policy during the Second Republic, and therefore Hobsbawm's portrayal and interpretation of the events at Casas Viejas in January 1933 found general acceptance. In January 1933 anarchist militants in Casas Viejas, believing themselves to be taking part in national insurrection, declared libertarian communism. In the ensuing gun battle with the civil guard several militants were killed in the home of a man known as Seisdedos and twelve more were subsequently rounded up and summarily executed by the republican police force known as the Assault Force. Hobsbawm's interpretation of the rising as a millenarian and spontaneous outburst of peasant anger, led by the charismatic local anarchist leader Seisdedos, became the standard description in subsequent histories of the Second Republic. For example, Raymond Carr wrote that, '... in Casas Viejas a local enthusiast staged one of those declarations of village independence characteristic of the millenarian tradition of rural anarchism'.[12] Paul Preston, in a similar vein, wrote that the rising was led by Seisdedos, and that in, 'a naïve millenarian fashion, he and his followers assumed that all the land would now automatically become communal'.[13]

The importance of Casas Viejas for the Second Republic is that it is generally accepted to have signalled the failure of the republic's land reform programme and the ending of the Socialist–Republican alliance on which the republic depended. It was thus a crucial event in the lead up to the outbreak of the civil war.[14] The role and policies of the anarchists during the Second Republic have traditionally been viewed as both a confirmation of the orthodoxy in relation to the origins and characteristics of the anarchist movement, and as a major destabilizing factor that undermined the positive, if cautious, attempt at democratic reform represented by the first governments of the Second Republic. In short, the anarchist movement, ideologically opposed to the republic and predestined to messianistic violence, launched a series of hopelessly naïve but destabilizing insurrections against a well-meaning and genuinely reforming administration, that achieved nothing but to exhaust both the republic and the anarchist movement itself.[15]

Rethinking Spanish Anarchism

Influenced by new approaches to the study of history researchers began to reconceptualize the methodological and interpretative bases of investigation into Spanish anarchism. In particular, researchers adopted a more cautious and critical approach to their use of official sources, conscious of the biases that official views of popular movements might contain. Indeed, historians of the European labour movements had began to question the usefulness of institutional approaches to the study of popular movements. Oral history offered one corrective, although there were limitations to its widespread use during the Francoist dictatorship.[16] Scholars also re-evaluated the orthodox explanations of the strength of anarchism in Spain, which appeared too determinist and schematic to account for the diversity of forms of organization and action that the anarchist movement took. This in turn has led to a re-examination of anarchist policy during the Second Republic, leading in turn to a reconsideration of the republic itself. The combined effect of this new research was to present new views of Spanish anarchism that decisively challenged the orthodox primitive rebel paradigm.[17]

Although criticisms of aspects of the primitive rebel thesis are long-standing, the intervention by Noam Chomsky is crucial to charting the rise of the revisionist critique of traditional views of Spanish anarchism. Chomsky's polemical article, published in 1969, was an influential critique of the methodology and analysis adopted by historians, particularly Gabriel Jackson, towards the anarchists. Chomsky argued that liberal and communist intellectuals adopted an élitist position when describing popular movements and mass participation in decision-making, emphasizing instead the necessity for supervision by those who possess knowledge and understanding. In short, Chomsky warned against the danger of academics adopting the attitudes of their own class in their analysis of popular movements such as Spanish anarchism.[18]

Chomsky's call for a reconsideration of the anarchist movement both influenced and came at the same moment when other historians began to review the traditional image of and explanations for Spanish anarchism. In a study of Catalan anarchosyndicalism, Joaquin Romero Maura cast doubt on the role of either ignorance or poverty in accounting for the strength of anarchism in Andalusia. He noted that neither were unique to that region, but neighbouring Estremadura, as impoverished structurally and socially as any province of Andalusia, was barren territory for the anarchist movement.[19] Other authors noted that the structure of property relations in Andalusia were not as uniform as the primitive rebel paradigm tended to suggest. *Latifundia* existed alongside other forms of landholding and usage and anarchism prospered in these regions also. Absentee landlordism or *latifundismo*, therefore, do not appear to be a necessary precondition or cause for the success of the anarchist movement in Andalusia. In his study of class relations in the Andalusian province of Córdoba, for example, Juan Martínez-Alier argued that the strength of anarchism in the province should not be explained in terms of the backwardness of the local economy. Agriculture in Córdoba was in the hands of a local bourgeoisie that was sufficiently knowledgeable and innovative to make the province known for the modernity and productivity of its agrarian sector. Martínez-Alier also questioned traditional descriptions of the Andalusian anarchist movement as being composed of almost servile peasants whose aspirations found outlet in periodic peasant *jacqueries*. Martínez-Alier noted that alongside the revolutionary tradition in Córdoba was a more reformist tendency in the workers' movement directed towards achieving higher wages and better working conditions. This tendency was increasingly evident from the turn of the twentieth century when the local peasants' movement more resembled the organizations of urban industrial workers in Spain than the primitive 'peasant revolutionary movements of the millenarian sort.' This was especially so during the *trienio bolchevique* of 1917–20 when most writers have suggested that anarchist millenarianism reappeared in southern Spain.[20] Martínez-Alier thus portrayed a rural workers' movement which, in seeking improvements in wages and conditions, pursued essentially rational and attainable goals. He emphasized the role of class consciousness, rather than the yearning for a return to a mythical pre-*desamortización* golden age, in explaining the strength of peasant anarchism in the province of Córdoba.[21]

Drawing upon these criticisms but pathbreaking in its own respect, Temma Kaplan's work on the anarchists of Jérez de la Frontera, in the province of Cadiz, one of the centres of anarchist support in Andalusia, pushed these criticisms forward. She rejected the idea that the anarchist movement in Andalusia could be characterized as a quasi-religious or millenarian protest. Andalusian anarchism, she argued, had a far wider class base than the primitive rebel paradigm suggested. In Jérez it was not the preserve of the classic landless labourers or *braceros* of the countryside, but included a broad range of social groups, including the proletarians, craftsmen and petit-producers of the local sherry industry. Nor was it primarily a movement of poverty and ignorance. Jérez was relatively prosperous and the anarchists sought to educate the local community. The local anarchist movement used a variety of populist appeals and strategies to mobilize this constituency in campaigns that had entirely rational conceptions of both the structures of exploitation and the mechanisms of oppression, and rationally conceived means and ends. Rather than violence being integral to southern anarchism, Kaplan argued that it was more often the response of the minority anarcho-communists to a State repression that labelled all resistance to the local élites as 'terrorism'. In contrast, the majority current of anarchocollectivism distanced itself from such violent action, and dedicated itself to building sustained labour and community based organizations with which to defend popular interests against encroachments by local élites. Kaplan concluded that the anarchists of Jérez were rational in terms of their understanding of their predicament and in their responses to it. It was the strength of anarchist organization rather than the millenarianism of the peasant community that was the key to the anarchists' mass mobilization, she concluded.[22]

From a similar perspective the most damaging critique of the old orthodoxy and methodology was made by Jerome Mintz in *The Anarchists of Casas Viejas*. Using oral history techniques in particular, Mintz reconstructed both the events of the Casas Viejas uprising of January 1933 itself, and more generally the sociology of Andalusian anarchism. Mintz directly challenged both the traditional view of the causes and events of January 1933 and the primitive rebel paradigm more generally. Mintz argued that the uprising at Casas Viejas was not an isolated, millenarian declaration of libertarian communism, led by the charismatic anarchist leader Seisdedos, of the traditional view. In fact, Seisdedos was not involved in the workers' movement and took no part in the uprising. Furthermore, the anarchists of Casas Viejas were participants in a botched national rising against the Second Republic rather than a spontaneous outburst of despair. Anarchism prospered in Andalusia, Mintz argued, not because of the millenarianism of the *braceros* but because it was adaptive to the aspirations and culture of the *braceros*.[23]

The work of these revisionist scholars has led to earlier interpretations being re-evaluated by some historians whose own work on Spanish anarchism fell within the primitive rebel paradigm. Raymond Carr, for example, conceded that,

> ... the observations in my own books on anarchist free love and vegetarianism are dismissed as the silly nonsense they are. Even the revered father of Andalusian agrarian social history, Díaz del Moral, takes a few hefty knocks for his bias in favour of the landlords and the vague racialism that attributes the sudden 'inexplicable' surges of peasant jacqueries – which can be explained by the rational aspirations of a depressed and repressed class – to Moorish blood.[24]

Kaplan and Mintz raised important questions about traditional interpretations of seminal events in the orthodox explanation of millenarian anarchism. The Jérez and Casas Viejas risings were initially both described by Hobsbawm as fitting in with the established pattern of revolutionary disturbances occurring when economic circumstances were at their most desperate, between January and March. Yet Kaplan and Mintz have shown that economic factors played little or no part in either rising. Jérez appears to have been an attempt to free imprisoned activists, whilst Casas Viejas was the response to a call for a nationwide revolutionary strike. With regard to the Jérez incident in particular, the research of Kaplan, and more recently George Esenwein, draws attention to the implications of the traditional methodological approach to the study of popular revolutionary movements. By relying almost entirely on official sources which labelled all anarchists as terrorists, in order to justify repression, historians have tended to reflect the 'official' view of events such as the Jérez uprising. Furthermore, by extrapolating from such specific events to generalized explanations of anarchism, it has been suggested that such histories have unconsciously replicated official perceptions of such popular movements.25

The structuralist explanation of the strength of Andalusian anarchism has also served to obscure the equally interesting and problematical question of the growth of the socialist movement in the rural south. If anarchism in Andalusia was the product of a distinct stage of historical development, then the penetration of socialism into anarchist strongholds would logically suggest that a new stage of historical development was underway. However, the research of Malefakis and Collier suggests otherwise. Socialism had failed to establish itself in the south until the dictatorship of Primo de Rivera allowed the socialist movement to take advantage of the repression of their anarchist rivals. The rapid growth of the socialist FNTT (Federación Nácional de Trabajadores de la Tierra) was the product of political rather than structural dynamics. With the declaration of the Second Republic and the promise of socialist-managed land reform, the FNTT expanded and quickly challenged the anarchists for dominance in traditional anarchist strongholds in southern Spain. Equally importantly, the southern rural socialists radicalized the Socialist Party (PSOE – Partido Socialista Obrero de España). The national leadership of the PSOE subsequently experienced great difficulty in containing the revolutionary impatience of the FNTT rank and file. In this respect, Collier's observation that the similarities rather than the differences between Andalusian anarchism and socialism are the more notable is significant.26

The revisionists have raised a number of important problems with the primitive rebel paradigm. Rural anarchism was not only, or even primarily, a movement of the most ignorant and impoverished rural proletariat. The work by Martínez-Alier, Kaplan and Mintz, among others, has emphasized the rationality of anarchist activity, with its emphasis on the building of permanent labour and community organizations through which to articulate and organize the interests and aspirations of rural workers. Their work has similarly challenged the tendency of the millenarian perspective, in a fashion that does more to mislead than illuminate, to extrapolate from the specific to the general.27

For the proponents of the view that Spanish anarchism was the product of a backward, underdeveloped society, the prevalence of anarchist strength in the most advanced regions of Spain is problematical and poses serious questions for the more determinist accounts of the development of labour organization and socialism in Europe. During the course of the first two decades of the twentieth century, Catalonia became the heartland of Spanish anarchism and eclipsed Andalusia in its importance. Unfortunately, general accounts of Spanish anarchism often failed to differentiate between rural and urban anarchism. Explanations originally conceived to account for the strength of rural anarchism tended to be applied to the qualitatively different setting of industrial Catalonia. Therefore, the strength of anarchism in Barcelona, in particular, was linked to the relatively backward and underdeveloped, small-scale, family owned structure of the production process of Catalan capitalism. Other contributory or causal factors included the general lack of political freedom and the pernicious influence of *caciquismo*, illiteracy, and the influx of Andalusian migrants into Barcelona who transmitted anarchism from a rural to an urban setting.

Familiarity with the industrial and social development of Catalonia illustrates the problems of the 'backwardness' thesis. Industrially, socially and culturally, the development of Catalonia was markedly different from that of Andalusia and most of Spain. Catalonia bore all the hallmarks of an advanced industrial society. Whereas Spain remained predominantly agrarian down to the 1930s, in Catalonia over 60 per cent of Catalan workers worked in industry, compared to only 27 per cent for Spain as a whole.[28] Socially and culturally Catalonia had experienced similar expansion and increasingly resembled the more advanced capitalist nations of Europe rather than the underdeveloped interior of Spain.[29] Politically too, Catalonia was the most advanced region of Spain.[30] In 1901, the Catalan regionalist movement, the Lliga Regionalista, successfully broke the mould of restoration politics and set out on the troubled road towards political autonomy from Madrid. Politics in Barcelona was subsequently noted for its degree of party representation and popular mobilization.[31] The success of Lerroux's Radical Republican Party in mobilizing working-class support in the first decade of the twentieth century should also caution us against interpreting the success of anarchism as being the product of the lack of conventional political freedom or the political corruption of the *turno pacífico*. Indeed, anarchism suffered more than most when constitutional guarantees were suspended.[32]

Accordingly several historians have questioned the argument that anarchism in Spain can be explained in terms of industrial backwardness or underdevelopment. As already noted, Catalonia was the most economically advanced region of Spain and this was the centre of anarchist strength.[33] Furthermore, anarchism was also to be found in the most advanced economic sectors of other regions. The CNT was thus able to penetrate those industries with the most advanced modes of production and subsequently a proletarianized (and therefore theoretically more socialist inclined) workforce, such as the coal miners of Asturias, the dockers in Gijón, the metal workers of Del Felguera, and the construction workers in Madrid.[34]

It is obvious that the structural explanations for the growth of Andalusian anarchism, which stress economic and social backwardness, are not applicable in the Catalan case. Recent research on other regions where the anarchist movement was strong lead to a similar conclusion. The Asturias is an area traditionally associated with the PSOE and its sister trade union federation, the UGT (Unión General de Trabajadores). By the turn of the present century, however, there was a significant anarchist presence in the region amongst the metal workers at La Felguera, the dockers at Gijón and later within mining workforce in the coalfield as well. In no respect were the Asturian anarchists comparable to the 'primitive rebels' of southern Spain, either in terms of their social and occupational origins or their praxis.[35] A similar picture emerges from two studies of the anarchist movement in Aragon. In this region it was the construction workers in Zaragossa, the fifth most important industrial region in Spain, who formed the backbone of what remained primarily an urban movement. The Aragonese CNT (the anarchosyndicalist trade union Confederación Nacional del Trabajo) would become second only to Catalonia in importance for the Spanish anarchist movement and the centre of the anarchist experiment in rural collectivization in the first years of the Spanish civil war. Both Casanova and Kelsey highlight political rather than structural factors in explaining the trajectory of the anarchist movement in Aragon. The intransigence of a local bourgeoisie assisted by a repressive state and the resulting intense polarization of local social relations, the greater vitality and acumen of local anarchist militants over their socialist counterparts, and the strength of *caciquismo* locally, which sapped the spirit of the political alternatives, are cited as reasons to explain the strength of the Aragonese anarchist movement.[36] The success of anarchist organization was not then necessarily, or even primarily, determined by the economic structure of a given region. And this conclusion accords with the findings of recent research on the labour movements in Europe which has cautioned against overemphasizing the relationship between social and economic structure and political and union affiliation.[37]

The CNT and the Second Republic

The traditional view of the relationship between the anarchist movement and the Second Republic emphasized the reforming potential of the Republic and the refusal of the anarchists to recognize that potential. With the leadership of the CNT usurped by the intransigent and ideologically driven fanatics of the FAI (Federación Anarquista Ibérica), the anarchist movement launched a series of hopeless revolutionary insurrections against the Republic, which discredited the government and helped drive the Right in Spain away from democracy. Recent scholarship on the anarchist movement during the Second Republic has questioned not just the orthodox presentation of the anarchists' response to the Republic but also the degree of the Republic's reforming achievement.

This view can be criticized for being ahistorical. The traditional viewpoint has a tendency to present the strategy and tactics of the anarchist movement as being largely static, of the movement being ideologically or psychologically constrained from evolving. One writer who has acknowledged the ability of the anarchist movement to evolve and mature is Robert Kern. Kern has argued that it was during the Second Republic that the anarchist movement came of age, advancing from what he describes as its previous form of primitive rebellion, directed largely against the monarchy and the Church, to develop new ideas and modernize itself, making a positive contribution to the debates on the future of Spain in the process.[38]

Nick Rider makes a similar point in his analysis of the FAI-led rent strike in Barcelona during 1931. Contrary to the view that the CNT only undertook explicitly revolutionary action which sought to provoke confrontation with the state as the prelude to social revolution, Rider argues that the FAI did not see the rent strike in these terms. Instead of responding imaginatively to what was commonly accepted was a major housing problem in the Catalan capital, however, the Republic resorted to a repressive 'law-and-order' approach that alienated the working class and illustrated the limits of reform. The response of the Republican state in Barcelona undermined the reformist elements within the CNT. Therefore, the anarchists' stance towards the Republic was thus less fixed or predetermined than the traditional viewpoint allows. The CNT was far more flexible and dynamic than originally conceived and it was the inability of the Republic to respond correspondingly that made confrontation inevitable.[39]

In a more ambitious critique, Graham Kelsey has similarly questioned the traditional description of the relationship between the CNT and the first administrations of the Second Republic. He questions both the extent to which the CNT in Aragon was ideology opposed to the Republic and the extent of the Republic's reformist and democratic commitment. The rapid expansion of the Aragonese CNT during the 1930s is presented as testimony not only of the extent of the social and economic problems confronting the masses but also of the anarchists' dynamic response to the challenge they presented. Far from adopting an ideologically based confrontational policy towards the new Republican regime, Kelsey has argued that the CNT in Aragon was 'neutral' to the regime and was increasingly moving towards a reformist stance. It was the inability of the Republic to respond in any other way but a repressive one towards the CNT's articulation of its members' grievances that halted and then reversed the reformist trajectory of the Aragonese CNT. It was this, rather than any predetermined ideological response or *faista* (member of the FAI) coup within the Aragonese CNT, that radicalized the anarchist masses in Aragon and made confrontation between the CNT and the Republican state possible.[40]

These studies present more open treatments of the anarchists during the Second Republic, ones that are more sensitive to the nuances of the experiences of the movement. The findings question traditional perspectives on both the relationship between the anarchist movement and the Second Republic and with regard to the nature of the Republic itself. Through their critical analysis of both the anarchist movement and the attitudes and actions of the authorities towards the anarchists, these historians have taken care to avoid replicating official views and descriptions of the movement.

Conclusion

With the decline of the postwar intellectual and political certainties the rediscovery of marginalized Left alternatives by those involved in the New Left and the 'New Social Movements' led to renewed interest not only in the Spanish anarchist movement itself but also in what were once considered to be the more 'exotic' aspects of the movement. Even after the formation of the CNT and its concentration on labour affairs, the Spanish anarchists never abandoned their wider societal approach to human emancipation.[41] This socio-cultural dimension of the movement and the radical social and political ideas generated by the anarchists (free love, criticism of the bourgeois family, concern for women's equality, participatory democracy, working-class self-education, ecology) particularly appealed to activists disillusioned with the conservatism and failure of traditional class organization in the West. The anarchist criticism of the bourgeois family and the emphasis on notions of sexual equality in anarchist propaganda attracted the attention of feminist scholars in particular. The founding of the *Mujeres Libres* ('Free Women') groups – the first of their kind in Spain – and the reforms instituted by the anarchist activist Frederica Montseny when minister of Health during the first year of the civil war, can be seen as testimony to the influence, and to the limits to that influence, that notions of sexual equality and women's emancipation had in the movement. The fact that women activists felt the need to establish the *Mujeres Libres* has led feminist historians to caution against presenting an overly optimistic account of the relationship between the anarchists and feminist ideas. Others have noted, however, that the anarchists' insistence on emancipation through participation and spontaneous intervention both precluded the provision of women's groups by organizations such as the CNT and formed a background against which women could organize. The very nature of anarchist organization, its fluidity, its organic links within the community, and its commitment to mass mobilization, created a favourable backdrop to such initiatives.[42]

This commitment to broader societal emancipation and the challenge it presented to the dominant culture is also important to an understanding of the anarchist movement and its relationship with the Spanish authorities. The questioning and flouting of traditional moral attitudes and practices arguably gave anarchism a means of influencing working-class culture and politics both beyond the formal confines of the organized labour movement and the confines of the dominant culture. It also opened the movement to new ideas, either political or from the avant-garde of the art world and elsewhere. The receptivity of the Spanish anarchists to the theories of French syndicalism in the decade after 1910 should caution against the view that the movement was static or timeless in terms of its thinking or strategy. Arguably the culturally dissident aspect of the movement served to isolate the anarchists and their working-class supporters from bourgeois society and so helped guard against reformism. This was reinforced by the reaction of middle-class Spaniards who linked anarchist praxis with criminality and threats to the social and moral fabric of Spanish society. This served to isolate the anarchist movement from bourgeois society and so helped guard against reformism. This is one factor, rather than the alleged millenarianism of the movement's constituency, which helps to explain the continuity and popular appeal of the movement's revolutionary commitment.[43]

In the early discussions of the Spanish anarchist movement there is an element to which a modern *leyenda negra* ('black legend') circumscribed analysis. Anglo-Saxon historians in particular thought in terms of the 'otherness' of Spain, and the anarchist movement was seen to epitomize that 'otherness'. Spanish development was considered to be different from that of mainstream Europe and there was an expectation that the Spanish would behave differently. The anarchist movement was evidence of both.

Research on Spanish anarchism has come a long way since the first generation of post-war historians began their work. Many of the earlier errors of fact and interpretation can be explained by the difficulty experienced by anyone attempting to research such a topic under Franco's dictatorship. Also, the approach and methodology of traditionalist history acted to replicate many of the 'official' attitudes and opinions towards anarchism. Yet also, we have to acknowledge that history says more of the period which the historian inhabits than it does of the subjects and period which s/he studies. With the collapse of Marxism and the intellectual certainties it provided, the study of popular movements has been liberated from often dogmatic schema that related political mobilization to socio-economic structure in a crude and inflexible fashion.[44] In fact, for Marxists there was a very good reason for rejecting such schema, since with the development of a post-fordist economy in Western Europe, the resulting socio-economic structure begins to look increasingly familiar to that which was once related to anarchism. According to structuralist theories, the future appears more anarchist than Marxist.

From today's perspective, with the diversification and globalization of the economy and the subsequent fragmentation of class structures, the anarchist method of organizing, which supplemented labour organizations with community structures in a more populist strategy, looks increasingly contemporary (see, for example, the anti-Poll Tax campaign in Britain). As do the more 'fanciful' concerns of the Spanish anarchists, with their emphasis on empowerment through participation and education, sexual equality and criticism of the bourgeois family, ecological considerations, and so on. Rather than being a premodern movement, Spanish anarchism looks premature. That the Spanish anarchists had one foot in the past is indisputable – we all do – but it also appears that they had one foot firmly moving forward to the future as well, which cannot be said for all movements once considered pristine models of modernity.

Notes

1 For an impressive history of this period, see E. Hobsbawm, *The Age of Extremes: The Short Twentieth Century 1914–1991* (London, 1994).
2 For an example, J. Joll, *The Anarchists* (London, 1979).
3 J. Díaz del Moral, *Historia de las agitaciones campesinas andaluzas* (Madrid, 1969).

4 G. Brenan, *The Spanish Labyrinth: An Account of the Social and Political Background of the Spanish Civil War* (Cambridge, 1943, second edn. 1990). See also Borkenau who saw anarchism as a religious movement which viewed the task of social transformation as a product of moral regeneration, F. Borkenau, *The Spanish Cockpit* (London, 1937, 1986), 21–4.
5 For an early application of such a Marxist model to Spanish anarchism, see H. Gannes and T. Repard, *Spain in Revolt: A History of the Civil War in Spain in 1936 and a Study of its Social, Political and Economic Causes* (London, 1936), 30.
6 E. Hobsbawm, *Primitive Rebels – Studies in Archaic Forms of Social Movement in the 19th and 20th Centuries* (Manchester, 1959, third edn. 1963), 80–4; idem, *Bandits* (Harmondsworth, 1969, second edn. 1972), 110–26; idem, *Revolutionaries* (London, 1973), 75; idem, 'Social Banditry', in H. Landsberger (ed.), *Rural Protest: Peasant Movements and Social Change* (1974), 142–57.
7 R. Herr, *An Historical Essay on Modern Spain* (Berkeley, 1977), 129.
8 S. Payne, *The Spanish Revolution* (London, 1970), 21–4.
9 Ibid., 31–4, 257; Herr, *Essay*, 129, 169; Borkenau, *Cockpit*, 21–4; A. Bar, *La CNT en los Años Rojos: del Sindicalismo Revolucionario al Anarcosindicalismo (1910–1926)* (Madrid, 1981), 14; W. Bernecker, 'The Strategies of "Direct Action" and Violence in Spanish Anarchism', in W. J. Mommsen and G. Hirschfeld (eds.), *Social Protest, Violence and Terror in Twentieth-Century Europe* (London, 1982), 88–111; R. Carr, *Spain 1808–1975* (Oxford, 1982), 420–44; G. Jackson, *The Spanish Republic and the Civil War 1931–1939* (Princeton, NJ, 1965), 19, 97; Joll, *Anarchists*, 12; G. Meaker, *The Revolutionary Left in Spain 1914–1923* (Stanford, 1974), 133–9. In their employment of religious imagery to describe and explain the anarchist movement, one is tempted to conclude that Anglo-Saxon historians used the symbolism of another example of the 'otherness' of Spanish society – its Catholicism – to comprehend anarchist 'otherness'. In this respect, if Spanish anarchism was 'Catholic', then Spanish socialism was more 'Protestant'. So pervasive has the primitive rebel paradigm been that even anarchist historians have succumbed: see M. Bookchin, *The Spanish Anarchists: The Heroic Years 1868–1936* (New York, 1977), 1-12; P. Marshall, *Demanding the Impossible: A History of Anarchism* (London, 1992), 453–5.
10 Carr, *Spain*, 420–44.
11 Ibid., 18, 31; J. Read, *The Catalans* (London, 1978), 173. Indeed, Gabriel Jackson argued that to understand the Catalan workers' movement it was first necessary to examine Andalusian anarchism, Jackson, op. cit., 19. For a recent expression of a similar viewpoint

see Antonio Bar's claim that the typical member of the anarchosyndicalist CNT was a semi-skilled manual worker employed in small- to medium-sized establishments, often with direct contact between worker and employer. His work environment was thus more personal and immediate than in the larger, more technically advanced factories where the UGT was more successful in organizing. Bar concludes that 'the real character of the CNT's membership is clearly revealed by the economic structure of those areas in the country in which the CNT was truly hegemonic', A. Bar, 'The CNT: The Glory and Tragedy of Spanish Anarchosyndicalism', in M. van der Linden and W. Thorpe (eds.), *Revolutionary Syndicalism: An International Perspective* (Aldershot, 1990), 135.

12 Carr, *Spain*, 625.
13 P. Preston, *The Coming of the Spanish Civil War* (London, 1978), 112.
14 E. Malefakis, *Agrarian Reform and Peasant Revolution in Spain: Origins of the Civil War* (New Haven, 1970), 305–6.
15 See variously, Brenan, Carr, Payne, Preston, Jackson, ops.cit.; H. Thomas, *The Spanish Civil War* (London, 1961, third edn. 1982).
16 R. Fraser, *Blood of Spain: The Experience of Civil War 1936–1939* (Harmondsworth, 1979, 1981).
17 For accessible reviews of recent research, W. Bernecker, 'Libertarian Communism and Social Revolution in the Spanish Civil War: The Collectivisation Movement 1936–1939: A Literature Report', *Iberian Studies* 9 No. 2 (1980), 43–53; P. Monteath, 'German Historiography and the Spanish Civil War: A Critical Survey', *European History Quarterly* 20 (1990), 255–83; J. Casanova, 'Anarchism, Revolution and Civil War in Spain: The Challenge of Social History', *International Review of Social History* 37 (1992), 398–404, and 'España, 1931–1939: República, protesta social y revolución', in J. Valdeón, (ed.), *Revueltas y Revoluciones en la Historia* (Salamanca, 1990), 135–50; M. Tuñón de Lara, 'Historia del Movimiento Obrero en España (un estado de la cuestion en los diez ultimos años)', in idem (ed.), *Historiografia Española Contemporanea* (Madrid, 1980), 231–50.
18 N. Chomsky, 'Objectivity and Liberal Scholarship', in J. Peck (ed.), *The Chomsky Reader* (New York, 1987), 83–120. The article was first published in N. Chomsky, *American Power and the New Mandarins* (New York, 1969).
19 J. Romero Maura, 'The Spanish Case', *Government and Opposition*, 5 No. 4 (1970), 456–79.
20 Indeed, Díaz del Moral studied Andalusian anarchism during the *trienio bolchevique*.
21 J. Martínez-Alier, *Labourers and Landowners in Southern Spain* (London, 1971), 289–98. For an illustration of the difficulties

presented to labour organization in the south by the attitude and actions of the Spanish state, see L. Gil Varón, 'Massacre and Cover-up: Río Tinto 1888', *Iberian Studies* 16 Nos. 1-2 (1987), 1-19.

22 T. Kaplan, 'The Social Base of Nineteenth Century Andalusian Anarchism in Jérez de la Frontera', *Journal of Interdisciplinary History* 6 No. 1 (1975), 47-70; Kaplan, *The Anarchists of Andalusia* (Princeton, NJ, 1977), 210-12. For other criticisms of the primitive rebel or millenarian thesis with regard to Andalusian anarchism, J. Martínez-Alier, 'Crítica de la interpretación del anarquismo como "Rebeldía primitiva"', in E. Sevilla Guzmán and K. Heisel (eds.), *Anarquismo y movimiento jornalero en Andalucia* (Córdoba, 1988), 169-73; J. Amsden, 'Spanish Anarchism and the Stages Theory of History', *Radical History Review* 6 (Fall 1978), 66-75; J. Casey, 'The Spanish Anarchist Peasant: How Primitive a Rebel?', *Journal of European Studies* 8 (1978), 34-43; C. Lida, *Anarquismo y Revolución en la España de XIX* (Madrid, 1972), 96; D. Castro Alfín, 'Anarquismo y jornaleros de la Andalucía del siglo XIX', in Sevilla Guzmán and Heisel, *Anarquismo*, 49-66. For a study that claims that the Andalusian anarchists displayed both rational and millenarian aspects, see J. R. Corbin, *The Anarchist Passion: Class Conflict in Southern Spain, 1810-1965* (Aldershot, 1993).

23 J. Mintz, *The Anarchists of Casas Viejas* (Chicago, 1982, 1994), 1-10. For a review of recent research on peasant movements, with particular reference to Spain, see J. Casanova, 'Sociedad rural, movimientos campesinos y colectivizaciones: reflexiones para un debate', in J. Casanova (ed.), *El Seño Igualitario: Campesinado y colectivizaciones en la España Republicana 1936-1939* (Zaragoza, 1988), 7-15.

24 R. Carr, 'Purity and Danger', *New York Review of Books* (23 September 1982), 54. See also Preston's recent revisions, in *The Coming of the Spanish Civil War* (London, second edn. 1994), 109.

25 G. Esenwein, *Anarchist Ideology and the Working Class Movement in Spain, 1868-1898* (Berkeley, 1989), 4, 174-84; Kaplan, 'The Social Base of Nineteenth Century Andalusian Anarchism', 48.

26 Malefakis, *Agrarian Reform*, passim; G. Collier, *Socialists of Rural Andalusia: Unacknowledged Revolutionaries of the Second Republic* (Stanford, 1987). Socialist organization and politics did not necessarily decisively affect the forms of action taken by the peasants in southern Spain. Peasants in the FNTT were not immune to taking spontaneous and relatively ill-organized action, as in the FNTT general strike of 1934. Malefakis notes (341) that little preparatory work had been undertaken by the union prior to the strike. See also Corbin, *Anarchist Passion*, 181.

27 For a recent criticism of such writers for a 'failure of objectivity', see M. G. Duncan, 'Spanish Anarchism Refracted: Theme and Image in

the Millenarian and Revisionist Literature', *Journal of Contemporary History* 23 (1988), 323–46.
28 J. Nadal, 'A Century of Industrialisation in Spain, 1833–1930', in N. Sánchez-Albornoz, (ed.), *The Economic Modernisation of Spain, 1830–1930* (New York, 1987), 63–74.
29 T. Kaplan, *Red City Blue Period: Social Movements in Picasso's Barcelona* (Oxford, 1992). With regard to the importance of illiteracy in explaining the appeal of anarchism, it would appear that illiteracy acted as a barrier to, rather than as a determinant of, union and political participation, M. Vilanova, 'Anarchism, Political Participation, and Illiteracy in Barcelona between 1934 and 1936', *American Historical Review* 97 No. 1 (1992), 96–120.
30 R. Kern, *Liberals, Reformers and Caciques in Restoration Spain 1875–1909* (Albuquerque, 1974), 29–30.
31 J. Harrison, 'The Regenerationist Movement in Spain after the Disaster of 1898', *European Studies Review* 9 (1979), 1–27.
32 Romero Maura, 'The Spanish Case', loc. cit., and, 'Terrorism in Barcelona and its impact on Spanish politics 1904–1909', *Past and Present* 41 (1968), 130–83; J. C. Ullman, *The Tragic Week* (Cambridge, Mass., 1968).
33 Romero Maura, 'The Spanish Case'.
34 A. Shubert, *The Road to Revolution in Spain: The Coal Miners of Asturias, 1860–1934* (Illinois, 1987), 115; idem, *A Social History of Modern Spain* (London, 1992), 133; P. Heywood, 'The Labour Movement in Spain before 1914', in D. Geary (ed.) *Labour and Socialist Movements Before 1914* (Oxford, 1989), 231–65.
35 A. Barrio Alonso, *Anarquismo y anarchosindicalismo en Asturias (1890–1936)* (Madrid, 1980), passim.
36 J. Casanova, *Anarquismo y revolución en la sociedad rural aragonesa 1936–1938* (Madrid, 1985), 1–25; G. Kelsey, *Anarchosyndicalism, Libertarian Communism and the State: The CNT in Zaragoza and Aragon, 1930–1937* (Amsterdam, 1992), 1–24.
37 Geary, *Labour and Socialist Movements*, passim.
38 R. Kern, *Red Years Black Years: A Political History of Spanish Anarchism, 1911–1937* (Philadelphia, 1978), 4–5.
39 N. Rider, 'The Practice of Direct Action: The Barcelona Rent Strike of 1931', in D. Goodway (ed.), *For Anarchism: History, Theory and Practice* (London, 1989), 79–105. For a discussion of anarchism and historical methodology, see Goodway's introduction to this collection.
40 'The rapidity with which this slide [to reformism] was first halted and then reversed is explained by and corresponds to the level of hostility displayed and repression employed by the first administrators of the Second Republic towards the country's anarchosyndicalist

organisation', Kelsey, *Anarchosyndicalism*, 2. See also Kelsey's essays, 'Anarchism in Aragon during the Second Republic', in M. Blinkhorn (ed.), *Spain in Conflict* (London, 1986), and 'Civil War and Civil Peace: Libertarian Aragon 1936–37', *The Anarchist Encyclopaedia*, Monograph 1 (November 1985).

41 A. Bar, 'The CNT: The Glory and Tragedy', 135–6.

42 M. Ackelsberg, '"Separate and Equal"? *Mujeres Libres* and Anarchist Strategy for Women's Emancipation', *Feminist Studies* 2 No. 1 (1985), 63–83; Ackelsberg, *Free Women of Spain: Anarchism and the Struggle for the Emancipation of Women* (Bloomington, 1991); T. Kaplan, 'Spanish Anarchism and Women's Liberation', *Journal of Contemporary History* 6 No. 2 (1971), 101–10; Kaplan, 'Other Scenarios: Women and Spanish Anarchism', in R. Bridenthal and C. Koonz (eds.), *Becoming Visible: Women in European History* (Boston, 1977), 400–21; A. Morcillo Gómez, '218 Feminismo y Lucha Política durante la II República y la Guerra Civil', in P. Folguera (ed.), *El Feminismo en España: Dos Siglos de Historia* (Madrid, 1988), 57–83.

43 Kaplan has recently examined the relationship between the anarchist movement and avant-garde artistic and cultural trends in Barcelona; see *Red City Blue Period*. For middle-class moral panics and resulting views of the anarchist movement, see C. Ealham, 'Crime and Punishment in 1930s Barcelona', *History Today* 43 (October 1993), 31–7; idem, 'Anarchism and Illegality in Barcelona, 1931–7', *Contemporary European History* 4 No. 2 (1995), 133–51; Sharif Gemie, 'Counter-Community: An Aspect of Anarchist Political Culture', *Journal of Contemporary History* 29 (1994), 349–67.

44 For an interesting discussion of the relationship between social structure and social and political change in the British case, see R. Price, *Labour In British Society* (London, 1986), ch. 1.

~10~
Harry Hearder: An Appreciation

DAVID BATES

(with additions by NICK CARTER and
ROBERT STRADLING)

This collection of essays was first projected some years ago and designed by friends and colleagues as an affectionate tribute to Harry Hearder. As is often the case with such enterprises, it was often delayed and waylaid; many and various were the vicissitudes encountered and the metamorphoses necessary to negotiate them. At first we struggled to conceal our plans from their object himself, hoping to enhance his eventual delight with the element of genuine surprise. This was perhaps an unrealistic, even misguided, aim. In the event (as the reader will discover below) it was Harry who sprang a surprise on the rest of us. At any rate, the onset of the final stages of his illness decided us to apprise him of the project, and we are content that, although he was never to see it in fully realized form, in the last year of his life, Harry derived some inner comfort from his awareness of the existence and progress of 'his' book. All those concerned offer it now to his memory not just as a set of essays on the themes of democracy and nationalism, but also as a reflection of values which were central to Harry's personal beliefs and the way he treated people, and also in grateful thanks for his example, encouragement and friendship over the years.

A native of Devon, Harry Hearder served in Italy in the later years of the Second World War. He took his first degree at the (then) University College of the South West at Exeter, and completed a doctorate at the London School of Economics in 1954. His academic career was spent in the employ, firstly of the LSE and secondly as Professor of Modern History at University College, Cardiff from 1967. Officially he retired in 1987, but he continued to teach in Cardiff on a part-time basis until 1993, offering his special subject on the Unification of Italy and a survey course of nineteenth- and twentieth-century European history. He never lost his affection for and contacts with the LSE, and this part of his life is given proper testament in these pages. But it was during his years in Cardiff that Harry came into contact with the majority of the contributors, either as departmental colleagues or undergraduates.

Harry joined what was in the 1960s a distinguished but rather undersized History Department which had established a solid reputation under the headship of the late Professor S. B. Chrimes. Its strengths were in the medieval period and in conventional areas of later British History. European History did not enjoy a striking level of commitment in terms of the curriculum or of research interests. Harry soon altered this profile. His initial impact, both intellectually and socially, is well remembered by many. His utterly ingenuous charm and generous sociability did much to foster a lively academic environment and the parties thrown by he and Anna were a byword across many disciplinary divides in the College. Extraordinarily kind, and always encouraging in the teaching environment, he was an inspiration and guide to generations of students. For the ablest he was a source of ideas shared freely with none of the temporal limitations to which undergraduates are now inured. On behalf of the more pedestrian he exercised his remarkable gift to build morale, seeking to develop their sensibilities to concept, issue and debate. No one had a keener belief that history happens in the seminar room as much as in the lecture theatre or in the pages of published texts. Set against the quality-dominated rigidities of the 1990s Harry's methods might now seem a little unorthodox, but in retrospect they represented all that was best in the liberal traditions of British higher education down to the 1970s.

In teaching, Harry was also positively inclined to the practice – then virtually the norm in university departments – of pursuing a range of thematic interests. It represented a highly effective prophylactic against the potential dangers of overspecialization: one increasingly discarded under the research pressures with which we are now so familiar, but which many are now rightly anxious to re-instate. Although he was uncharacteristically jealous of his constitutional title of 'Professor of Modern History'

– a description not to be understood in the Oxbridge sense – for many years Harry taught a popular option on 'The Italian Renaissance' in addition to his more contemporary courses. He was perhaps not one of the world's great lecturers when it came to heavily-subscribed 'run-through' courses. But unlike many who enjoy such a reputation, he was approachable and always helpful. He possessed a gentle but at the same time, deceptively subversive, sense of humour which undergraduates loved. They also appreciated his willingness to get involved in the social side of university life. Amongst other things, Harry played in staff vs. students cricket matches, he got involved in Lucky Jim-style escapades at conferences, and he ran annual historical-cum-social trips to Rome in which he acted as an expert courier. Just as important to the students was the fact that Harry genuinely cared about them. He always attended graduation ceremonies to chat to mums and dads, reassuring them about their child's abilities and experiences, and was known to provide flattering job references in which (so some colleagues avow!) the subjects concerned would have had difficulty in recognizing themselves.

He was a superb research supervisor. Despite the very good impression he gave of an absent-minded professor, he never missed a meeting, and was always ready to discuss and initiate progress. He gave early and invaluable advice regarding what to read, who to talk to, where and how to research. In the writing process which so many find agonizing, Harry's editorial skills were greatly appreciated – as was the speed with which he read and commented upon draft chapters (usually within a few days of receiving them).

But Harry's activities were never confined within the universities he served. A long-standing member of the Labour party and of the United Nations Association, he worked prodigiously for both causes. At the heart of his commitment was an opposition to oppression and tyranny, a belief that human life was valuable and that its condition could and should be constantly improved. As academic and writer he joyfully accepted that his responsibilities extended to the wider communication of his subject and sought to make his own and others' work accessible to a range of reader-groups. His best publications were general textbooks, exemplified in his often reissued *History of Europe 1840–80* and his more recent *History of Italy*. Yet he always pursued fresh research. It was typical of his self-effacing nature that (in the surprise referred to above) he left a new scholarly article, the existence of which seems to have been unsuspected by his friends and family, to be revealed posthumously in the pages of the *International History Review*. Through two successful series for Longman, and via his work at national level in the Royal Historical Society and the Historical Association, he sought to stimulate and enable the writings of others – usually, though with some notable exceptions – drawn from the younger generations of scholarship.

Harry always saw the positive in people – even if he was aware of their failings. A sentence from his last historical study – a biography of Cavour – illustrates this very nicely. Harry wrote of Cavour: 'His virtues, like his vices, were essentially human ones. It is this which makes a study of his life, his career, his beliefs and his motives, such an agreeable one.' Over twenty years ago Harry co-edited a *festschrift* for his boss, Stanley Chrimes, who was retiring. In a fascinating essay which he contributed to the volume, he carefully examined King George V's exercise of his key constitutional responsibilities in the two crises of 1926 and 1931. Personally an opponent of monarchy in any guise, it was no sense of deference to the different opinion held by the volume's dedicatee that drew Harry to conclude in favour of the king's comportment. He attributed George V's success in avoiding political partisanship to 'a simple and almost boyish sense of fair play'. Considered reflexively, these words explain not only Harry's particular historical judgement but also his character and activity in general. In sum, Harry Hearder's life enriched humanity, the humanities, and many humans: into the bargain, he did not neglect to enjoy it himself.

INDEX

Abraham, William, MP ('Mabon'), 14, 108, 111, 116, 117, 118–20, 123
Alabama dispute, 71, 82 fn. 11
Albinana, Dr Jose Maria, pro-Nazi Spanish conservative, 164–5
Alcala-Zamora, Niceto, first President of the Spanish Republic, 139, 140
Alexander II, Tsar, 56, 70
anarchism, 15–16, ch. 9 *passim*
Andalusia, 198–200, 201, 203–6, 208
Ansaldo, Juan Antonio, 172–3
Ashley, W. J., 98, 100
Austria, 49, 50, 51, 53–5, 56, 58–62
Azaña, Manuel, Spanish Republican politician, 10, 14–15, ch.7 *passim*, 180

Beethoven, Ludwig van, 18 fn. 19, 19, 21, 23, 25, 29, 30–2, 35, 36
Fidelio, 25, 30
Bentham, Jeremy, 73, 74
Berlioz, Hector, 38–9
Birmingham (UK), 92, 93, 102
Brace, William, MP, 108, 112, 119
Brenan, Gerald, 135, 198
The Spanish Labyrinth, 135, 152 fn. 8
Britain, 7, ch. 3 *passim*, 67, 68, 71, 74, 81, 93–105, 167, 177
Butterfield, Herbert, 8–9; *see also* Whig interpretation of History.

Caballero, Ernesto Gimenez, Spanish surrealist and

Falangist, 164, 165, 166, 167, 170
Casas Viejas rising (1933), 136, 140–1, 199, 201, 204–5
Catalonia, 140, 173, 200–1, 203, 207–9
Cavour, Camillo Benso di, prime minister of Piedmont from 1852, 12, 52–4, 55–8, 60–3, 222
CEDA, Spanish Catholic anti–Republican, authoritarian party, 170, 171, 177, 183
youth movement backs FE da las JONS, 180
Chamberlain, Joseph, British radical and Liberal Unionist politician, 12–13, 15, ch.5 *passim*
'Unauthorised Programme', 92–3
Charles X, King of France, 21, 33
Chomsky, Noam, 202–3
City of London, 85–6, 87–8, 90, 91, 94, 96, 102
Clarendon, Lord, British Foreign Secretary 1855–8, 52–3, 56
Cobden, Richard, 75, 91–2
Cold War, 3–4, 196, 197
Confederacion Nacional del Trabajo (CNT), 140, 208, 209–11
Conservative Party (British), 12, 93–6
Cowley, Lord, British ambassador to Paris 1858–9, 57, 58–61, 62–3
Cymru Fydd ('Young Wales' movement), 13–14, 107, 117–25

Eliseda, Marquis de La (Francisco Moreno y Herrera), temporary

financial backer of the Falange, 170–1
European Community, 3–7
European Union, 3, 6, 18 fn. 19
Evans, Isaac, 119, 120

Falange, ch.8 passim
Falange Espanol,
  formation of, 167, 168–71
  links up with JONS, 1701
  FE de las JONS 171–2, 174–5, 180, 181, 183, 186
fascism, 15, 103, 159, 165, 166–7, 169–70, 175
Ferdinand I, King of the Two Sicilies, 21, 26
France, 6, 7, 10–11, 22, 23, 36, 37, 49–51, 52, 53–4, 56, 57–8, 60–3, 67–8, 75, 77, 81, 167, 173; see also Louis Napoleon
Franco, General Francisco 134, 136, 142, 147, 150, 158 fn. 7, 159–61, 164, 165, 166, 173, 178–9, 182–3, 184–8
French Revolution, 11, 49, 138–9

Garcia Valdecasas, 167, 169
Germany, 6, 19, 20–1, 24, 25, 26–38, 40, 41, 43, 68–9, 72, 76, 77, 78–9, 87, 98, 99, 100, 166, 170, 171, 185
Gil Robles, Jose Maria, Spanish Catholic and conservative politician, 177, 179
Gladstone, William Ewart, British Liberal Prime Minister, 51, 93
Guarigha, Raffaele, pro-Falange Italian Ambassador to Spain in 1934, 168, 171

Halliday, Thomas, South Wales working-class politician, 114–15, 116, 117–18
Hague Peace Conferences (1899 and 1907), 76–7
Hewins, W. A. S., 98–100
Hitler, Adolf, 11, 161, 166, 171
Hobsbawm, Eric, 198–200
Hudson, British minister at Turin 1858–9, 52, 59, 63

International Postal Union, 69–70
International Telegraphic Union, 69–70
Italy, 4, 7, 11–12, 19, 22, 27, 28, 39–40, 43–4, ch. 3 passim, 168–9, 170, 175–6, 177, 185; see also Piedmont.

Jerez insurrection (1892), 199, 205–6

Kaplan, Temma, 204, 205, 206
Keynesianism, 5, 7, 102
Koestler, Arthur, 8, 9, 11, 14
  The God that Failed, 9, 17 fn. 15

Labour Party (British), 102–3, ch. 6 passim, 196
Largo Caballero, Francisco, Spanish Republican Prime Minister 1936–7, 181, 185, 187
Las Juntas de Ofensiva Nacional–Sindicalista (JONS), 165, 167, 168, 170–1, 174–5, 180–1
Lloyd George, David, Welsh Liberal politician, 117, 120–4
Liberal Party (British), 12, 92, 102, ch. 6 passim
Liberal Unionists 12, 93, 94–5
Lizst, Franz, 35–6
Louis Napoleon, from 1852 Napoleon III, Emperor, 50, 54, 56–60, 63

Malmesbury, Lord, British Foreign Secretary 1858–9, ch.3 passim
Martinez-Alier, Juan, 203–4, 206
Martinez Barrio, Diego, President of the Cortes, 183–4
Marxism 148, 213
Mazzini, Giuseppe, Italian revolutionary nationalist, 12, 39–40, 49, 51
Metternich, Klemens von, Prince, 21, 24, 29, 43, 50
Mill, John Stuart, 97–8
  Principles of Political Economy and Taxation, 97–8
Mintz, Jerome, 204–5, 206

Index

Mola, General, Spanish anti-Republican, 180, 181
Moltke, Helmuth von, Count, 79–80
Mosley, Sir Oswald, 10, 102–3
Mozart, Wolfgang Amadeus, 24–5, 26
Mussolini, Benito, 161, 168–9, 175–6, 179; see also fascism, Italy

Napoleon I, Emperor, 11, 19, 26, 70, 143
National Fair Trade League, 87–8
Nazism, 3, 5, 164, 171, 175
Nicholas II, Tsar, 76–7
Nietzsche, Friedrich, 9–10, 138, 148

Ortega y Gasset, Jose, 142, 143, 144, 147–8, 166, 167
Agrupacion de la Republica and, 144, 167
Orwell, George, 8–11, 14, 15
Nineteen Eighty-Four, 9–10, 150

Palmerston, Henry J. T., Lord, 50–3, 55, 56
Partido Socialista Obrero de Espana (PSOE), 140, 206, 208
Piedmont, 49, 51, 52–3, 55, 56, 58, 60–2
Prieto, Indalecio, Spanish socialist politician, 160–1, 162, 184–5, 188
Primo de Rivera, Jose, Spanish Falange leader, 15, ch. 8 *passim*
Primo de Rivera, General Miguel, Spanish dictator 1923–30, 143, 155 fn. 42, 161, 162, 164

Ramos, Ramiro Ledesma, Spanish Falangist, 160, 164, 168, 170, 171, 173, 174–5
Ricardo, David, 86–7, 97
Principles of Political Economy and Taxation, 86–7
Richards, Thomas, MP, 108, 12, 113, 116

Rossini, Gioacchino, 11–12, ch.2 *passim*
Barber of Seville, The 20, 23–4, 44
Stabat Mater, 37–8
Ruiz de Alda, Julio, Spanish aviator and Falangist, 168, 170, 174
Russia, 7, 56, 68, 70, 76

Salisbury, Robert Gascoyne-Cecil, 3rd marquis of, British Conservative Prime Minister 1895–1902, 92, 94
Schindler, Anton, 36–7
Smith, Adam, 97–8
Social Darwinism, 80–1
Sotelo, Jose Calvo, Spanish conservative politician, 163, 178, 179, 181
Southworth, Herbert, 167, 186, 188
Soviet Union 3, 5, 11, 177, 196
Schumann, Robert, 33–5
Spain, 8, 10, 14–16, chs. 7–9 *passim*
Suner, Ramon Serrano, Spanish Falangist and advisor to Franco, 175, 178, 180, 182, 185, 187

Tariff Reform 12, 13, 84, 90, 94–103
Tariff Reform League, 95, 99, 100, 101
Thomas, D. A., south Wales coalowner and opponent of Cymru Fydd, 121–2, 123, 124
Treasury, H. M. 94, 95
Treaty of Rome, 5, 6

Union General del Trabajores (UGT), 140, 208
United States of America, 71, 72, 73, 74, 76, 87, 99, 100, 101

Victoria, Queen, 55, 59

Wagner, Richard, 29, 37–8, 41–3
Lohengrin, 38, 41
Wales, 13–14, ch. 6 *passim*; see also Cymru Fydd

Weber, Carl Maria von, 21–4, 27–8,
    30–1, 40, 41
  Der Freischutz, 27–9
  Euryanthe, 30–1
Weber, Max Maria von, 28, 29, 30,
    42

Williams, John, M P , 108, 112, 119
Whig interpretation of history, 3–4,
    8–9, 11

Subscribers to this Volume

Matthew Anderson, London
Robin Attfield, Cardiff
Pat and Toby Barrett, Hereford
David Bates, Glasgow
Derek Beales, Cambridge
Andrew Belsey, Cardiff
J. M. Bourne, Birmingham
F. R. Bridge, Leeds
Nick Carter, Leicester
Julia Cornelius, London
Emma Cownie, London
Steve Davis, South Cave, E. Yorks
D. Dilks, Cottingham
Michael Lawrence Dochrill, Cheam
E. W. Edwards, Cardiff
Robert Evans, Oxford
William J. Fishman, Harrow
David Gillard, Melrose
George Gillespie, Cardiff
Richard Griffiths, Reading
Lin Howells, Cardiff
Meirion Hughes, Cardiff
Anthony M. Johnson, Cardiff
J. Gwynfor Jones, Cardiff
Robert J. Knecht, Birmingham
Clive H. Knowles, Cardiff

Subscribers

John Law, Swansea
Peter Lowe, Manchester
H. R. Loyn, Cardiff
J. R. Mac Cormack, Halifax, Nova Scotia
Andrew MacLennan, Harlow
Eddie May, Leicester
Scott Newton, Cardiff
Jonathan Osmond, Cardiff
Robert Oresko, London
F. V. Parsons, Glasgow
Paul Preston, London
John Percival, Cardiff
Gwynedd O. Pierce, Cardiff
Brian Holden Reid, London
Maria Rosa Saurin de la Iglesia, Urbino
Dai Smith, Cardiff
Bruce B. Solnick, Lennox, Mass.
Bill and Rosemary Stephens, Leeds
Robert Stradling, Cardiff
David P. Turner, Newcastle upon Tyne
Donald Cameron Watt, London
Katharina Weigand, München
Chris Williams, Cardiff

Department of History, University of Wales Swansea
Welsh Centre for International Affairs, Cardiff